D1713184

The Other Economy

THE
OTHER
ECONOMY

PASTORAL HUSBANDRY ON
A MEDIEVAL ESTATE

KATHLEEN BIDDICK

UNIVERSITY OF CALIFORNIA PRESS
BERKELEY • LOS ANGELES • LONDON

University of California Press
Berkeley and Los Angeles, California

University of California Press, Ltd.
London, England

Copyright © 1989 by The Regents of the University of California

Library of Congress Cataloging-in-Publication Data

Biddick, Kathleen.
The other economy: pastoral husbandry on a medieval estate /
Kathleen Biddick.
p. cm.
Bibliography: p.
Includes index.
ISBN 0-520-06388-0 (alk. paper)
1. Pastures—England—Midlands—History.   2. Animal industry-
England—Midlands—History.   3. Animal culture—England—Midlands-
History.   4. Agriculture—Economic aspects—England—Midlands-
History.   5. Peterborough Abbey—History.   I. Title.
HD1641.G7B53   1989
333.3′22′0942651—dc 19   88-32906
                                                        CIP

Printed in the United States of America

1   2   3   4   5   6   7   8   9

To my first mentors, Suzanne Wemple and Maristella Lorch, and to the community of women at Barnard College (1967–1971)

CONTENTS

FIGURES

TABLES

xi

PREFACE

Fernand Braudel's recognition "that there was not one but several economies" in preindustrial Europe bequeathed to historians unanswered questions about power and resources. Braudel brilliantly described the framework of such heterogeneous economic activity—material life, the market, and capitalism—without specifying their linkages. Historians now face the challenge of linking the political structure of local resources with their everyday use in these multiple economies. This study returns to the traditional genre of medieval-estate studies to explore such missing links. The rich literature on seigneurial agriculture notwithstanding, historians know little about the local use of resources by agrarian institutions.

A return to estate studies is timely. The growing debate over the historical formation of European agricultural regions raises fundamental questions about the changing practices of medieval agrarian institutions and processes of regionalization. Geographers mean by regionalization the spatial linking and unlinking of symbolic, social, political, and economic resources. Without an understanding of institutional resource-use, the tensions between the reproduction of agrarian institutions and regionalization risk going unrecognized.

The chapters that follow emphasize, in particular, the study of pastoral resources. They offer the first systematic analysis of pastoral resource-use on a medieval seigneurial estate, the estate of Peterborough Abbey. The findings question the subordinate, dependent position accorded to pastoral husbandry in prevailing models of medieval economic development. The study, although local, also bears on the debate over feudal power and the market in European agricultural development. To conserve their power as agrarian lords, the abbots of Peterborough actively but selectively participated in the market at the same time they strove to conserve "costless" consumption of everyday subsistence goods.

Such findings urge enlarging the debate on medieval agrarian innovation and productivity to include questions of consumption. Efforts to understand estate economies in their own terms will reward us with a greater appreciation of their paradoxically resilient and brittle participation in medieval regional economies.

I began the study of the local pastoral economy of Peterborough with its archaeology.[1] The archaeological tutelage I received at the Fengate excavations, Peterborough, continues to influence deeply my historical approach to medieval productivity and development. I wish to acknowledge here those colleagues and institutions that supported the archaeological prehistory of the project presented in this book. An anonymous donation made to the Center for Medieval Studies, University of Toronto supported my first research trip to European excavations. A Canada Council doctoral fellowship and funding provided by the Royal Ontario Museum enabled me to undertake archaeological research at the Fengate sites under the direction of Francis Pryor, who generously supported my study of the excavated animal bones. Hans-Peter Uerpmann of the Institut für Urgeschichte, Universität Tübingen took time out from his research to introduce me to computers and shared his program for analysis of archaeozoological material. The Cohon family helped me to complete that analysis upon my return to the United States.

Over the years conversations with Christopher Evans, a colleague from the Fengate excavations, have challenged me to enlarge my conceptions of archaeology and history. Edmund King offered invaluable suggestions in the early stages of the historical parts of this project, and I am grateful to him for the loan of microfilms and transcripts of materials. The archivists and staff of the Northamptonshire Record Office continued such support as I worked with the Peterborough Abbey documents. A Mellon Fellowship in History at Stanford University offered me a much-appreciated opportunity to think more about consumption and markets. Colleagues in the Stanford Social Science History Workshop under the direction of Paul David were particularly helpful.

When the time came to write this book, the University of Notre Dame granted me a semester's sabbatical and generously supported subvention costs. Without that material support my scholarly labors could not have appeared in their present form. Bruce Campbell's dedication to issues of historical development encouraged me through several drafts of this manuscript. I am grateful for the time he took out from his own work to share with me the benefits of his comparative perspective. The anonymous readers for the University of California Press who went over the penultimate version of the manuscript offered me helpful reviews for which I am thankful. I have had excellent advice, and what errors remain, factual or judgmental, are mine alone.

Other colleagues intervened at crucial moments, and I am particularly grateful to Pamela Falkenberg, Robert Franklin, Mary Gordon, Maryanne Kowaleski, and Albion Urdank, colleague and husband, for tender concern and constructive criticism. Finally, I wish to express my gratitude to Ambrose Raftis, who introduced me to a way of seeing history vibrant with a Cezanne-like vision of everyday forms. That vision continues to sustain me.

INTRODUCTION

THE OTHER ECONOMY

The comparative world histories of Fernand Braudel, E. L. Jones, and Immanuel Wallerstein characterize Europeans as uniquely "carnivorous," distinctive in commanding "more working capital per head than Asians, mainly in the form of livestock," and claim that "the emphasis on cattle in Europe led to the extensive use of animal muscular power as an engine of production."[1] In such textbooks, domestic animals mark a profound difference between Western and Eastern agrarian technology. Yet, startlingly enough, no historians have written a history of European livestock husbandry.

Paradoxically, historians have marginalized pastoral history while considering it a central feature of European agrarian history. In contrast with an abundant literature devoted to cereal agriculture, only a scattering of data exists for European pastoral husbandry.[2] Such fragments, dispersed in histories of estates, technology, and innovation, or in special studies of groups such as the Cistercians or areas such as the Spanish *mesta*, do not begin to answer basic questions about European livestock husbandry.[3] The demography of herds and flocks, changing household practices of consumption, and marketing of pastoral resources all await their histories.[4]

Evolutionary models still exert enough power on economic history to divert attention from pastoral husbandry. The progress which nineteenth-century political economists attributed to the advent of the plough, namely, sedentariness, cereal surpluses, and differentiation of town and country, superseded pastoral husbandry.[5] In such evolutionary schemata, pastoralism—things having to do with animals—preceded cereal agriculture. An abiding identification of the pastoral with the primitive and marginal, and often with women's work, short-circuited historical study of European pastoral husbandry. Historians, as inheritors of this tradition, have rendered European pastoral economies historically invisible and "other" so as to sustain linear narratives of European progress.

Although they are based on little data, purported relations of

1

pastoral and cereal husbandry have figured prominently in models of medieval and early modern European agricultural development. Rather than study pastoral husbandry, economic historians have simply assumed that it depended on cereal agriculture. Assuming that expanding cereal cultivation necessarily contracted pastoral production, historians predicted trends in herd demography and pastoral production from their observations of cereal acreage and yields.

The medieval economic historian Michael Postan used such a priori logic to formulate his well-known thesis of a pastoral crisis in thirteenth-century England, a critical moment for demographic history and the "high-farming" era of English agrarian lordship. Without actually studying livestock husbandry, he argued that grazing resources diminished as arable land grew in the thirteenth century; herds, consequently, declined in numbers. Less livestock produced less manure and consequently impoverished cereal production. Soils deteriorated in the older, richer cultivated areas and destabilized on newly ploughed marginal lands. Cereal yields declined in such conditions, and reduced productivity contributed to the demographic crisis of the fourteenth century. Postan argued that only "purely pastoral areas"—uplands, marshes, woodlands—escaped this rigid equilibrium.[6] He thus derived the pastoral from, and subordinated it to, the cereal sector:

> So inherent was the shifting frontier between grass and grain in the very process of medieval growth and reclamation that most readers will be prepared to take it for granted. What is less self-evident is that in the course of the thirteenth century and perhaps even earlier the frontier not only approached but in many ways crossed its limits of safety, and that by the end of that [century] and the beginning of the following century, in corn-growing parts of the country taken as a whole, pasture and the animal population had been reduced to a level incompatible with the conduct of mixed-farming itself.[7]

Even the scanty available evidence disproves such a rigid equilibrium between pastoral and cereal agriculture and the neat separation of pastoral and mixed-farming areas. The rising costs of pasture during the thirteenth century, which Postan attributed to scarcity, could have resulted from increased demand for pasture as wool prices rose and sheep flocks grew.[8] Historians have also failed to find the correlations between livestock and cereal yields required by Postan. In a study of arable productivity on demesnes in thirteenth- and fourteenth-century Norfolk, Bruce Campbell found high cereal yields together with low ratios of livestock to arable acreage. These rich Norfolk yields approached the so-called revolutionary levels recorded for the seventeenth-century Netherlands.[9] Campbell compellingly argues that institutional arrangements, lordship over labor, and market dependence, rather than any simple equilibrium between pastoral and arable resources, produced such high yields.

Students of field systems have not found that the development of open-field systems synchronized with population growth, as the Postan model postulated. They contend that the open-field system of the English Midlands had matured—had, indeed, grown somewhat inert—by the twelfth century, almost a century before the peak of population growth and arable expansion that Postan had posited.[10] They further argue that open-field arrangements actually slowed population growth rather than registered its onslaught in the thirteenth century. Studies of transitions from two- to three-course rotations have also shown little synchronicity with Postan's demographic timetable and have pointed to the influence of other factors, especially the growth of market dependence, on the adoption of intensive cereal rotations.

Examples from the literature on medieval technology also contradict the simple linkage between demography, cereal agriculture, and livestock advanced by Postan. John Langdon has published evidence of a dramatic increase in the horse population in thirteenth-century England and relates such increase to a growing demand for speedy haulage among both peasants and lords.[11] As their economies became increasingly oriented to the market, peasants and lords expanded production of oats, not to feed themselves but to fuel horse transport.

The intensification of flock management as English wool exports reached their medieval zenith at the end of the thirteenth century also suggests complex links between agrarian lordship and the medieval world economy.[12] During the late thirteenth century the Florentines wrested dominance of the English wool trade from the Flemings.[13] English royal finances grew increasingly entwined in interregional indebtedness and foreign exchange based on wool. The extent to which royal and seigneurial indebtedness stimulated production of large flocks and thereby served as the impetus for new management techniques deserves attention. The assumption of simple pastoral dependence on the cereal economy precludes any attempt to study more complicated relationships between different herding strategies, cereal agriculture, and the medieval world economy.

The available evidence on the pastoral economy, although scattered, already suggests that lords and peasants responded to and shaped complex dynamics in their pastoral economies. Historians have much to learn from the systematic study of such dynamics. This book pioneers an in-depth analysis of pastoral husbandry on a medieval estate. It asks the most basic question: How did relations between pastoral and cereal activities change throughout the history of the estate?

TOWARD A HISTORY OF EUROPEAN
PASTORAL HUSBANDRY

The economic activities of the estate of Peterborough Abbey offer answers to this question.[14] I have deliberately chosen to explore an estate rather than a geographical region because the institutional approach offers the best chance to focus on a nuanced study of poorly known household strategies for pastoral resource-use. Founded as a frontier monastery straddling the edge of the English peat fens and the undulating uplands of the eastern Midlands of England, Peterborough Abbey controlled manors in areas conventionally considered highly arable and highly pastoral.[15] Such a blend of resources makes this estate an ideal laboratory for questioning Postan's fundamental conceptualization of "pastoral" and "arable" and their interrelationships.

The sources for the pastoral economy of Peterborough Abbey vary in quality and quantity. Archaeological findings offer the chief evidence for the Abbey's early economic history. The Domesday inquest and a royal survey provide insight into the Abbey's resources and their changing deployment over the late eleventh and early twelfth century. The Pipe Rolls, records of the royal Exchequer, shed light on the estate's economic relationships to the Crown and facilitate a political understanding of its changing agrarian organization over the twelfth century. Manorial accounts preserved for the entire estate provide the richest source of systematic evidence for herd demography and productivity and the Abbey's coordination of resources to achieve its reproductive strategies at the turn of the fourteenth century.

Since no scholar has written a history of European pastoral husbandry, this study pioneers a methodology for analyzing pastoral activities. The method goes beyond the partial model offered by studies of cereal agriculture, which have concentrated almost exclusively on the narrow issue of gross productivity—that is, the yield of grain from seed or per acre.[16] Such a narrow approach ignores everyday political and economic use of local resources. It leaves unaddressed, first, the political formation of resources (who developed what resources for whom?) and their changing forms of deployment within and beyond households. The method developed here, a broader one capable of analyzing the complexities of pastoral activity, explores the links between consumption, production, and exchange of pastoral resources, livestock, and their products.

The study has grappled with defining the terms *consumption, production*, and *exchange* appropriately for a medieval monastic household.[17] Modern conceptions, which valorize production and oppose it to consumption, do not apply to multistranded medieval economies with their Braudelian links to material life, the market economy, and capitalism. This study applies *consumption* to ways of using resources in the household. It defines resources broadly to include not only those derived from the environment (material forces and produced goods) but those more intangible resources produced from harnessing human activities, such as authority and social control.[18] *Exchange* refers to ways of circulating resources beyond the household and *production* to ways of making things for consumption and exchange. For discussion of change over time, the term *reproduction* figures strongly. Reproduction includes ways of ensuring the replacement of resources. The interplay of such definitions suggests the difficulties involved in simply or arbitrarily isolating, opposing, or hierarchizing these processes in the study of preindustrial societies.

The study yielded a rich and diverse history of the Abbey's pastoral economy. The right of Dark Age abbots to "eat off the land," to collect resources and food from different parts of their estate, linked Peterborough's first abbots to their pastoral resources. The act of consumption literally embodied or symbolized their lordship. As the monarchy developed and increased its demands over the twelfth century, and as the commercialization of the medieval world economy intensified, the Abbey grafted the production of cash crops onto the trunk of consumption. Such hybridization of old forms of consumption and new forms of exchange bore bitter economic fruit.

The Abbey wielded its seigneurial power to redistribute land and pastoral resources on the estate to coincide with new productive strategies. Paradoxically, the market tempted the Abbey as a source of cash as it threatened the Abbey's autonomy in replacing resources on its estate.

The nature and context of the Abbey's control over pastoral resources thus changed over time; control over resources bound agrarian lordship to ecology, to the physical world.[19] By considering the effects of politics on ecology, this study extends beyond the confines of the estate to broader questions of power and resources in medieval agricultural development.

Readers will wonder about the typicality of the pastoral economy of Peterborough Abbey. With such a poorly known subject as the European pastoral economy, it is difficult to know in advance what comparative measures offer the best insight into typicality. Wherever possible, comparisons have been made with published data from other estates, especially Winchester and Westminster, and Bruce Campbell's regional study of Norfolk demesnes. The comparisons underscore the selectivity of different estate strategies. Such selectivity precludes statements about tradition and typicality until further study illumines the changing range of reproductive strategies practiced by different estates and regions.

In their pursuit of rich and thick description of the pastoral economy of Peterborough Abbey, the chapters that follow seek to enlarge the ways in which we talk about preindustrial agrarian institutions. The study achieves such a goal to the extent that it restores hitherto invisible and marginalized forms of economic activity to historical vision and resonates to the extent that it inspires sustained appreciation of the multiple vanishing points of such economic activity.

Part I
THE FRAMEWORK OF LORDSHIP
OVER RESOURCES

1

CONSUMPTION AND PASTORAL RESOURCES ON THE EARLY MEDIEVAL ESTATE

LORDSHIP AND RESOURCES

From its foundation in the seventh century the abbots of Peterborough Abbey expressed their agrarian lordship through consuming resources. The Domesday inquest and a royal survey of the estate made in 1125, a generation after the Norman Conquest, offer the earliest comprehensive documentation for management of its resources. A discussion of that written evidence forms the core of this chapter. Evidence for formative phases of resource use during the seventh through tenth centuries comes from the archaeological record. Although archaeologists cannot yet precisely define local arrangements, their excavations so far have revealed important shifts in the regional framework of the estate economy during the early medieval period. Historians can better appreciate the transformations of lordship occurring in the eleventh and twelfth centuries by considering the early medieval archaeology of the Abbey's regional economy.

The Regional Framework of the Mercian Estate

The Anglo-Saxon Chronicle attributes the Abbey's foundation to Wulfhere (A.D. 657–674), under whose rule the Mercians gained dominance over petty kingdoms of southern England.[1] Wulfhere appointed Seaxulf (d. A.D. 691), the first recorded Abbot of Peterborough, or Medeshamstede, the monastery's Anglo-Saxon name, as Bishop of the Mercians. Peterborough's abbots remained politically prominent as Mercian power grew over the eighth century. They frequented the court of Offa (A.D. 757–796), the most powerful leader of the Mercian dynasty. As an important Mercian foundation, the

Abbey headed a confederation of monasteries in the late seventh century. The houses of that confederation, which linked the Abbey with the political heartland of the Mercians in the West Midlands and a trading outlet near London, appear in figure 1.[2]

The archaeological record offers a perspective on the regional framework of this Mercian estate. The foundation of the monastery marked a political effort to stabilize a locale that had undergone much change since the fifth century.[3] The archaeological remains of pagan Saxon settlement in the Peterborough area during the fifth and early sixth century have an ephemeral, frontier quality.[4] Not until the seventh century, coincidental with Mercian interest in the eastern Midlands and the activities of the Christian mission, do archaeological remains grow more complex and substantial. Excavations of a mid-seventh-century nunnery founded on the site of a Roman palace complex at Castor, two miles (3.2 km) west of Peterborough, uncovered a prestigious ecclesiastical occupation associated with a substantial domestic settlement.[5]

So far archaeologists have excavated only one Mercian rural settlement in the Abbey's vicinity.[6] At Maxey, a site located six miles (9.6 km) north of Peterborough, excavation uncovered timber-framed buildings, pits, postholes, and ditches. A series of large pits and slag deposits offer ambiguous evidence for industrial activities, possibly the tanning of hides and smelting of ore for exchange at emporia, such as London, or Dorestad across the Channel. These emporia had begun to develop vigorously during the opening phase of the monastery's growth.[7] Mercian interest in trade and monasteries coincided. They used their monasteries as reception centers for messengers and ambassadors who facilitated diplomatic and commercial exchange.[8]

The regional distribution of local stone quarried at Barnack, some eight miles (12.8 km) northwest of Peterborough, shows the role of sacred centers in consumption and distribution. Barnack stone found its way into Mercian workshops that produced the sculptural friezes found at Peterborough, and nearby Castor, Fletton, and Breedon-on-Hill, Leicestershire.[9] The sculptural tradition bound the regional religious centers symbolically.

The Mercian Abbey of Peterborough enjoyed access to a range of political and ecological resources. Although the Abbey's foundation in the mid-seventh century predates the earliest surviving English land charters, grants to ecclesiastical foundations preserved from the

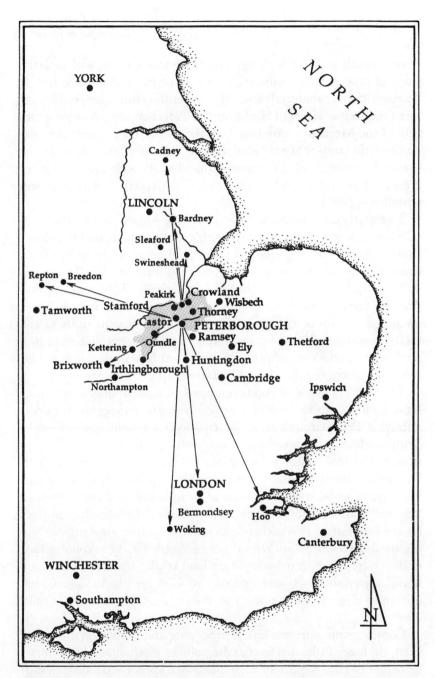

Fig. 1. Mercian Peterborough. The arrows point to monasteries of the confederation headed by Peterborough. Stippling marks the conjectural territory of the Mercian Abbey. The other names refer to important locations of the early medieval period mentioned in the text.

later seventh century typically endowed monasteries with a large
tract of land loosely bounded by rivers or extensive woodlands.[10]
Garbled charter materials from the eleventh century do recall fragments of such a Mercian land grant to Peterborough. A reconstruction of the Mercian estate based on these charters suggests that the
Abbey held lands that extended deep into the peat and silt fens to its
east and also controlled extensive upland to the west along the river
Nene.[11] The conjectural territory of the Mercian Abbey is represented in figure 1.

The spotty documentary evidence for the Abbey's actual management of such resources with their arable and pastoral potential shows
that the collection of *feorms*, or renders of goods and services from
estate centers, served as the organizational framework.[12] The feorm
had its origins in a chief's right to "eat off the land," a consumption
practice typical of societies organized as complex chiefdoms.[13] Based
on the collection of renders from different settlement units of the
estate, a system of feorms coordinates the subsistence resources in a
territory with the consumption needs of lordship. Consumption, and
not production, regulated social relations and resource use.[14]

The actual details of goods rendered in feorms, only rarely preserved, offer clues to the ecology of early estate management. Fortunately, a Peterborough lease for two lives for holdings located in
Sempringham and Sleaford, Lincolnshire, includes such instructions.[15] The lessee owed a food rent deliverable in three parts. First,
he had to render annually some woodland products; sixty wagons
(fothers) of wood, twelve wagons of brushwood, and six wagons of
faggots.[16] The second part of his feorm reserved the following supplies
for the monastery: two casks of clear ale, two cattle for slaughter, six
hundred loaves of bread, ten mittan of Welsh ale. The Abbot, "lord
of the church," collected a separate food render from the lessee: one
horse, thirty shillings, and one day of food rent including: fifteen
mittan of clear ale, five mittan of Welsh ale, fifteen sesters of mild
ale.[17]

Consumption of feorms linked processing and storage on the estate.
First, the lessee processed food at the point of production. The monastic center did not require storage space for unprocessed food or a staff
to process it. The lessee had to malt barley, grind grain, and bake
loaves of bread. The ubiquitous ale required in food renders actually
served as storage of barley.

Mercian power that supported Peterborough Abbey relied on wider economic relations that grew more fragile as the ninth century progressed. Politics and agrarian organization shifted profoundly in England in the mid-ninth century.[18] The political dominance of the Mercians collapsed. Lay magnates extended their local lordship in the countryside and assumed a defensive stance. They built the first fortified manorial complexes during this period and contested control over land and other resources.[19] The same magnates who were busy defending their holdings also erected their own churches, thus deflecting sacral power from the monasteries to themselves.[20]

Local competition for power and land stimulated regional agricultural development in the East Midlands over the later ninth century. Archaeologists have excavated a rare iron ploughshare, part of a heavy medieval plough, from a late Saxon context at the small town of St. Neots, Huntingdonshire, not far from Peterborough.[21] In his fortified manorial complex the ninth-century lord of Goltho controlled weaving activities on the scale of Carolingian *gynecea*.[22] Such local magnates purchased the new, wheel-turned pottery produced in pre-Conquest regional centers of Stamford, Northampton, and St. Neots.[23]

In the midst of such political and economic transformation in the East Midlands, Peterborough Abbey lay in ruins. The Anglo-Saxon Chronicle reports that in A.D. 869 the Danes "came to the monastery at *Medeshamstede* and burned and demolished it, and slew the abbot and monks and all that they found there, reducing to nothing what had once been a very rich foundation."[24] So far we know little more about Peterborough in the later ninth and early tenth centuries than this "sleeping beauty" story.

At the time of the great monastic revival in the mid-tenth century, the fen-edge of the eastern Midlands served as the bulwark for important royal refoundations.[25] Bishop Aethelwold's campaign there had as its objective the landed endowment of the Benedictine abbeys of Peterborough (966), Crowland (966), Ely (970), Ramsey (971), and Thorney (972).[26] He restored Peterborough Abbey to its former royal splendor and dedicated "a basilica there furbished with suitable structures of halls, and enriched with surrounding lands."[27]

Within twenty years the Abbey joined in the economic boom of the later tenth century. For a brief period the Abbey controlled a mint. The Abbey was well positioned as a small economic center near the

regional town of Stamford, which ranked eighth among English
towns according to its known number of moneyers.[28] Over the century between its refoundation and the Norman Conquest, the Abbey
succeeded in filling in its holdings in Northamptonshire and adding
some properties in Lincolnshire.[29] Under Abbot Leofric (1052–1066)
chroniclers called Peterborough the "Golden Borough": "more than
any man before or since he [Leofric] enriched the Abbey of Peterborough with gold and silver, with vestments and land."[30] At the
time of the Domesday survey, the valuation of the estate amounted to
323 pounds of silver and ranked the Abbey among the top thirty
English estates in its gross value.[31]

DOMESDAY RESOURCES:
THEIR EXTENT AND MANAGEMENT

Peterborough Abbey rebounded after its refoundation. It enjoyed a
comparable range of resources, but managed them no longer as a
territorial unit but through manors scattered in the landscape.
Between the Domesday survey in 1086 and the survey of 1125 the
Abbey had subinfeudated some properties.[32] The following discussion
considers only those properties over which the Abbey retained control
in the Domesday generation.[33] Figures 2 and 3 show the locations of
the Abbey's manors.

The Setting of the Domesday Manors

The eastern perimeters of the estate of Peterborough Abbey in the
Domesday generation extended into the adjacent peat fens. The
monasteries of Peterborough, Thorney, Crowland, and Ramsey did
not fight for sharp definition of their fen boundaries until the thirteenth century.[34] The river Nene bounded the estate to the south.
Several manors (Boroughbury, Castor, Fletton, Alwalton, Warmington, Oundle, Irthlingborough) hugged its banks. To the west, the
Welland River formed an estate boundary. Northern holdings of the
estate lay along transportation routes to the town of Lincoln and to
the north. This slice of the East Midlands defined by the scattered
manors of Peterborough Abbey roughly coincided with the Mercian
territory over which it had wielded power. The ecology of its agrarian

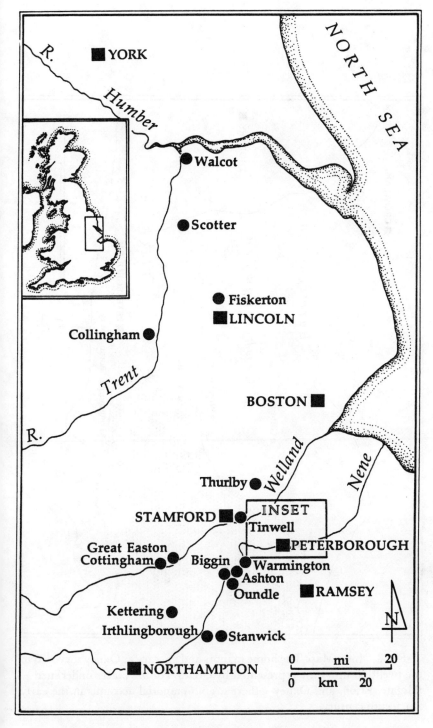

Fig. 2. The twelfth-century estate of Peterborough Abbey. The manors controlled by the Abbey are marked with circles, except for the home manors of the Abbey, which are represented in the inset map.

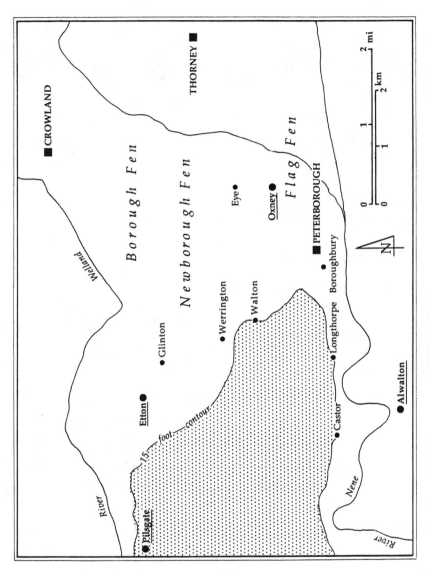

Fig. 3. Inset Map: The home manors and vaccary at Oxney surveyed in the twelfth century are represented by circles. For the places underlined— Pilsgate, Etton, and Oxney—there are no manorial accounts in the early fourteenth century.

lordship, control over fen, river meadows, woodlands, and diverse soil-types, had not altered radically.

Fen

From the eastern borders of the monastic precincts the peat fen stretched to the horizon. The Abbey's home manor of Boroughbury and the manors of Glinton, Werrington, and Walton lay along the margin of the fen on the slightly elevated gravel terraces of the river Nene (6–21 m OD). Within the fen the manor of Eye and the cell at Oxney, resting on gravel and clay ridges, rose as islands above the surrounding peat.

The classification of peat fen as a pastoral resource depends upon the history of its local management. Fen vegetation is as sensitive as woodland to human intervention.[35] During dry periods unmanaged peat fen reverts to a dense growth of brush and small trees, a vegetation known as carr. Typically, the woody growth is composed of alder (*Alnus*), ash (*Fraxinus*), hazel (*Corylus*), buckthorn (*Rhamnus catharticus*), elm (*Ulmus*), dogwood (*Cornus sanguineus*), raspberry (*Rubus idaeus*), and oak (*Quercus*). The ground surface of brushwood-peat or carr is firm enough for the tread of livestock. The habitats of fen-edge woodland and carr, therefore, do not differ radically as rough forage. When fen carr grows dense, it becomes impenetrable to cattle, sheep, and horses, thus diminishing its use as rough pasture. Only pigs, with their ability to crash through bush, benefit from foraging on the herbaceous ground cover of dense carr.

Grazing and mowing effectively coax fen's botanical succession away from dense carr and enhance the growth of reeds and rushes, vegetation commonly associated with fen flora.[36] Regular cropping at intervals of one to two years and four to five years respectively maintains the mixed sedge (*Cladio-Molinetum*) and litter (*Molinetum*) habitats characteristic of mown fen. Under wet conditions—and the medieval fenland grew wetter over the thirteenth and fourteenth centuries—peat fen reverts to reed swamp (*Phragmitetum*) and pure sedge (*Cladietum*). Drainage can deflect succession to such swampy conditions.[37]

The Domesday Book ignores the Abbey's fen resources.[38] It recorded only 140 acres (57 ha) of meadow for the Abbey's fen-edge manors of Boroughbury, Glinton, and Werrington. In the eighteenth century the antiquarian John Bridges estimated that the common fen, Borough Great Fen, adjoining Peterborough, measured six thousand acres (2,429 ha), and the *Victoria County History* records half that acreage.[39]

The 1125 survey fails to evaluate either fen or meadow resources. It does, however, list labor services. Those required of peasants living along the fen-edge reveal aspects of fen management in the early twelfth century. Peasants on the manors of Glinton, Walton, and Werrington rendered carriages of rushes (*junci*) to the Abbey. Such renders show that the Abbey's peasants mowed fen on a four-to-five-year cycle. Peasants on the manors of Werrington and Walton carried carriages of fodder (*herbae*) to the Abbey. A shorter mowing regime of one to two years produced the mixed sedge (*Cladio-Molinetum*), typical fen fodder. The labor services show that the Abbey relied on its peasants to mow parts of the fen on regular cycles of different rhythms to produce different fodder crops. Some of the renders listed in the 1125 survey also hint at the use of other fen resources, such as water birds. The Abbey received ducks and geese from peasants in the manor of Glinton, the only manor listed with a fowler in 1125.

As a fen landlord the Abbey also enjoyed the products of fish and eels from the fen rivers and streams. The Domesday Book states that the Abbey had one boat on Whittlesey Mere, the largest freshwater lake in England until its drainage in 1851.[40] The Abbot had sublet another boat, a fishery, and fishermen from Thorney Abbey in exchange for wood and pigs from the upland behind Peterborough. The Domesday survey valued at eighty shillings a fen fishery belonging to Peterborough Abbey, a value that exceeded any one of its mills, markets, or woodlands. The 1125 survey reveals much less about the Abbey's fisheries. It reports only that the Abbot collected fifteen shillings in fish from three fishermen in Boroughbury and six shillings for a fishery in Glinton.

Neither survey accounts for the vast quantities of fen eels collected by the Abbey, which other documents mention. According to a tenth-century foundation charter of the neighboring Abbey of Thorney, Peterborough Abbey was entitled to eight thousand eels from the fen fisheries at Upwell, Outwell, and Elm located east of Peterborough, near Wisbech.[41] These eel renders came from locations that once stood at the edge of the more extensive fen territories attached to the

Mercian estate of Peterborough Abbey. Their collection probably harks back to earlier territorial arrangements.

The written sources offer only a fragmentary picture of the Abbey's fen management. The scale and intensity of the Abbey's utilization of the fen remains uncertain. Statistics for the Abbey's demesne livestock recorded in the survey of 1125 (to be discussed further in chapter 2) do not suggest that its dairying or sheepherding, which would later dominate the fen and fen-edge, had developed much beyond small-scale production in the early twelfth century. Perhaps underutilization of its fen resources contributed to their absence from valuations of the estate. Some producers, however, must have supplied the nearby looms of Stamford textile industry with wool and Stamford households with food.[42] The written documents tell us even less about the utilization of local fen resources by the Abbey's peasants.

Meadow

The manors of Peterborough Abbey enjoyed good riverside locations that provided the estate with 1,515 acres (613 ha) of Domesday meadows.[43] Geographically the Abbey's holdings of assessed meadowlands were quite dispersed. The greatest concentration of meadow resources lay furthest from the Abbey. Its more distant manors, which served as staging points to the north (Thurlby, Collingham, Fiskerton, Scotter, Walcot), possessed 61.4 percent (930 acres) of the assessed holdings.[44] Its home manors (Boroughbury, Longthorpe, Castor, Glinton, Werrington, Pilsgate, Fletton) husbanded only 17.8 percent (271 acres) of assessed meadow. Slightly less than a quarter of the Abbey's assessed meadows lay on its western Northamptonshire manors. Figures 4 and 5 show the distribution of meadow on the Abbey's estate.

Medieval farmers usually mowed meadows for hay. From mid-December to early summer, they enclosed meadows to protect the production of the hay crop. They mowed the hay from mid-June to July. Then, depending on management, livestock grazed the mown meadows, unless a second hay crop was to be taken in late August.

Farmers can also choose to graze meadows with their stock rather than mow them.[45] The decision to mow or graze riverside meadows depends on seasonal strategies of matching livestock populations with

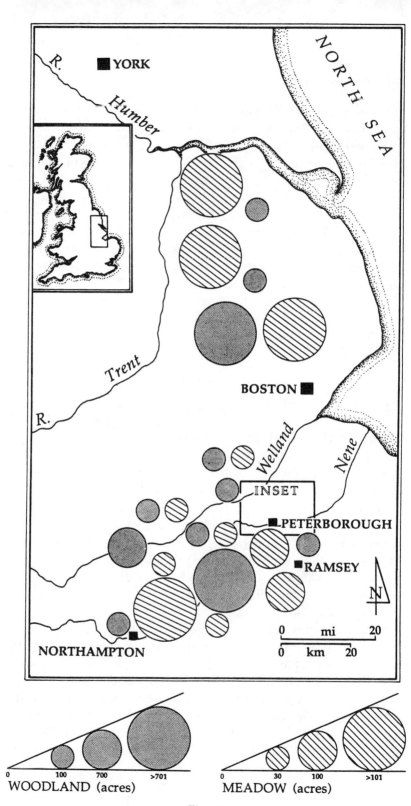

YORK

NORTH SEA

R. Humber

Trent

R.

BOSTON

Welland

Nene

INSET

PETERBOROUGH

RAMSEY

N

NORTHAMPTON

0   mi   20

0   km   20

WOODLAND (acres)

0   100   700   >701

MEADOW (acres)

0   30   100   >101

Fig. 4

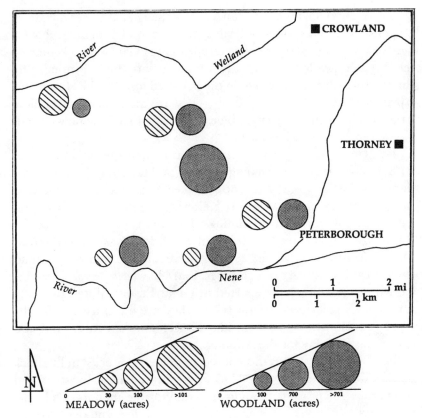

Fig. 5

Figs. 4 and 5. The meadow and woodland resources of the Abbey recorded in the Domesday Book.

pastoral resources. Mowing and storage of hay for winter fodder implies a pastoral economy where the number of animals exceeds winter pasture and one in which movements of livestock can be coordinated with storage locations. If farmers graze meadows in the summer, they must store some other source of fodder for the winter or move the animals to winter pasture. The decision to mow or graze depends, too, on who controls the resource and on the demands of the livestock economy. Medieval farmers usually restricted the grazing of alluvial meadows to cows and horses. Dairy cows, in particular, had special need to feed on the early spring flush sprouting in alluvial meadows, when other forage was scarce.

Low-lying river-meadows can also be managed as water meadows by constructing a system of drains, weirs, and channels. Archaeologists have found evidence of water meadows in late Saxon Winchester.[46] Water meadows are usually associated with sheep farming. The sheep, especially ewes, are let on the irrigated meadow in March and April to graze on the spring flush. They are then removed to allow irrigation for a July hay crop. Livestock then grazed the new growth of late summer, the aftermath.

The Domesday survey assesses meadow acreage on the estate, without comment on its management. The 1125 survey rarely mentions meadow acreage or meadow-related activities such as mowing in its list of peasant services. At Kettering the survey does mention extra meadow worth fifteen shillings. To give a comparative value for this figure, 6,048 acres (2,419 ha) of stocked (*oneratur*) woodland at Oundle in 1086 were valued at twenty-five shillings. Tinwell also had extra meadow valued at six shillings. Extra hay (*et de feno de super plus*) valued at six shillings is reported at Great Easton. When the 1125 survey does record mowing services, they are owed usually by the Abbey's sokemen. At Glinton and Fiskerton, sokemen mowed and carted hay one day for the Abbot.

The Domesday survey did not record demesne or peasant livestock on the Abbey's manors. The 1125 survey lists demesne livestock and the number of peasant ploughs on many of the manors. Only the weakest associations between the numbers of demesne oxen, or the estimated number of peasant oxen, or the total of demesne and peasant oxen and the Domesday meadow acreage can be found when those values are plotted. The estimated number of peasant oxen correlated most closely with meadow acreage, but in this case there was only a 13 percent probability that the correlation was significant. Such statistics belie a linear relation between pastoral resources and tillage on the estate in the early twelfth century.[47]

Woodland

The Abbey controlled nine times more woodland than meadow, according to the Domesday survey. Figures 4 and 5 illustrate the distribution of woodland on the estate. In toto, the Abbey controlled 13,880 acres (5,619 ha) of woodland, which included 1,390 acres (563 ha) of woodland for pannage and 310 acres (125.5 ha) of underwood in 1086.[48] Its manors in western Northamptonshire, especially those located on the eastern and western edges of Rockingham Forest, had access to over two-thirds (8,814 acres or 63.5 percent of total woodland acreage) of the Abbey's woodland resources. Through its home manors the Abbey controlled another 3,366 acres, or 24.2 percent, of its woodland. On the northern manors, where the Abbey had access to so much meadow, it husbanded only 1,700 acres, or 12.2 percent, of its total woodland resources compared with 61 percent of its meadow.

The Abbey dominated much of the woodland of Northamptonshire, which by 1086 covered only 8.8 percent of that county.[49] According to thirteenth-century surveys, the forest bounds of Rockingham Forest enclosed 16,822 acres (6,729 ha), much of it woodland. In 1086 the Abbey controlled 50 percent of that area through its manors on the perimeter of the forest. By the early twelfth century the Abbey had begun to retain its woodland when it leased its manors (*Et abbas tenuit boscum in sua manu*). At Oundle it assarted over 400 acres (162 ha) of woodland by 1189 to create its great cereal grange, La Biggin.[50]

Medieval woodlands were managed as renewable resource.[51] Fellers husbanded an upper tier of woodland, composed of timber or standard trees such as oak, ash, and maple, on a thirty-year cycle, and a lower tier of underwood or coppice, usually sallow (*Salex*), oaklings (*Quercus*), and hazel (*Corylus*), on a seven-to-twenty-one year cycle. The cropped underwood provided faggots for firewood and rods used for weaving wattles for housing, fences, folds, and so on. Underwood also provided raw material for charcoal makers. Such practices kept the woodland in a constant process of reproduction and harvest.

Topographically, grassy swards and heaths for grazing flourished in the mosaic composed of woodland in different stages of regeneration. The requirements of coppicing conflicted, however, with herding pigs on autumn mast, a practice often associated by our textbooks with medieval woodlands. Coppiced plots must be herbivore-proof during their early stages of regeneration, since cattle, pigs, and other browsers can do great damage to new, tender shoots. The small pigherds recorded in the 1125 survey are consistent with a picture of the Abbey as a manager of coppiced woodland and the keeper of pigs on a modest scale.[52]

As the center of a complex household and developer of a monumental building program in the twelfth century, the Abbey consumed timber and other woodland products. From the manors located within a seven-mile radius (11.3 km), it received 129 carriage-loads of wood as an annual render from its peasants, who also rendered oats and fowl for their right to collect firewood in the Abbey's woodland. As a rule of thumb one acre (0.40 ha) of twenty-year coppice yields about twenty carriageloads of bulky bundles of firewood.[53] Thus the render represents only about 12.5 acres (5 ha) of coppice ready for harvest. If the Abbey used a ten-year cycle for coppicing, it would have a total area of 125 acres (50 ha) of its woodland under coppice. This measure reflects, of course, the Abbey's customary right to extract wood renders from its tenants and not the total productive capacity of its woodland resources. The woodlands of the Abbey also lay close enough to the town of Stamford to fuel the greedy kilns of the Stamford pottery industry.[54] If the Abbey redirected to Stamford the carriages of firewood collected by its peasants, they would support about three hundred firings.

Arable

As a cereal cultivator the Abbey had its share of good and bad soils. Lighter gravel and drift deposits characteristic of the Nene and Welland river terraces served as an arable focus for most of its Soke and Northamptonshire manors.[55] The higher-lying soils sloping up from the river terraces may be divided into two basic types: (1) lighter soils of limestone, cornbrash, and sand; (2) heavier soils of different clay deposits. Dry, light soils of cornbrash found at Castor, Long-thorpe, Alwalton, Pilsgate, and Walton; the Lincolnshire limestones of Cottingham, Tinwell, and Great Easton; and sands at Collingham and Scotter can produce good crops, but their porosity makes them very susceptible to summer drought. Arable in the central part of the Soke, where few streams run off from the Welland and Nene, was particularly vulnerable to dryness.[56] The threat of parched crops reduced the potential value of soils composed of cornbrash and limestone. These dry areas also posed problems for summer pastur-ing, since herds required convenient sources of water.

The second type of soil, the clays, characterized the higher-lying parts of the manors of Warmington, Oundle, Ashton, Aldwincle, Stanwick, Irthlingborough, Pytchley, and Fiskerton. The tractability of the clays could vary from the lighter clays at Fiskerton to the very sticky boulder-clays of the middle Nene Valley at Irthlingborough, Oundle, and Aldwincle.

The Domesday survey and the survey of 1125 shed light on the Abbey's management of its arable resources. They record information on demesne and peasant ploughs and labor services owed by the Abbey's peasants. The arable resources of the estate could not be utilized without the labor of the Abbey's tenants; therefore, an analysis of those labor services opens discussion of their management.

The Abbey's Peasants and Its Use of Their Resources

The basic pattern of peasant labor services rendered on the estate was already in place in the early twelfth century.[57] Topographical studies of Northamptonshire charters show that the headlands and furrows of field systems had extended to parish boundaries by the twelfth century.[58] The agrarian landscape had taken on its medieval shape, and lordship had staked its claims to human resources within this developed landscape. In what ways had labor services become part of the political ecology of the estate of Peterborough Abbey?

Peasants owed week work and ploughing services to the Abbey. Ploughing services were a greater capital investment for the peasant, since they required not only their time but their ploughs and plough animals. The survey of 1125 defines ploughing services differently on different manors of the estate. On some manors ploughs of the village appeared for the Abbey a specified number of times for winter, spring, summer, and fallow ploughings; or the ploughs had to plough so many acres. Sometimes these types of ploughing services were combined on manors.

When ploughing services were expressed in acres, a virgater commonly had to plough one acre. At Eye and Boroughbury, tenants had to plough two acres and four acres respectively. The Abbot also reserved the right to call for ploughing boons (*precaria*), or days where all ploughs were expected to work for him, at his call. The number of precaria owed to the lord varied from manor to manor.

A specific example best illustrates how the Abbey matched human resources with the requirements of managing its arable resources. On the manor of Kettering, the manor with the most peasant ploughs in 1125, and a heavy burden of three days of week work, the Abbey expected twenty-two village ploughs to plough four acres (1.6 ha)

Table 1. Estimated Rent per Virgate, Week Work, and Ploughing
Services: Peterborough Abbey Estate: 1125 Survey

Manor	Est. Rent/ Virgate s.	Week Work	Ploughing[a]			By Total Acres	
			Gn	Wn	Sp	Fl	Sm
Boroughbury	1.02		(4)				128
Longthorpe	0.55	3					16.5
Castor	0.69	3					54
Glinton	0.35	3					27
Werrington	0.66		10x				
Walton	1.09	3	6x				
Eye	1.23		3x				26
Pilsgate	0.85	3		1	1		
Fletton	0.63	1				6x	6.5
Alwalton	0.35	1					9
Warmington	1.86	3			15x		68.5
Oundle	0.80	3		2x			10
Aldwincle	—	—	no details on labor services				
Stanwick	—	—	no details on labor services				
Irthlingboro'	—	—	no details on labor services				
Kettering	2.13	3		3x	4 + 3x	3x	
Pytchley	0.70	3		1 + 3x	1 + 3x	1x	
Cottingham	0.50	2[b]	2 + 6x				
Great Easton	0.83	2			1x		26.3
Tinwell	1.21	2					34
Thurlby	4.12	2[c]	1				
Collingham	4.00	1		1x			
Fiskerton	2.67	2		.5 + 1x	3x	1 + 1x	
Scotter	3.18	2		1x	1x		
Walcot	—						
Etton	0.71	3					36
Gosbeckirke	—						24

Source: *Chronicon Petroburgense.*

[a] Ploughing services recorded by appearance listed as 1x etc.; ploughing services listed by acres to be ploughed by virgaters and half-virgaters appear as 1 etc. Gn = during the year, no season mentioned; Wn = winter; Sp = spring; Fl = fallow; Sm = summer.

[b] (3x—Aug.)

[c] (4x—Aug.)

each for summer sowing. This service amounted to ploughing 88 acres (35.6 ha). The Abbey also required its peasants at Kettering to plough thrice in winter, thrice at the summer sowing, and thrice in the summer. Estimating the amount ploughed per day in the heavier winter and spring ploughing at 3.5 rods, the villagers cultivated then 115.5 acres (46.7 ha).[59] Thus, in total, the Abbey had 225.5 acres (91.3 ha) of demesne ploughed by its peasants at Kettering. This figure comes reasonably close to the sown area of the Kettering demesne over the period 1280–1310 when the Abbey planted a mean acreage of 271 acres (109.7 ha) in a winter-spring rotation of rye and oats.

The Abbey could convert its labor resources into cash as a way of collecting them. The patterns of commutation reflect both management decisions and differences in wealth and demand for labor on individual manors. On those manors where the Abbey had already commuted much peasant labor for cash payments, peasants worked only one or two times a week, except during the busy days of August, and they rarely ploughed. The Abbey charged higher rents per virgate on such manors: Thurlby, 4.12s.; Collingham, 4.00s.; Scotter, 3.18s.; and Fiskerton, 2.67s. As early as the turn of the twelfth century the Abbey decided that cash commutation was cheaper than surveillance when considerable distances were involved. The manors of Scotter (68 miles—110 km), Collingham (49 miles—79 km), and Fiskerton (45 miles—73 km) were each not less than forty-five miles (73 km) distant from the Abbey. Thurlby, located only thirteen miles from the Abbey, is an exception to this rule; but the Abbey viewed Thurlby as part of its staging system to the north and treated it as a northern manor.

These four manors do not exhaust the list of manors with weekly labor services of less than three days. Three other manors, Tinwell, Great Easton, and Fletton, also fell into this category. Peasants on these manors paid middle-range rents of 1.21s., 0.83s., and 0.71s. respectively. In addition to two days of week work, peasants at Tinwell owed light ploughing services of one acre (.40 ha) per virgate. Here soil conditions influenced the calculation for commuting labor services. Tinwell was located on lighter soils of the Lincolnshire limestone, and the Abbey itself kept plough teams composed of only six oxen, instead of the normal complement of eight. The rent per virgate at Tinwell is probably lower, since there was less actual labor

in the arable sector to commute. Great Easton and Fletton provide an
alternative picture of rent and labor services. Peasants owed light
week work, but the Abbot still collected a form of ploughing service
that was unique to these two manors. Peasants had to sow a portion
of the area that they ploughed with their own seed. The cost of seed
increased the cost of ploughing services for peasants and probably
accounted for the lower rent per virgate on these two manors.

The remaining manors owed to the Abbey the heavy render of
three days of week work. Rents varied from 2.13*s.* per virgate to a low
of .35*s.* The variation in rent on manors with three days of labor
service may be explained by variations in wealth on the different
manors and by differences in the additional labor extracted by the
Abbot. For instance, Kettering, with the highest rent of 2.13*s.* for the
manors with heavy week work, has every appearance of being one of
the Abbey's wealthiest manors. The forty Kettering villeins are full
virgaters, and they had the highest ratio of villeins to villein ploughs
(1 : 0.55). Kettering villeins owed no labor services beside week work
and ploughing services, according to the 1125 survey. Their high rent
reflected their wealth and also masked commuted carrying services.
Manors where peasants paid low rent per virgate, such as Glinton
(0.35*s.*), owed heavy carrying services to the Abbey. Peasants at
Glinton had to ferry the Abbot where he wished, and for every plough
they had to carry three carriages of timber (*lignum*) to Peterborough.
They also dried two carriages of firewood and transported them to
the Abbey. The Abbey collected carrying services from its nearby
manors; therefore those rents were lower.

The pattern of labor services recorded in the 1125 survey highlights
the Abbots's logic of resource use. By 1125 the Abbey had already
established basic expectations for consuming labor services. Within
these limits the Abbey could play off collecting them in cash or in
actual service. The costs of supervision clearly bothered the Abbey.
On those manors some distance to the north, it collected the labor
services mostly in their cash equivalent. The Abbey could increase
labor services further only by defining the amount of work to be
accomplished within a unit of time—a Tayloresque piecework approach—or by defining the given units of time more closely, that is,
that a day of work required service from a specified starting time to a
specified stopping time.[60] If the Abbey wished to increase its total
units of labor service collected, it could do so only by increasing

human resources on the estate. The Abbey's growing need to consume labor would, therefore, affect the demography of its peasantry.

CONCLUSION

The Domesday survey and the survey of 1125 offer a limited view of the ecology of the estate of Peterborough Abbey. Activity in the arable and the woodland can be pieced together best. Fundamental aspects of labor structure and the Abbey's use of its human resources were in place at the turn of the twelfth century. The Abbey managed its human resources the most intensively. It husbanded its woodland too, but had already begun converting some of it into arable. The surveys leave fenland resources largely unaccounted for. Such neglect camouflages the Abbey's development of its fen islands of Eye and Oxney as well as incipient definition of fen boundaries among those communities sharing this resource.

Only further archaeological investigation into the allocation and management of resources in the regional economy over the seventh to the twelfth century can provide a much-needed sense of scale and process to regional development sketched here from the sparse written documentation and excavation results available now.

Fundamental questions of early medieval agricultural development await archaeological exploration. What was the storage capacity of this economy? When did the large granaries and hay barns, which begin to be written about in the mid- to later twelfth century, first appear as regular installations in the countryside?[61] Who provisioned the growing towns of Stamford and Northampton? Did these towns stimulate specialization in animal and crop husbandry in the Peterborough area?

The surveys of the Domesday generation do cast doubt that the estate functioned as a large-scale producer in the countryside. Peasants, therefore, enjoyed greater access to resources during the eleventh and twelfth century than they would in the thirteenth century, when agrarian lords directly managed their demesnes. The scale and nature of demesne production was crucial to the well-being of the peasant economy. The following chapter further explores documentary sources for evidence of the scale of demesne economy as the problem of scale awaits ongoing archaeological research to supply a more secure context.

2

THE SCALE OF CONSUMPTION AND PRODUCTION ON THE ESTATE OF PETERBOROUGH ABBEY IN THE DOMESDAY GENERATION

VALUATIONS AND DEVELOPMENT

The Norman conquest of England expressed itself fiscally in increased valuation of estates, ideologically in the burden of monumental public building, and economically in regional shifts in town development.[1] By the early twelfth century, lords of English estates found themselves competing more intensively with kingship for resources. Traditional methods of managing estates, which relied on farmers of manors to provide lords with sustenance and some cash, gave way to direct management of seigneurial estates by the end of the century.[2] The effects of these changes on resource management will be the subject of this chapter.

A chapter from the *Leges Henrici Primi* (1114–1118) describes how agrarian lords evaluated their manorial resources in order to negotiate farming arrangements in the early twelfth century. An estate agent reviewed and adjusted the notional value of a manor upon termination of a leasing arrangement. On the basis of this information he set a new value on the *redditus*, or "rent," for the next lease:

> When the manor is returned to the lord, inquiry must be made of the herdsmen concerning the beasts, their number and kind, and of the other servants about matters which are their particular concern, that is, whether individual items are maintained in full quantity and of equal value; they must be questioned about increase in the number of men and cattle, about whether the manor has decreased in value in respect of demesne land and tenants, pasture or woods, about whether any occu-

pant has increased his due payments or whether anyone has unjustly withheld them; about what is held in the granaries and what has been sown.[3]

The emphasis on "assessing" individual items in their "full quantity and equal value" tells us much, but not nearly enough, about the relations of accounting and valuation in the early twelfth century. How did agents pass from counting heterogeneous physical units to assigning a value in a single unit of currency?[4] The instructions do not reveal whether accountants distinguished spheres of production from those of consumption in their valuations.[5] The few leases preserved from the twelfth century suggest that the length of leases grew shorter and their bids grew more competitive as the function of money and the market changed.[6] Commercialization of leases could threaten the consumption arrangements typical of such farming leases. Close study of the surveys can show some of the tensions between consumption and such commercialization prior to the decision to abandon farming leases.

The Domesday survey recorded values for the manors of Peterborough Abbey in 1066 and 1086. In the 1125 survey, every manor of the estate, with the exception of Fletton, paid a cash rent (redditus), a form of valuation. Ten manors also rendered grain to the Abbey.[7] The change in valuations for manors over the Domesday generation can be used to explore whether or not development of resources contributed to increased rents.

The valuations of the manors of Peterborough Abbey display a typical pattern of increase over the Domesday generation.[8] Overall, valuations increased by 60 percent between 1066 and 1086. By 1125, Peterborough manors paid a redditus 79 percent higher than the valuations of 1086, a striking increase.

The increases between 1086 and 1125 were not distributed evenly. Table 2 groups manors according to different ranges of increase. Manors experiencing the highest increases in fiscal valuations at or greater than 200 percent constitute a diverse group. Glinton, a fen-edge manor, five miles (8 km) from the Abbey, with its Domesday *appendicia* (or dependency), Etton, underwent an increase of 300 percent, as did Cottingham, located on the edge of Rockingham Forest some twenty-four miles (38.6 km) from Peterborough. Returns from Pilsgate in the western Soke, ten miles (38.6 km) distant

Table 2. Change in Valuations and Demesne Ploughs, 1086–1125

	Change in Valuations Δ% 1086–1125	Change in Demesne Ploughs 1086–1125	Demesne Ploughs to Peasant Ploughs 1086	Demesne Ploughs to Peasant Ploughs 1125	Δ% Peasant Ploughs 1086–1125	Δ% Peasant Population 1086–1125
Increase > 200%						
Boroughbury		−1	1:0.4	1:375	650	13
Glinton & Etton		2	1:1.66			162
Cottingham		0	1:5.0	1:3.0	−40	−42
Pilsgate		0	1:11.0	1:10.0	−9	45
Increase > 100% < 200%						
Pytchley		2	1:4.0	1:4.0	100	158
Great Easton		0	1:4.0	1:6.0	50	19
Kettering		3	1:10.0	1:5.5	120	56
Scotter		0	1:2.75	1:5.25	91	−7
Collingham		0	1:7.0	1:7.0	0	6
Tinwell		0	1:3.5	1:6.0	71	17
Werrington and appendicia		0	1:3.8	1:4.0	5	21

	Increase	< 100%	> 15%	
Aldwincle	1	1:4.5	1:2.5	11	54
Stanwick	−1	1:1.08	1:4.5	177	59
Irthlingboro'	0	1:2.5	1:2.5	0	−9
Decrease					
Alwalton	0	1:3.5	1:3.5	0	52
Longthorpe	0	1:2.0		0	39
Warmington	0	1:2.0	1:4	100	34
Thurlby	−1.5			0	−33
No change					
Castor & Ailsworth	0				14
Oundle	0	1:3.0	1:3.0	0	−3
Fiskerton	0	1:5.0			−2
No information					
Fletton		1:3	1:3.0	0	18
Ashton		1:3			
Ambiguous					
Walcot		1:2.6			

Source: See n. 7 to this chapter.

from the Abbey, and Boroughbury, the home manor just outside the monastery precincts, increased 250 percent and 200 percent respectively.

An increase in the number of demesne ploughs did not account for the leap in valuations on the Abbey's manors. Gains and losses of demesne ploughs over the Domesday generation are also set out in table 2. On the twenty-two manors for which we have comparable information, the Abbey made a net gain of only 6.5 ploughs over its Domesday ploughs. The Abbey actually lost ploughs on its demesnes of Boroughbury, Irthlingborough, and Thurlby; nor does its small gain in the number of ploughs correlate well with its "growth" manors.

If the Abbey wished to increase the value of its manors, it could have relied on expanding its commercial resources, especially tolls and market rents, which contributed substantially to income on some manors. At Glinton and Boroughbury the rents from tolls account for 17 percent and 20 percent of their cash renders respectively. The population of trades- and craftspersons, presumably the fifty-five men listed at Boroughbury, paid lucrative rents of 71*s*. 2*d*., or 13.5 percent of the total manorial rent. At Oundle the value of the market increased from 25*s*. to 83*s*. (37 percent) over the Domesday generation; however, the actual rent of the manor had not increased to reflect the increased revenue from the market. Oundle's Domesday value and its 1125 redditus were the same.

Much of the increase in manorial values came not from growth of demesne cereal production or commercial income, but from growth in tenant productivity and some expansion of the Abbey's pastoral activities.[9] The addition of peasant ploughs and the increase in peasants recorded on the manors between 1086 and 1125 are set out in table 2. At Boroughbury, a manor undergoing revenue increases, peasant ploughs multiplied 7.5 times (from two to fifteen ploughs). The manors of Glinton and Etton saw the greatest increase in the peasant population over the Domesday generation. The number of peasant cultivators more than doubled from twenty-six to sixty-eight persons. Such a sharp rise could reflect the fact that the Domesday survey subsumed Etton under Glinton as an appendicia and the 1125 survey valued Etton separately. Unfortunately, it is not possible to corroborate population growth among the peasantry with their increased productivity at Etton and Glinton, since the 1125 survey failed to record peasant ploughs on the two manors.

The 1125 survey does show that Glinton and Etton were comparatively well endowed with livestock. In the early twelfth century Etton herded the largest sheep flock in the Soke of Peterborough, and Glinton kept horses and to a lesser extent pigs. Growth and specialization in the pastoral resources on the two manors, as well as an increase in the peasant population, contributed to the increase in their valuations.

Demesne livestock at Pilsgate undoubtedly added to its high valuation as well. Neither demesne nor peasant ploughs increased there over the Domesday generation, although the peasant population increased by 45 percent (from 38 to 55 peasants). With the second largest sheep flock in the Soke in 1125 and as one of two manors (the other being Etton) on the estate with a shepherd, Pilesgate shows signs of a demesne undergoing pastoral development. Its high valuation suggests how lucrative livestock could be. Located five miles (8 km) from the town of Stamford along the Barnack Road, both Pilsgate and Etton could supply wool to the Stamford textile industry.

Over the Domesday generation the valuation of the manor of Cottingham increased at the high rate of 300 percent, even though the manor lost one-third of a hide to predatory royal constable Robert de Olli. The manor also lost four peasant ploughs and the peasant population declined by 37 percent between the two surveys.[10] Woodland resources of 504 acres (204 ha) in Rockingham Forest greatly enriched Cottingham, where the Abbey stocked its largest herds of pigs and goats. The growing value placed on pastoral resources contributed to the increased valuation of this manor.

On the thirteen other manors, where cash rents increased substantially, the overwhelming contribution to increased productivity came from the increase in peasant ploughs over the Domesday generation. Table 2 lists the ratio of demesne ploughs to peasant ploughs and the percentage changes between 1086 and 1125 in peasant ploughs and in the peasant population. For those manors where comparisons between 1086 and 1125 are possible, the Abbey added four ploughs, raising the number of its demesne ploughs from 46 to 50, an increase of 8.7 percent. On the same manors the number of peasant ploughs rose from 157.5 to 214.25, an increase of 35.8 percent. Such figures probably underestimate growth. For instance, table 2 indicates that peasant ploughs declined at Fiskerton. Failure to mention the ploughs of the Domesday sokemen in 1125 probably contributed to the observed decline, as well as the waste of the Conquest, which had not yet been fully restored. At Pilsgate, where the Abbey has half of its holding, three out of six hides, peasant ploughs decreased by only 9 percent.

The figures from 1086 to 1125 also indicate that the peasant population grew over the Domesday generation. It is notoriously difficult to compare people counted in either survey; so the figures can be taken only as general guidelines to an order of magnitude. For those manors that appear in both surveys, the population increased by 38 percent (765 to 1,053) in line with the increase of ploughs already observed (36 percent). The rate of population growth and increase in ploughs on individual manors varied, however. The "growth" manors, Glinton with Etton (162 percent) and Pytchley (158 percent), absorbed a good portion of the observed population growth.

The rent income of the Abbey increased over the Domesday generation. Some growth occurred on those manors where the Abbey developed its pastoral and commercial resources. Peasants greatly increased productivity in the arable sector through their demographic increase and the ploughs they added to exploit the resources of the manor. The Abbey itself did not develop its own demesne agriculture aggressively over the Domesday generation. It increased its own demesne ploughs at a modest rate compared to the increases among its peasants.

There were tensions in such a pattern of development. The Abbey's pastoral development required pasture, but so did the peasants' plough oxen, upon whose increase the Abbey gained increased revenue. At some point the Abbey would have to choose between its own pastoral development and development of the peasant sector. The Abbey's short-term strategies for developing its revenues, which relied on its peasants, would ultimately conflict with allocation of its pastoral resources.

FOOD RENTS AND THE SCALE OF
DEMESNE PRODUCTION

Variations in the growth of valuations on the estate over the Domesday generation indicate that the manors developed unevenly. The pattern of uneven development camouflages some of the regular dues that Abbey collected from all its manors, such as portions of its food rent. The Abbey expected to feed its household with liveries of food sent from its manors. Given the size of the Abbey's household in 1125 and its provision of hospitality, such food liveries or their cash equivalents were substantial. In 1125 the surveyors enumerated 114 members of the monastic household. The Abbey had to satisfy the consumption needs of sixty monks and a number of Abbey servants working in the bakehouse (9), brewhouse (6), kitchen (7), tailorshop (4), piggery (1), church (2), infirmary (5), and leper hospital (13 lepers and 3 servants), as well as those permanently employed in the Abbey's building program, including a mason (1), stonehaulers (2), and an overseer of the works.

The Abbey fed its household through a system of food rents collected from its manors. By 1125 the Abbot had commuted to money renders a good portion of the food owed by its manors. Only the manors of Thorpe, Castor, Glinton, Etton, Werrington, Walton, Alwalton, Fletton, Warmington, and Oundle sent grain shipments to the Abbey. As an accounting convenience during the vacancy of the Abbot's office, the surveyors of 1125 placed a cash value on the renders collected in kind in order to generate a grand total of revenues expressed in cash. The value of grain collected in kind from the manors constituted 25.5 percent (£97 12s. 0d. out of £382 5s.) of the total of revenues collected by the Abbey in 1125. To what extent did the balance of the total (74.4 percent) represent surplus over and above the consumption needs of the Abbey?

To answer this question it is useful to examine the annual consumption of food by a Benedictine abbey in the early twelfth century. No such annual food budget exists for Peterborough Abbey. Fortunately, the archive of the neighboring Benedictine monastery, Ramsey Abbey, has preserved a schedule of its annual food farm at the turn of the twelfth century suitable for comparison.[11] Ramsey manors lay along the fen and clay lands just south of Peterborough. Domesday surveyors comparably valued both estates. The details of the Ramsey schedule can help to reveal what lies hidden behind the screen of commuted food farms listed in the Peterborough survey of 1125.

The Ramsey schedule of food rents lists the grain and livestock collected annually by the monastic household. The Abbey collected the food in monthly installments from a manor or a group of manors organized to yield a monthly render. The value of the Abbey's annual food farm can be calculated from the schedule, which gives the cash equivalent of each item of food composing the monthly rent. A detailed itemization of the food renders and their values may be found in appendix 1.

The annual cash equivalent of the monthly food renders, including monthly renders in money, amounted to 4,981 shillings. Processed grain in the form of fine flour for bread, baked loaves, flour of second grade, malted grain for drink, and oat fodder constituted 34 percent of the annual value. Meat did not form a significant portion of the food render, as was proper in an observant Benedictine house.[12] Secondary animal products (lard, cheese, butter, eggs) ranked second in their contribution (22 percent) to the value of the annual food rent, lard being almost as important as malt grain in the valuation. Ramsey Abbey also collected a monthly cash payment of 80 shillings, which comprised 20 percent (960/4, 981*s*.) of the total annual value of the renders collected from Ramsey manors.

The figures for the annual food rent collected by Ramsey Abbey offer a context for evaluating the cash rents collected by Peterborough Abbey in 1125. The rents collected at Peterborough break down as shown in table 3.

Peterborough Abbey collected one-quarter (1,952/7,645*s*.) and Ramsey one-third of their respective incomes in grain. A comparison of Peterborough's total cash render (7,645*s*.) with the cost of Ramsey's annual consumption renders (4,981*s*.) shows that Peterborough Abbey collected cash in excess of 53 percent of the consumption budget proposed by the Ramsey figures. Peterborough Abbey thus

Table 3. Cash Renders (*Redditus*) and Cash Equivalents for Grain Renders: 1125 Survey

	£	*s.*	*d.*	
Cash Render	284	13	4	(5693.3*s*.)
Grain render	97	12	0	(1952.0*s*.)
Total	382	5	4	(7645.3*s*.)
Vacancy				
King's share	212	5	4	(4245.3*s*.)
Abbey	170			(3400.0*s*.)

enjoyed a return from its estate in excess of approximately 50 percent over annual consumption values of a comparable monastic neighbor. The king recognized such profitability during the Peterborough vacancy of 1125. He reserved 55 percent of the Abbey's annual cash rents (4,245.3s. out of 7,645.3s.) for himself, leaving the Abbey with 3,400s., or 68 percent (3,400s. out of 4,981s.) of the estimated amount of money it required for consumption. The king thus directed the surplus of the estate to himself in the vacancy.

The cereal and livestock products consumed annually by Ramsey also provide interesting guidelines to the minimal level of demesne production required to feed a monastic household in the early twelfth century. To such figures can be added the expectations of surplus indicated in the Peterborough Survey. Calculations for the acreage and livestock required to produce the food consumed by the monks of Ramsey appear in appendixes 2 and 3 and are summarized in tables 4 and 5. The farmers on the manors of Ramsey Abbey had to harvest between 1,300 and 1,700 acres of land, depending on two- or three-

Table 4. Estimated Acreage Required for Annual Consumption and Surplus at Rate of 50 Percent

	2-course Rotation Range (Consumption-surplus)	3-course Rotation
Wheat	658–987	494–741
Barley	256–384	192–288
Oats	256–384	192–288
	1,170–1,755 acres	878–1,317 acres

Source: See appendix 2 for calculations.

Table 5. Estimated Number of Livestock Required to Produce Products in Ramsey Food-Farm Schedule

Product	Amount	Number of Animals
Lard	120 pensae 17,280 lb.	8,640 pigs
Cheese	120 pensae 17,280 lb.	197 cows or 1,970 ewes

Source: See appendix 3 for calculations.

course rotation, to produce the required amount of grain for consumption and a surplus of 50 percent over consumption needs. With fifty-two demesne ploughs recorded in the Domesday survey, Ramsey Abbey could have easily cultivated demesne land to the extent of the above estimate. There was one Ramsey plough for every 37.5–41 demesne acres, with double ploughing of the fallow included.

Figures for demesne ploughs of Peterborough Abbey show that the Abbey too could have managed cereal agriculture at a scale comparable to the calculation for Ramsey. Given the acreage required to satisfy consumption (1,300–1,700 acres) the sixty-two demesne ploughs listed in the 1125 survey would have worked between 28 and 34.4 acres respectively, depending on whether the rotation was two-course or three-course. The ratios of demesne ploughs to acreage on both estates approximate the scale of peasant agriculture, where the virgater ideally worked a 30–40-acre (12–16 ha) holding with one plough.

The quantities of secondary animal products consumed annually according to the Ramsey food schedule provide a base from which to extrapolate the size of the herds necessary to yield renders of cheese and lard. (See appendix 3 for calculations and table 5 for a summary.) To produce 17,280 pounds of lard, Ramsey Abbey would have to have herded 8,640 pigs. To produce the same weight of cheese, the Abbey would have to have herded 197 cows or 1,970 ewes or combinations thereof.

The survey of 1125, which lists demesne livestock, enables the historian to compare such levels of consumption with the size of the demesne herd. Statistics on manorial livestock drawn from a royal survey of manors held in wardship in 1185 also offer some comparison of the scale of livestock husbandry on lay estates in the same century just as lords were turning to direct management.[13]

THE SCALE AND ORGANIZATION OF LIVESTOCK HUSBANDRY[14]

Tables 6 and 7 compare the number of livestock on the Peterborough Abbey estate with those on lay estates held in wardship in 1185. The figures show that the Abbey was better stocked. The surveyors of 1185 frequently commented, however, on the understocking of estates and recommended restocking. With such recommendations an estate in

Table 6. Demesne Livestock on the Peterborough Abbey Estate, 1125: Summary Statistics

Livestock	n	mean	s.d.	c.v.	total
Ploughs	25	2.5	0.96	38	62
Oxen	26	17.2	8.8	51	462
Cows	27	4.5	4.4	97	123
Calves	27	3.0	2.8	93	81
A. Otiosa	27	3.2	4.3	134	87
Horses	27	0.8	0.89	111	21
Pigs	27	28.6	29.1	102	773
Sheep	27	59.3	93.4	158	1,601

Source: *Chronicon Petroburgense*, 157–166.
Key to column headings: n = number of manors involved in calculation; mean = average; s.d. = standard deviation; c.v. = coefficient of variation expressed as a percentage; total = total number for 1125 survey.

Table 7. Summary Statistics of Livestock on Estates Held in Wardship, 1185

Livestock	n	mean	s.d.	c.v.	total
Ploughs	54	1.1	1.3	118	60.75
Oxen	ploughs only listed				
Cows	55	1.9	4.8	253	102
Calves	sample too small				
A. Otiosa	not listed				
Horses	55	0.9	1.8	200	48
Pigs	55	2.4	5.5	229	134
Sheep	55	37.6	78.5	208	2,069

Source: *Rotuli de Dominabus*.
Key to columns: as in table 6.

1185 would have herded on average one and one-half times more
sheep than the average Peterborough manor. The greater expectations for stocking levels of sheep in the later twelfth century will be
explored shortly. Most striking are the variations in the number of
different livestock present on Peterborough and the more scattered
lay manors of the 1185 survey. The coefficient of variation, almost
double the mean in most cases, renders the mean an ambiguous index
of comparison. Variation itself can help us to understand better how
the Abbey coordinated herding among its different manors.

Cattle

Consumption depended on the Abbey's herding enough plough oxen
to draw its demesne ploughs. The Abbey maintained a strict equilibrium between the number of oxen on each manor and demesne
ploughs.[15] Manors located on lighter limestones and gravels held
demesne plough teams composed of six oxen. The majority of manors
kept the standard eight-oxen team. The total number of oxen on the
estate numbered 462 for the sixty-two demesne ploughs. The mean
number of oxen on the estate in the first decade of the fourteenth
century, 529, represented only a 20 percent increase over the twelfth-
century herd.[16] The Abbey had already established the scale of its
oxen husbandry by the early twelfth century. Peasant oxen, based on
the number of peasant ploughs on the Abbey's manors, clearly outnumbered those on the demesne by a ratio of three to one in the early
twelfth century.

The Abbey followed a complex strategy for herding its cows. On
most of its manors it maintained just enough cows to produce oxen for
demesne ploughs. On over half of the manors, cows numbered less
than one quarter of the oxen herd. Seven manors without a cow herd
had to rely on the market or other manors to supply them with their
oxen. To ensure the supply of draft beasts on the estate, the Abbey
kept three herds of breeding cows at the manors of Eye, Oxney, and
Alwalton. Specialization in dairying activity could be expected on
the three breeding manors. The herd of 123 cows on the Peterborough estate in 1125 was not large enough to provide enough milk
to produce the 17,280 pounds (6,472 kg) of cheese collected annually
in the Ramsey food farm. Even in the early fourteenth century with
a herd of dairy cows numbering just under two hundred, Peter-

Table 8. Working and Breeding Cattle on the Manor of Castor[a]

Year	Oxen	Cows	Calves
1125	32	7	3
1301	34	15	11
1308	45	22	11
1310	47	10	8

Sources: 1125 survey; Fitzwilliam Account Rolls, 2388, 233, 2389.
[a] The proportions of oxen, cows, and calves are similar: chi square at 6 degrees of freedom $= 9.8 < 12.5$ (0.05).

borough Abbey produced approximately 15,000 pounds (6,818 kg) of cheese, butter, and milk and marketed 50 percent of the yield of dairy produce. The Abbey very rarely milked its ewes in the early fourteenth century. In the twelfth century the Abbey must have milked both sheep and cows to produce enough cheese for consumption.

The Abbey continued to use breeding manors to supply stock to its manors in the fourteenth century. The ratio of oxen to cows maintained on the manor of Castor illustrates the continuity of management practices on an "equilibrium" manor, where just enough cows were kept to produce the requisite oxen (table 8). On the manor of Castor the proportion of oxen, cows, and calves remained similar over two centuries even with an overall increase in demesne cattle.

The Abbey kept bulls on seven of its manors located in different geographical areas of the estate. On average, one bull served fifteen demesne cows, a better ratio than that for the fourteenth century, when one bull served eighteen cows. The presence of two bulls at the breeding manor of Eye underscores its specialization as breeder of demesne cattle for the estate.

Historians regard the *animalia otiosa* enumerated in the 1125 survey as young cattle.[17] On the Peterborough estate no manors without cows kept animalia otiosa. Their association with cows supports the link between breeding and young stock. Their distribution on the Peterborough manors also suggests links with carrying and hauling, although their claim to leisure (*otiosa*) belies such a connection. Every manor responsible for grain shipments to the Abbey kept animalia otiosa. Such animals were most heavily concentrated (74/87) within seven miles (10.4 km) of the Abbey, where carriage services were heaviest. Manors within this radius supplied the Abbey not only with grain but with wood and other materials, such as building stone. Interestingly enough, Boroughbury, the home manor just outside the Abbey precincts, kept no animalia otiosa. The carriage of goods on the estate moved toward the Abbey precincts. Carriage did not emanate from the Abbey, which had not yet entered the economy as the direct producer and distributor of surplus it would become in the next century.

Horses

The Abbey did not rely much on horses for ploughing and hauling in the early twelfth century.[18] Horses, including draft horses (*auri* [*affri*, *averi*]), younger horses (*pulli*), wild horses (*equi indomiti*), and a harrow horse (*herciator*), were in low supply. Kettering, the manor with the most ploughs (four demesne and twenty-two peasant ploughs), possessed the greatest number of draft horses: three auri. Of the five manors without draft horses, three were located on the western edge of the estate on lighter limestone soils. These manors (Great Easton, Cottingham, Tinwell) kept the smaller plough teams of six oxen. The remaining two, Thurlby and Fiskerton, were still recovering from the depredations of the Conquest, which might explain their failure to keep any horses.

Only five young horses were counted on the manors, apart from the young horses running in the wild herd. Their location on different manors displays an incipient specialization in horse breeding. Warmington, the one manor on the Northamptonshire manors with a young horse, later served as the horse-breeding center for that area of the estate in the fourteenth century. The wild horses and their offspring at Glinton on the fen-edge and the young horse nearby at Etton also anticipated the Abbey's use of its fen pastures as a breeding ground for horses in the fourteenth century.[19]

The horse husbandry of the Abbey is most striking for its comparative underdevelopment.[20] In 1125 the Abbey possessed one horse (26 : 462) for every eighteen demesne oxen (including the categories: auri, pulli, herciator) compared to one horse for every 1.78 oxen in the fourteenth century.[21] This remarkable expansion of horse husbandry took place within a framework already in place in the twelfth century. The fen pastures served as the locus for horse breeding. Only one manor outside the orbit of the home manors, Warmington, bred horses for manors further afield. The market also played a role in the Abbey's recruitment of carriage horses in the fourteenth century. A revolution in horse husbandry on the estate occurred after the 1125 survey.

Pigs

With its generous endowment of Domesday woodland (13,880 acres), Peterborough Abbey had the capacity to herd the 8,000 pigs required to produce the great amounts of lard required by the Ramsey food farm. The statistics for a demesne herd numbering 773 pigs recorded in 1125 show, however, that the Abbey was a modest pig-keeper. The strategy of managing woodland resources extensively by collecting pannage already conflicted with the more intensive management of coppiced woodland practiced on the estate by the early twelfth century.

The distribution of pigs on the estate bore little relation to the Abbey's woodland resources in the early twelfth century.[22] The Abbey already managed its pig herd intensively through sty management rather than extensively in a pannage system. Swineherds tended the pigs at the manors of Glinton, Kettering, and Castor. The Abbey also employed a swineherd, presumably for its own piggery, within its precincts. The surveyors claimed that the swineherd at Castor tended both pigs and sheep, but they recorded no demesne sheep there. By the fourteenth century the Abbey altered the scale of its pig husbandry by doubling the size of its demesne herd.

Sheep

The scale and geography of sheepherding on the estate in the early twelfth century differed radically from management in the late medieval period. Of the twenty-seven manors with demesne animals in 1125 only sixteen kept sheep flocks. In the twelfth century the Abbey herded no sheep on the fen-edge where during the fourteenth century they would be concentrated in large numbers.[23] In 1125 the Abbey herded its flock on higher-lying manors of Castor, Etton, and Pilsgate located in the central Soke. The Abbey had not yet turned its attention to developing its fen pasture on the scale that would support the local transhumance typical of its later more intensive sheep husbandry.

The surveyors recorded the greatest concentration of demesne sheep on the western Northamptonshire manors—a pattern that persisted at the height of sheep farming in the fourteenth century. The manor of Etton alone supported a breeding population composed of *arietes* (rams), *oves* (sheep), and *agni* (lambs). Shepherds watched the largest sheep herds at Kettering (300 sheep), Etton (280 sheep), and Pilsgate (180 sheep).

All the other entries in the survey simply describe the sheep as *oves* and do not enumerate milking ewes (*oves cum lacte* or *oves lactantes*). A contemporary survey of the English estates of the Abbey of Holy Trinity, Caen, does enumerate milking ewes, and they made up just under fifty percent of the flock (1,010/2,144 sheep).[24] If Peterborough Abbey milked a proportionate number of its own sheep, then its dairy could have produced at levels commensurate with those of the four-teenth century, when dairy cows provided the Abbey's main source of dairy products.

Management of the twelfth-century sheep flock differs most from early fourteenth-century sheep husbandry in its lack of specialization. It is likely that the Abbey relied on its sheep flock more for dairy products than for wool in the early twelfth century. By the fourteenth century the demesne flock chiefly produced wool. By integrating fen pastures into the pastoral cycle of sheepherding over the thirteenth century, the Abbey was able to increase its flock size. Increasingly, the Abbey rationalized flock management so as to satisfy different re-quirements of its wethers, ewes, yearlings, and lambs. Such coordina-tion of resources with different subgroups of the flocks represents the technological accomplishment of demesne wool production in the high-farming era.

Goats

Goats figured more prominently on the estate in the early twelfth century than they would two centuries later.[25] The surveyors ex-pected one hundred goats to be stocked at Cottingham, the manor on the edge of Rockingham Forest, where they also expected the largest Abbey pig herd. The association of goats with pigs at Cottingham and

Walton suggests some scrubby woodland there. Goats and pigs can thrive on scrub. At Kettering, a manor on the perimeter of Rockingham Forest, the peasants had to pay a render of one penny for their billy goats and a half penny for their nanny goats. The Abbey's goat herd still grazed at Cottingham in the fourteenth century, and the Abbey milked the nanny goats to prepare goat cheese.

The survey teaches a compelling lesson about the organization of the livestock economy on the estate in the early twelfth century. The Abbey produced to consume in the early twelfth century. Its consumption needs in the arable sector determined the size of its ox herd. Cows bred to reproduce the oxen. The Abbey did not rely heavily on horses to supplement draft power on the estate. The contribution of the Abbey's sheep flock to either dairy or wool production was modest too in the twelfth century. The annual harvest of wool would have been just enough to clothe the sixty monks with new garments.[26] The Abbey also managed pigs for consumption. Its woodland was already too valuable to be used simply as a source of pannage. The higher expectations for dairy production in the early twelfth century, based on estimates from food-rent schedules, suggest several economic interpretations. The pastoral economy at large, both demesne and peasant sectors, may have been more dairy-oriented in the earlier period.

THE SCALE OF OTHER FORMS OF PASTORAL CONSUMPTION

The Abbey did not restrict itself to consuming only the fruits of its own demesne economy. It tapped into the peasant economy by collecting renders in pastoral and cereal goods. The peasants on the estate owed the Abbey a combination of customary food renders, wood dues, and a heavy feast-day rent for the celebration of Saint Peter's Day.[27] The Abbey had commuted some of the peasant renders for cash by 1125. Table 9 lists renders it still collected in kind. The sums indicate that the Abbey collected a goodly amount of food and craft surplus from its peasants.

Peasant renders, like the monthly food rent already observed, emphasized processed foods and materials. Peasants baked grain into loaves and wove wool and hemp into cloth.[28] They prepared *disci*, either some food render or pottery vessels; the meaning is uncertain.

Table 9. Peasant Renders Listed in the Survey of 1125

Render	St. Peter's Day	Customary wood dues	
rams	59		
wethers	5		
sheep	6		
cows	5		
chickens	179	670	129
other birds		16 ducks, 11 geese	
dishes	115		
eggs	760	4,545	660
bread	2,700	91	107
oats (skeps)		73 + 3 bu.	108
salt		27 modii	
cloth (ulnae)	65 wool, 18 linen		

Source: *Chronicon Petroburgense.*

In any case the peasant food rents, in particular the feast-day rent, looked back to a world of consumption in which many households cooked, collected, and processed for their lords.

CONCLUSION

A study of the scale of production required to meet the expectations of annual consumption on a twelfth-century monastic estate has yielded important insights. The manors of Peterborough Abbey yielded a cash return 50 percent in excess of annual consumption requirements calculated from the monthly food-rent schedule of its neighbor at Ramsey. Even with such a surplus the scale of cereal and pastoral husbandry on the estate was modest. First and foremost, the Abbey appeared as a consumer and not a producer in the early twelfth century. The Abbey also relied heavily on the peasant sector, the small-scale producers, for its sustenance and surplus.

The Abbey began to shift this framework of lordship over the twelfth century as it developed a fierce appetite for cash. To acquire the denarii produced by the king and his moneyers the Abbey found that it had to produce on an ever-expanding scale, one that outstripped its long-standing methods of producing to consume. By the end of the twelfth century the Abbey turned to direct management of the estate to control better the links between production and markets. The markets linked the Abbey into a new world, which Braudel has called "the medieval world economy"; the link transformed the character of medieval agricultural production in England.[29]

3
FROM CONSUMPTION TO PRODUCTION: PETERBOROUGH ABBEY IN THE THIRTEENTH CENTURY

INDEBTEDNESS AND ESTATE MANAGEMENT

The monastic community of Peterborough Abbey produced to consume in the early twelfth century. An analysis of its move toward
large-scale production and direct management must account for
changes in consumption. A growing demand for money combined
with indebtedness and inflation to transform money as a medium of
consumption and production in medieval society over the twelfth
century.[1] The transformation of money in the twelfth century is more
easily grasped at the regional level first. Its impact on one agrarian
estate, Peterborough Abbey, can then be considered.

English kings began to search for new sources of money over the
twelfth century as traditional revenues, such as county farms, settled
inertly at their customary limits. The fiscal valuation of military
services based on the fee, the inauguration of tallages levied on
English towns, the implemention of high fees for settlements and writs
in the king's court, and the shift of the taxation base away from land
to movable wealth, all served to drain money from town and country
into the king's coffer at a quickening tempo.[2] The king in turn
dissipated this revenue on war.[3] Paying mercenary troops, erecting
and maintaining castles, settling alliances with money pacts, and
supporting a growing bureaucracy, all increased the costs of administrative kingship in England over the twelfth century.

As the demands of English feudal government on its lords and
peasants mounted, European trading networks underwent depression and realignment.[4] Silver grew scarcer for coinage and trade wars

flourished.[5] To satisfy the new levels of demand for money in the world economy, credit and finance developed at a European scale over the twelfth century. On the basis of fragmentary early evidence it is not possible to measure the scale of interregional or international indebtedness; it is possible, however, to examine qualitatively the early techniques used by merchants to indebt agrarian lords. Such techniques created a new set of economic relations between creditor and debtor in the twelfth century and impinged on agricultural production in England.

By the mid-twelfth century, English agrarian lords were contracting debts by taking advance payment from merchants for crops and animal products, especially wool.[6] Most impressive were the activities of the Flemish financier, William Cade, who advanced them money and then collected in kind. The economic relations created by such contracts are crucial to understanding agricultural development in England in the twelfth century. First, such loans, really instruments of trade, drew the agrarian producer into vertical links with financiers who monopolized the exchange of agricultural products from production points to the distribution points of the industrializing sectors they represented.[7] If English lords spent the cash advances before their creditors collected in kind, they were induced to commit future crops to the same merchant. The relation produced a structure of indebtedness whereby creditors pushed agrarian producers further into cash-cropping.

English agrarian lords grew structurally indebted over the late twelfth and early thirteenth centuries.[8] They increased the scale of their production to compensate for the costs of their borrowed money; agrarian loans were more costly than commercial loans.[9] Increased scale of production also ensured the increased flow of borrowed money. Structural indebtedness locked the English agrarian sector into cash-cropping grain and wool for the expanding industrial sector of Flanders. As a response to this structural change, English agrarian lords moved abruptly toward direct management of their estates.[10] The older agrarian arrangements of farming out estates and collecting food or its cash equivalent were unsuited to new forms of agrarian indebtedness and its demands for large-scale production.

The Abbey of Peterborough was vulnerable to such economic transformations. Its monks grew familiar with debt over the twelfth century. The chroniclers of the Abbey first comment on debts left by

abbots upon the death of Martin of Bec (1132–1154). His successor,
William of Waterville (1155–1175), "settled all the debts of Abbot
Martin to the amount of three hundred silver marks (£200) except
the sixty marks (£40) of interest which by the Abbot's effort our lord
the king ordered to be pardoned."[11] The interest rate represented
20 percent of the principal. The actual interest rate for the loan
depended on the time involved, which we do not know.

William left his own debts of more than 1,500 marks.[12] Locally, the
same William advanced money. He kept lands of a certain Ives of
Gunthorpe until "the Abbacy should receive therefrom sixty marks"
a good example of a vif-gage.[13] During his abbacy William also faced
the growing fiscal demands of the Crown. The continuous series of
Pipe Rolls, preserved from 1159, furnish information on the royal
charges on the Abbey and the Abbey's payments on these charges.[14]
In figure 6 the annual fiscal renders demanded of Peterborough
Abbey by the Crown are plotted along with the Abbey's annual
payment on those demands. Over the period 1159–1218 (for which
edited Pipe Rolls are available) the royal levy on the Abbey increased. The Abbey did not meet these demands and emerged as a
chronic debtor to the Crown. The king did not regard benignly the
failure of the Abbey to pay. Exercising his feudal prerogative, the
king seized the Abbey upon the death of its Abbot in 1177 and again
in 1210 and used the seizure as an occasion to funnel the Abbey's
income into the royal treasury. In 1177, for instance, the king seized
23 percent of the Abbey's annual income from the estate and did not
reduce the debt of the Abbey accordingly.

The Pipe Rolls also reveal that the Abbey owed money to Aaron of
Lincoln, a leading Jewish financier in twelfth-century England.[15]
Upon his death in 1191, the king confiscated the Abbey's debts to
Aaron and charged the Abbey one hundred pounds for settling them.
The total sum of the Abbey's debts to Aaron is not known. The
discounted debt of one hundred pounds ranked the Abbey fifth
among twenty-eight Northamptonshire debtors whose debts to
Aaron ranged from twenty shillings to 493.5 pounds. Even deeper
debts lay in the Abbey's future. In the abbacy of Robert of Sutton
(1262–1274), Peterborough owed £4,324 18s. 5d., almost twice the
debt of Canterbury Cathedral Priory in 1254, when their debt stood
at £2,168.[16]

The Abbey had harvested money as a chief crop of its estate in the

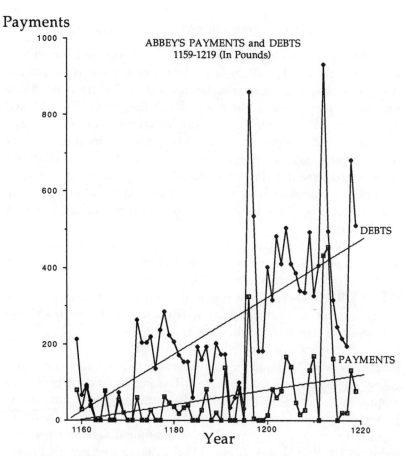

Fig. 6. The Abbey's payments and debts to the royal treasury as recorded in the Pipe Rolls, 1159–1219.

early twelfth century. By the end of the century the Abbey was a sharecropper of money. The king deflected a growing share of the crop to his treasury, and a good part of the crop was burdened by the surcharge of debt. The purchasing power of English money also changed over the later twelfth century.[17] By 1200 the Abbot could buy 30 percent less with the money returns from the estate. The Abbey faced a choice between continuing to consume cash returns from its estate as a sharecropper and undertaking the direct production of grain and animal products. Along with other English agrarian lords, the Abbey chose the latter course.

REORGANIZATION OF ESTATE MANAGEMENT

The Peterborough evidence for reorganizing agrarian lordship in response to the fiscal problems of the late twelfth and early thirteenth century is meager. It consists of the chronicle of Robert of Swaffham and the vacancy entries in the Pipe Rolls for the years 1176, 1210, and 1211.[18] The Abbey still farmed out its manors over these years; nevertheless, the fragmentary sources do indicate a marked intensity in developing agrarian resources on the estate.[19] Before taking over direct management of the estate, the Abbey experimented with agricultural innovations pioneered by the Cistercians and attempted to augment its production in the interstices of the manorial framework of the estate.

The Abbey's adaptation of some Cistercian innovations can be pieced together from the chronicle of Robert of Swaffham, who took up the narrative history of the Abbey with the abbacy of Benedict (1177–1193). Robert, who wrote in the mid-thirteenth century, had a keen interest in the managerial activities of Peterborough's abbots and reported regularly on their agrarian efforts.

Swaffham recounts that Abbot Benedict (1177–1193), in obvious imitation of the Cistercians, set up the grange of Novum Locum (later called La Biggin) on the border of Rockingham Forest in Northamptonshire.[20] Benedict had pieced the grange together from over six hundred acres of assarted land and managed it, as the Cistercians managed their own, "independent of communal agriculture and of servile labor."[21] Abbot Andreus (1194–1199) shared Benedict's predilection for Cisterican technology; early references to local windmills appear during his reign.[22]

Peterborough Abbey also participated in the rush to acquire houses and storage space in the towns, a policy which Cistercians vigorously pursued.[23] For over 250 marks, Abbot Acharius (1200–1210) purchased a house in London.[24] At that price, the house was undoubtedly stone-built and its undercroft could serve as a storage space for wine and other goods which the Abbey bought and sold in London.

The Abbots of Peterborough followed the Cistercians too in developing the storage capacity of their manorial properties. First notice of granaries (*horea*) appear in the chronicler's treatment of the abbacy of Robert of Lyndsey (1214–1222), who erected granaries at Novum

Locum, Oundle, Thorpe, and Boroughbury itself.[25] The Peterborough documents do not mention if the granaries were stone-built. Given its attentiveness to Cistercian innovations, the Abbey would have been acquainted with the great Cistercian masonry barns built on their granges over the early thirteenth century.[26]

The chronicle sources hint at several steps taken by the Abbey to create an economy of scale on their estate. The obituary of Abbot Walter (1233–1245) shows the measure of such an enterprise: "He left behind an abbey that had all things in good order, namely in the stocking of horses, oxen, cows, sheep, and all livestock in the greatest number, and in many places he left behind grain for three years."[27]

The vacancy accounts of 1176, 1210, and 1211 entered on the Pipe Rolls offer an opportunity to estimate the change of scale in the Abbey's agrarian enterprise. Production estimates calculated from the 1125 Survey and the vacancy accounts are set out in table 10.[28] The returns for 1176 suggest some agricultural stagnation on the estate at the opening of the last quarter of the twelfth century, marking a possible hiatus as feudal demands and indebtedness weighed on traditional methods of consumption.

The figures for 1211 dramatically contrast with those of 1176. Agricultural enterprise on the estate crossed a threshold in the first decade of the thirteenth century. The estimated area of demesne devoted to cereal agriculture and the income from grain sales more than doubled. The bill for necessary expenses, a category that included wage stipends for servants and the cost of upkeep for ploughs and other agricultural tools and buildings, mounted for the Abbey. Both grain sales and expenses increased faster than the rate of inflation at the end of the century.

The purchases of ploughs and livestock in the vacancy accounts also suggest a radical leap forward in scale. In 1176 the vacancy managers purchased four horses for the mill. Between the Feast of the Annunciation (25 March) and Michaelmas (29 September) 1210, the managers bought three horses, seven oxen, and sixteen ploughs. They bought an additional sixteen oxen and two plough horses in 1211. The Abbey increased its sheep flock by three-fifths over the twelfth century. Its sheep herds would double again by the end of the thirteenth century.

Demesne agriculture also crossed a threshold in the balance of its cereal and pastoral sectors. In the vacancy account of 1176 the Abbey

Table 10. Comparative Statistics for the Estate Economy: Twelfth
and Early Thirteenth Century

Redditus Assisus Rents	*s.*			
1125	5,693.33			
1176–77	5,626.83			
1210–11	6,070.00			

Cereal Sales	*Total Sales* *s.*	*Price/q*	*Est. Acreage*[a] 2 course	3 course
1125			1,755	1,317
1176–77	245	1 *s.* 2½ *d.*	694	521
1210–11	3,744.50	3 *s.* 7 *d.*	3,586	2,690

Wool Sales	*s.*	*Sheep flock*[b]	
1125		1,701	
1176	192.33	1,421 est.	
1211 + cheese	240.00	2,297 est.	
hides	60.67		

Necessary *Expenses*	*s.*
1176–77	910.42
1210–11	1,043.83

Purchases of *Ploughs Livestock*	*s.*
1209–10[c]	100.10
1210–11	123.50

Pasture Sales	*s.*
1176	151.58
1210–1211	824.83

Table 10 (continued)
Source: Chronicon Petroburgense; Pipe Rolls, 26 Henry III, 12 John, 13 John.

[a] Acreage for 1125 estimated as discussed in appendix 2. Acreage for 1176 and 1210–11 estimated by dividing grain sales by wheat prices appearing in David L. Farmer, "Some Price Fluctuations in Angevin England," Economic History Review, 2d ser., 9 (1956–57): 34–43 and J. Z. Titow, English Rural Society, 1200–1350 (London, 1969). The quantity of wheat was then transposed into acreage according to the calculations set out in appendix 2 under the assumption that sales represented 50 percent (at minimum) of yield.

[b] Flock size estimated by dividing wool sales by annual mean price of 14 pounds of wool taken from T. H. Lloyd, The Movement of Wool Prices in Medieval England, (Cambridge, 1973) and multiplying by average fleece weight of 1.25 pounds.

[c] The figure includes sales of cheese and hides.

made more money from its pastoral sector with the sales of wool, hay, and herbage (343.9s.) than from the sale of grain (245s.). In 1211 the pastoral sector contributed only one-third of the combined cereal and pastoral income. A shift in the balance of pastoral and arable occurred in spite of a great increase in the sale of hay and pasture on the estate. The increase in sales of herbage undoubtedly reflected the activities of Abbot Acharius (1200–1210) in developing the fen pastures east of the Abbey. He drew up boundaries in the peat fen between Peterborough and neighboring Crowland Abbey and paid King John one hundred marks (£66.6) "pro habenda pastura,"[29]

Agricultural production on the estate transformed in scale over the century separating the 1125 survey and the vacancy account of 1211. Such dramatic shift in the allocation of resources on the estate could not help but severely affect the peasant sector of agricultural production.[30] Prior to the late twelfth century the scale of demesne agriculture on any one of its manors did not depart radically from that of the peasant sector. Now the Abbey engaged in agrarian production in plantation-owner style. A sense of the consequences of the new demesne agriculture for the peasantry can be gained by comparing a survey of demesne manors in the Soke of Peterborough and Lincolnshire drawn up by the Abbey in 1231 with the 1125 survey.[31]

The peasant sector of the English agrarian economy was not immune to the structure of agrarian indebtedness that locked itself into place by the thirteenth century. The social and economic value of land changed in the peasant household as a peasant land-market developed in England by the middle decades of the thirteenth century.[32] The courts developed the common law of villeinage as they sought to define the legal status of the peasantry over the same period.

Peasants on the Lincolnshire manors of the Peterborough Abbey estate challenged their status in an early villeinage plea in 1169–70.[33] The Abbey's peasants had cause for concern about their status, since the Abbot managed to increase rents and in many cases services of its unfree tenants over the twelfth century.

The demographic and economic fortunes of the Abbey's peasants changed between the surveys of 1125 and 1231. The survey of 1231 itself may be taken as evidence of the Abbot's desire to define more closely the holdings of his peasants.[34] Figures for the peasant population on the home manors of the Abbey in 1125 and 1231, along with the rents collected, are set out in table 11. The number of virgaters on the home manors increased 32 percent (101/133) over the century. At the same time the number of half-virgaters decreased by 44 percent (58/32). The pattern of decline in the population of half-virgaters and the increase in the number of full-virgaters repeats itself on every home manor with the exception of Glinton, which experienced the greatest overall growth of all the home manors.

On the manor of Eye the thirteen half-virgaters of 1125 had disappeared. In their place in 1231 stood fifteen full-virgaters, owing a full complement of rents and services. The Abbey had upgraded the labor services of its peasants at Eye with the upgrading of their status. In 1125 half-virgaters at Eye were subject to no week work. They each ploughed two acres and further ploughed three times a year. In 1231 the full-virgaters at Eye performed a full complement of labor services. They owed three days of work a week to the Abbey along with carrying, mowing, and boon services. The Abbey also managed to increase their ploughing services. Eye virgaters were to plough three acres in 1231 and owed ploughing services on an additional five occasions. In 1125 the peasants at Eye were developing a frontier manor of the Abbey on an island in the peat fen. By 1231 the manor had fully matured and the Abbey extracted a full complement of labor services from its peasants.

The sharpest increase in the peasant population occurred among the smaller landholders. The number of tofters increased by 209 percent (34/105). The tofters held their tofts with either crofts or one to two acres of land attached to the toft. They provided a growing pool of labor service for the peak periods of seigneurial demand during haymaking and harvesting. The typical burden of labor service for the Abbey's tofters involved two days of summer work, usually mowing and lifting hay, and two days of autumn work.

Table 11. Peasants and Their Rents on the Home Manors of
Peterborough Abbey: Surveys of 1125 and 1231

Home Manor	a	b	c	d	e	f	g
Boroughbury[a]							
1125	32	12	15	—	—	59	45
1231	35	9	20	10	—	74	84.5
Longthorpe							
1125	12	6	6	—	4	28	17
1231	17	3	10	6	6	42	57.7
Eye							
1125	—	13	—	—	1	14	16
1231	15	—	14	—	—	29	40.9
Castor & Ailsworth							
1125	25	4	6	—	14	49	26.1
1231	27	2, 4	13	3	—	49	51.8
Glinton							
1125	13	8	6	—	26	53	23.7
1231[b]	14	12	32	6	17	81	130.5
Werrington							
1125	11	8	1	—	17	37	24
1231	12	4	16	—	24	56	59.4
Walton							
1125	8	7	—	—	4	19	20.9
1231	13	2	—	4		19	55.3
Total							
1125	101	58	34	—	66	259	172.7
1231	133	32, 4	105	29	47	350	480.1

Sources: *Chronicon Petroburgense*; Peterborough Black Book (see n. 31 to this chapter).
I am grateful to Edmund King for sharing his transcript of the survey.
Key to column headings: a = virgaters; b = half-virgaters; c = tofters; d = plotholders; e = others; f = total tenants; g = total rents.
  [a] The burgesses and serjeants of Peterborough are excluded from the 1125 figures.
  [b] Figures excluded peasants at Northborough.

A new type of smallholder, plotholders, appeared in the 1231 survey. Typical of the plotholder was Agnes Pudding of Boroughbury manor, who held two acres of land from the Abbot for the annual rate of two pennies. Presumably these peasants were assarters and the source of the Abbey's casual hired labor in the great period of demesne expansion in the early thirteenth century.

A comparison of the two surveys shows that the number of peasants holding virgates on the home manors of the Peterborough Abbey estate increased slightly over the twelfth century while half-virgaters declined. Assarting activities undertaken by peasants on the home manors could account for the growth of the number of customary virgate holdings. More puzzling is the sharper decline of the "middling peasants," those holding half-virgates. Half-virgaters did not replace themselves over the century, nor did assarting tofters advance into this category. The patterns suggest that the Abbey manipulated the status of its customary tenures over the twelfth century by labeling half-virgaters as virgaters in order to increase the collection of rents and services.[35] The Abbey encouraged tofters to settle on its home manors, since it could collect labor services and rents from them. The appearance of small plotholders was undoubtedly related to the Abbey's increasing demand for casual hired labor. The 14 percent increase in its necessary expenditures observed in the vacancy accounts (see table 10), which included wages to hired labor, is easily matched by contribution of 32 percent made by the plotholders to the increase in customary tenants over the century.

The Abbey succeeded in raising its rents with such demographic strategies. The surveyed population of customary tenants on the home manors increased by 31 percent over the century. At the same time the Abbey increased its customary rent roll by 150 percent (172.6s./430.6s.). The town of Peterborough also served as a growing source of rent for the Abbey over the twelfth century. In 1125, seventy-two townsmen paid the Abbey 71s. 2d. in rents. In 1231 an unspecified number of Peterborough burgesses paid five times this amount (360s.).[36]

Not only did the Abbey extract more rent and labor, it also transferred pastoral and arable resources away from the peasant sector to the demesne.[37] By 1231 the Abbey had almost quadrupled the scale of its agricultural production.[38] It would double this scale again by the turn of the fourteenth century. The account rolls preserved for the estate in the early fourteenth century enable the historian to study in detail the organization of this economy of scale.

THE PROBLEMS OF SEIGNEURIAL HIGH FARMING AND PASTORAL HUSBANDRY

Economic historians have traditionally divided English seigneurial farming into four phases: (1) a pre-twelfth-century period of direct demesne farming; (2) the dissolution of demesne farming over the twelfth century; (3) seigneurial "high farming" between 1200 and 1325 marked by rationalized, profit-conscious direct management of the demesne; (4) a period of demesne leasing by rentier landlords over the later fourteenth and fifteenth centuries.[39] Historians have associated economies of scale with direct management of demesne farming.

So far this study has argued that there was no primal phase of large-scale demesne production prior to the twelfth century.[40] English agrarian lords farmed out the manors of their estates and consumed cash and food collected from their farmers. Such arrangements can be documented for the estate of Peterborough Abbey as early as the eighth century. Factors more complicated than gradual population growth and inflation transformed the scale and management of seigneurial farming at the end of the twelfth century. The structural indebtedness of English lords pushed them into direct management of agrarian production on a scale hitherto unknown.

Historians have regarded the thirteenth century as the period of high farming for English agrarian lords.[41] The feats of scale and the growth of agrarian bureacracry to monitor production have impressed historians and undoubtedly inspired the term *high farming*. High farming has invoked praise and criticism. The chief critique of high farming is consistent with the prevailing demographic model of agrarian development.[42] According to the model, cereal agriculture in both the demesne and peasant sectors expanded over the thirteenth century as population grew. Such expansion reduced available pastoral resources; thus the pastoral sector contracted. Fewer livestock produced less manure for the upkeep of soil fertility. The vicious cycle of expansion in the cereal sector and contraction of the pastoral sector resulted in the great famine of the second decade of the fourteenth century.

No studies of seigneurial pastoral husbandry exist to verify such a model of high farming. The chapters that follow examine in detail how one high-farming estate, Peterborough Abbey, organized its pastoral sector in the first decade of the fourteenth century, the zenith of the high-farming era. The study utilizes the detailed information recorded in the livestock sections of manorial account rolls to establish the demographic characteristics of the Abbey's herds and its production and consumption of secondary products including traction, dairy products, hides, wool, and meat.[43] A general introduction to the herds of the Abbey will establish a context for the detailed discussion of the management of each domesticate.

At the turn of the fourteenth century the estate of Peterborough Abbey herded 1,293 cattle, 4,718 sheep, 269 horses, and 1,394 pigs and tended 1,160 hens, 992 chicks, 2,582 doves, 729 geese, 128 capons, and 65 ducks. Since the survey of the estate in the early twelfth century, the cattle and pig herds had doubled their numbers and the number of horses and sheep had tripled. The Abbey farmed 4,906 acres (1,986 ha) in 1300–01, over four times the area estimated in 1125. Peterborough's acreage compares with an estimated 8,373 acres under cultivation by Canterbury Cathedral Priory, 4,835 acres by Westminster Abbey, and 6,969 acres by the Bishop of Winchester in the early fourteenth century.[44] Gross livestock numbers had increased on the estate, but so too had the area of demesne arable expanded. The livestock ratios devised by Postan and Titow provide a means of comparing the changing proportions of livestock to cereal acreages.[45]

The livestock ratios calculated for the estate of Peterborough Abbey along with comparative figures available from the estate of the Bishop of Winchester and seigneurial demesnes in Norfolk are set out in tables 12 and 13. Fluctuations in the size of seigneurial sheep flocks drive the thirteenth-century ratios up and down. The low animal ratios for eastern Norfolk reflect the relative unimportance of sheep raising in that fertile corn-growing area without access to extensive rough pasture.[46] The ratios for horses and cattle remain static. Early modern historians have devised methods of calculating livestock ratios that are less susceptible to fluctuations in size of sheep herds. Tables 12 and 13 list livestock ratios calculated according to the latter method.

The livestock ratios for Peterborough Abbey and the Bishop of Winchester were comparable. For both the Abbey, with access to fen

Table 12. Comparative Livestock Ratios[a] (livestock per 100 acres under seed)

	a	b	c	d	e	f
Peterborough Abbey						
1125	57	1.5	58.5	30.3	88.8	1,317
1300–01	26.2	5.4	31.8	24.0	55.8	4,906
1307–08	29.6	6.3	35.9	39.9	75.9	5,228
1309–10	29.7	6.8	36.6	44.2	80.8	4,985
Mean	28.5	6.1	34.8	36.0	70.8	5,039
Winchester						
1209–1270			21.8	39.5	61.5	12,732
1271–1299			23.3	38.0	61.3	11,159
1300–1324			26.5	49.1	75.7	9,613
1325–1349			23.2	51.8	75.0	8,024
Eastern Norfolk						
1255–1350					34.8	
Westminster Abbey						
1300–24					31.2	

Key to column headings: a = livestock ratio for cattle; b = livestock ratio for horses; c = livestock ratio for cattle and horses; d = livestock ratio for sheep; e = composite livestock ratio for cattle, horses, and sheep; f = acreages involved.

[a] Livestock ratios calculated according to J. Z. Titow, *Winchester Yields* (Cambridge, 1972), appendix L, where cattle and horses, regardless of age, are counted as one unit, and sheep, regardless of age, are counted as a unit of 0.25, and pigs are not counted at all. For Peterborough Abbey the livestock ratios are based on estate totals for Peterborough Abbey. The Winchester figures are based on totals calculated from *Winchester Yields*, appendix L. The grand animal ratio for demesnes in eastern Norfolk is taken from Bruce M. S. Campbell, "Agricultural Progress in Medieval England: Some Evidence from Eastern Norfolk," *Economic History Review*, 2d ser., 36 (1983), table I. Westminster ratio calculated as the mean of twelve manors over the period 1300–1324 as listed in Table III.c in David L. Farmer, "Grain Yields on Westminster Abbey Manors, 1271–1410," *Canadian Journal of History* 18 (1983). Figures for 1125 taken from chapter 3. *Animalia otiosa* are included among cattle. Wild horses (*equi indomiti*) are excluded from the equids for 1125.

Table 13. Livestock Ratios for Peterborough Abbey Calculated according to Methods Used by Early Modernists[a]

	a	b	c	d	e	f
Peterborough Abbey						
1300–01	12.6	9.4	3.2	9.0	2.8	37.0
1307–08	14.5	14.5	4.6	17.1	3.6	54.4
1309–10	14.4	14.2	5.1	17.6	3.6	54.8

Key to column headings: a = livestock ratios for bulls, oxen, and bovecti and iuvencae; b = livestock ratios for cows, boviculi, geniculae, annales, vitulae; c = livestock ratios for horses; d = livestock ratios for sheep; e = livestock ratios for pigs; f = composite livestock ratio.

[a] Livestock ratios per 100 acres under seed calculated according to livestock units used by J. A. Yelling, *Common Field and Enclosure in England, 1450–1850* (London, 1977), 159, with the modification that bovecti and iuvencae were grouped with bulls and oxen, since medieval accountants do not regularly distinguish males (steers) from females (heifers) in this category; likewise, immature cattle—boviculi (bullocks) and geniculae (younger heifers)—are grouped with cows, yearlings, and calves. The acreage used in the these calculations appears in column f of table 12.

pasture, and the Bishop, who controlled stretches of downland pasture, sheepherding played an important part in their pastoral economies. The high animal ratios reflect the importance of sheep.

The figures in tables 12 and 13 also point to important shifts in Peterborough's pastoral economy. The animal ratio was higher in the twelfth century, suggesting that the estate economy was more pastoral in its emphasis. Relative to the cereal acreage, the Abbey herded more oxen and horses and fewer sheep than it did in the fourteenth century.

The proportionately higher number of oxen on the twelfth-century estate makes sense, since oxen served the dual purpose of ploughing and haulage. Not until the latter twelfth and the thirteenth century did lords rely extensively on horses for vehicle transport. The shift in economic emphasis among the different domestic animals on the estate over the two centuries appears more clearly when the ratios of different animals to oxen are compared over time. These ratios are set out in table 14. Relative to the number of oxen, the number of cows, horses, and sheep increased over 100 percent in the two centuries. The growth of these herds reflects the diversification and

Table 14. Ratio of Cows, Horses, and Sheep to Oxen:
Peterborough Abbey

	a	b	c	d
1125 ᶜ	86.5	1:3.75	1:4.2	1:0.28
1300–01	26.2	1:1.45	1:1.36	1:0.07
1307–08	29.6	1:1.42	1:1.46	1:0.05
1309–10	29.7	1:1.44	1:1.30	1:0.05

Sources: Figures for 1125 compiled from the *Chronicon Petroburgense* and figures for the fourteenth century compiled from estate account rolls: Fitzwilliam Account Rolls, 2388, 233, 2389.
Key to column headings: a = ratio of cattle per 100 acres under seed; b = ratio of cows to oxen; c = ratio of horses to oxen; d = ratio of sheep to oxen.

growing commercialization of dairying, transport, and wool in the estate economy.[47]

The changing composition of livestock in the herding economy of the estate characterizes a pastoral sector of some dynamism and complexity and dispels any notion of linear relations between animal and cereal husbandry. The relations of the Abbey's cereal yields to livestock units and other inputs further underscore the diverse and multiple links between the cereal and pastoral sectors.

CEREAL PRODUCTION AND ANIMAL HUSBANDRY

In the first decade of the fourteenth century the Abbey sowed approximately five thousand acres with grain. Wheat and oats occupied half of the total acreage and the crops of barley, dredge (a mixture of oats and barley used in brewing), rye, and legume the rest. Summary statistics for the acreage sown on the estate and sowing rates appear in tables 15 and 16. Bruce Campbell has shown that seeding rates tended to reflect local practices.[48] Compared with recent findings for demesnes in eastern Norfolk, the Abbey tended to sow wheat and rye moderately, barley thinly. On half of its manors it sowed oats moderately and on the others heavily. Seedings rates for legumes varied most from place to place but tended to grow heavier through the decade.

Table 15. Summary Statistics for Cereal Acreage on the Estate of
Peterborough Abbey

	a	b	c	d	e	f
Acreage 1300–01						
mean	77.6	34.9	29.2	23.7	17.6	30.5
s.d.	45.1	26.7	20.0	26.9	11.1	15.9
c.v. as %	58	77	69	113	63	52
n	21	21	20	16	16	21
total	1,633	733	584	616	281	1,500
1307–08						
mean	72	38.5	31.4	30.5	21.3	62
s.d.	39.5	25.4	16.0	29.4	11.1	40.7
c.v. as %	55	66	52	96	52	66
n	22	22	17	14	21	22
total	1,583	847	534	428	447	1,363
1309–10						
mean	70.7	40.4	32.2	32.0	24.5	57.6
s.d.	41.0	23.5	17.4	25.6	19.0	37.4
c.v. as %	58	58	54	80	78	65
n	20	21	16	14	21	21
total	1,414	847	515	448	511	1,209

Source: Fitzwilliam Account Rolls, 2388, 233, 2389.

Key to column headings: a = wheat; b = barley; c = dredge; d = rye; e = legumes; f = oats.

Key to row headings: mean = mean acreage; s.d. = standard deviation; c.v. = coefficient of variation expressed as percentage; n = number of manors involved in calculation.

Cereal yields can be calculated from manorial accounts in two ways. With continuous series of account rolls the sowing of one year can be matched with the harvest recorded in the subsequent account. With discontinuous series, such as the Peterborough accounts, the historian must rely on the calculations of yields to seed scribbled by medieval auditors in the margins of grain accounts.[49]

Table 16. Summary Statistics for Seeding Rates on the Estate of Peterborough Abbey (bushels per acre)

1300–01						
mean	2.4	4.0	4.4	2.5	2.4	5.1
s.d.	0.37	0.09	0.6	0.1	0.4	0.7
c.v. as %	15	2	14	5	17	7
n	20	21	20	16	16	21
1307–08						
mean	2.5	3.9	4.6	2.5	2.6	5.5
s.d.	0.05	0.2	0.5	0.1	0.3	0.6
c.v. as %	2	5	13	1	11	1
n	21	23	15	14	20	22
1309–10						
mean	2.5	4.0	4.5	2.5	2.7	5.5
s.d.	0.01	0.02	0.55	0.18	0.46	0.53
c.v. as %	1	1	12	7	17	10
n	19	21	16	14	21	21

Key to column and row headings: as in table 15.

Auditors of Peterborough Abbey made such marginal notes in 1307–08 only, for the manors of Boroughbury, Eye, and Fiskerton. That year the Abbey experimented with increasing yields by extra manuring and weeding on the manors of Boroughbury and Eye. At Fiskerton it followed its normal policy of collecting labor services for manuring and weeding and added no special inputs. Apart from such special efforts taken to increase yields, the Abbey's special interest in 1307–08 might have come from the cumulative pressure of harvest failures of barley and oats in 1305 and of barley in 1306. The manors of the Winchester estate, mostly located in south-central England, experienced serious harvest failures for these cereals in those years.[50]

The Abbey's yields per seed and per acre appear in table 17 along with comparative data available from eastern Norfolk, Westminster, and Winchester demesnes and from the recommendations of the *Husbandry*, a thirteenth-century agricultural manual. The Abbey enjoyed yields at Boroughbury well above average. Its barley yield of 28.3 bushels per acre exceeded the demesne maximum for eastern

Table 17. Cereal Yields of 1307: Manors of Boroughbury, Eye, and Fiskerton

	Wheat	Barley	Yield per Seed Dredge	Rye	Oats	Peas
Husbandry	5	8	6	7	4	6
Boroughbury	6	7	4	—	—	6
Eye	5	—	—	7	—	—
Fiskerton	4	4	—	6	—	—
Westminster 1300–24	2.9	3.8	3.6	3.1	2.1	3.2
E. Norfolk pre-1350	4.6	3.0	—	3.6	2.6	2.7
Winchester 1306–07	4.0	3.2	—	—	2.2	—

	Wheat	Barley	Seeding Rates per Acre (bushels) Dredge	Rye	Oats	Peas
Husbandry	not stated for each type of grain					
Boroughbury	2.49	4.00	4.95	—	—	2.34
Eye	2.57	—	—	—	—	—
Fiskerton	2.50	4.00	—	2.49	—	—
Westminster 1300–24	—	—	—	—	—	—
E. Norfolk pre-1350	2.90	4.90	—	2.60	5.20	2.90
Winchester 1306–07	not available					

	Wheat	Barley	Yields per Acre (bushels) Dredge	Rye	Oats	Peas
Husbandry	not stated					
Boroughbury	15.78	28.32	20.70	—	—	14.80
Eye	12.85	—	—	—	—	—
Fiskerton	11.00	15.68	—	14.94	—	—
Westminster	not available					
E. Norfolk pre-1350	13.60	14.80	—	12.70	13.10	7.40
Winchester 1306–07	9.44	11.84	—	—	10.08	—

Sources: Dorothea Oschinsky, ed., *Walter of Henley and Other Treatises on Estate Management and Accounting* (Oxford, 1971), 418–419; for the Peterborough manors: Fitzwilliam Account Roll, 233; Westminster manors: Farmer, "Grain Yields on Westminster Abbey Manors, 1271–1410"; Norfolk manors: Bruce M. S. Campbell, "Arable Productivity in Medieval England," *Journal of Economic History* 43 (1983): 379–404; Winchester manors: calculated from Titow, *Winchester Yields*.

Norfolk and came close to the harvest maximum there of 29.5 bushels per acre. The Abbey worked hard for such high yields on its home manor of Boroughbury in 1307–08. First, the Abbey used 22 percent of the labor services rendered that year for harrowing, manuring, and weeding, inputs that helped to increase yields. The Abbey, however, regularly used such labor services as table 18 and figure 7 illustrate.[51] In 1307–08 the Abbey supplemented its regular labor inputs with extra manuring and weeding. It spent a considerable amount of money on collecting manure in the town (46s. 9½d.) and spreading it on the fields (6s. 6d.). It also spent an additional sum (33s. 8d.) on hired weeders. An index of the Abbey's investment in improving yields, based on converting labor services to their local cash value (5d.) with the Abbey's extra cash investment in manuring and weeding, shows the Abbey's effort to improve yields. In 1300–01 the Abbey invested 0.92d. an acre on improving Boroughbury yields. It increased investments by 192 percent in 1307–08 when it spent 2.69d. per acre on yields. In 1309–10 the investment fell to 1.53d. per acre.

The home manor of Boroughbury had livestock ratios much lower than the average for the estate (table 19) and closer to the low livestock ratio of 34.8 recorded for demesnes in eastern Norfolk prior to 1350. The strategies followed to achieve high yields at Boroughbury are reminiscent of those described by Bruce Campbell for eastern Norfolk, where expenditures on manure and weeding produced high yields.[52] In 1307–08 the Abbey certainly invested in high yields by recruiting and paying laborers to manure and weed and probably

Table 18. Labor Services: Manor of Boroughbury

	1300–01	1307–08	1309–10
Winter Works			
Total Owed	4,797	4,797	4,797
Acquitted	1,840	1,711	1,923
Sold	156	71	446
Summer Works			
Total Owed	2,090	2,090	2,090
Acquitted	924	788	893
Sold	0	0	0

Table 18 (*continued*)

	W	S	W	S	W	S
Field Preparation	122 3.4%	0	188 4.3%	0	106 2.9%	0
Weeding	0	110 3.1%	166 3.8%	0	0	0
Manuring	619 17.3%		617 14.2%		557 15.4%	
Reaping		528 14.8% 264 acres		400 9.2% 200 acres		365 10.0% 182.25 acres
Winnowing	117 3.2%		0		36 0.9%	
Mowing	0	332 9.3%	54 1.2%	678 15.7%	0	832 22.9%
Thatching, Turves	14 0.3%		40 0.9%		0	
Hedges, Dikes	130 3.6%		168 3.8%		81 2.2%	
Woodland	246 6.9%		149 3.5%		154 3.8%	
Streams	75 2.1%		152 3.5%		139 4.2%	
Sent to Abbey	925 25.9%	153 4.2%	1,438 33.3%	224 5.2%	1,305 36.0%	0
Stubble	33 0.9%					
Miscellaneous	116 3.2%	11 0.3%	43 0.9%		50 1.3%	
Total	3563[51]		4317		3625	

Source: Fitzwilliam Account Rolls, 2388, 233, 2389.
Key to column headings: W = winter; S = summer.

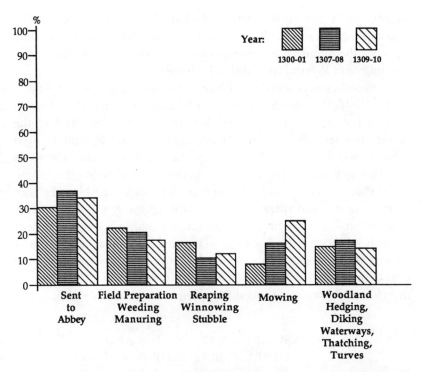

Fig. 7. The use of labor services collected on the manor of Borough-bury. The graph depicts what percentage of the total labor services collected the Abbey devoted to different agricultural activities. The use of labor services sent to the Abbey precincts itself is not specified.

Table 19. Boroughbury Livestock Ratios (per 100 cultivated acres)

	1300–01	*1307–08*	*1309–10*
Boroughbury	32.5	31.9	30.4
Estate	55.8	75.9	80.8

Source: Fitzwilliam Account Rolls, 2388, 233, 2389.

supervised labor services more closely on this manor just outside its precincts. Proper rotation of legumes could also have enhanced yields. Unfortunately, such rotations cannot be reconstructed from the discontinuous Peterborough series.[53] The Abbey planted only 7 percent of its demesne acres with legumes at Boroughbury, compared to an average of 14 percent for eastern Norfolk. The strategies pursued at Boroughbury to achieve high yields thus place the manor somewhere between the intensive practices of eastern Norfolk and extensive low-yielding ones Westminster and Winchester.

At the other manors where the accountants had also noted yield to seed in 1307–08—the fen manor of Eye and the manor of Fiskerton, located just outside Lincoln—yields were respectable. At Eye the Abbey invested 1.86*d.* per acre to improve yields in 1307–08. It hired labor to weed and to collect and spread manure in addition to its usual budget of labor services. At Fiskerton the Abbey relied solely on such labor services to cultivate its crops. Although the Abbey did hire workers to dig and spread marl at Irthlingborough in 1307–08, it entered no marginal notations about the manor's yields. It spent some money at Irthlingborough on digging and spreading marl and feeding the horses used in marling. Perhaps the Abbey marled some part of the sixty-five acres taken out of cultivation since 1300–01 and therefore did not show immediate interest in return on yields.

CONSUMPTION OF GRAINS AND
THE PASTORAL SECTOR

The Abbey used its grain to feed the monastic household, its *famuli* (employed agricultural staff), and some of its livestock, especially horses. Such strategies of consumption linked different grains in different ways to the pastoral sectors of the estate economy.

The Abbey planted between 4,906 and 5,228 acres of demesne and harvested between 62,980 and 81,190 bushels of cereals and legumes (table 20). Figure 8 illustrates the proportions of grains consumed by the Abbey, its famuli, and its livestock. In the year 1300–01 the Abbey consumed 44 percent of its total harvest, its livestock another 21 percent, and its manorial workers 10 percent. Of the amount of grain fed to livestock that year, almost two-thirds (62 percent) fattened livestock for slaughter and consumption by the household or fed the riding horses of its stables, animals that marked the Abbot's status as an agrarian lord. The Abbey used the remaining quarter of its total harvest for seed corn and sales. Together the grain eaten by the monastic household and the grain that fattened livestock produced a consumption rate for the household of 57 percent of the annual harvest in 1300–01. Historians have tended to ignore the

Table 20. Consumption, Production, and Exchange of Grain on the Peterborough Abbey Estate[a]

Bushels	CONSUMPTION	% of Yield			PRODUCTION	% of Yield			EXCHANGE	% of Yield		
		1300-01	1307-08	1309-10		1300-01	1307-08	1309-10		1300-01	1307-08	1309-10
WHEAT Yield	ABBEY	61	63	77	SEED	27	25	26	BUY	14	4	27
1300-01 12,760	ANIMALS	.04	0	2	WORKERS	11	17	15	SELL	22	8	6
1307-08 16,054		61	63	79		38	42	41		+8	+4	-21
1309-10 13,864												
OATS Yield	ABBEY	0	0	0	SEED	38	40	36	BUY	6	8	6
1300-01 19,256	horses	28	27	24	Other anim.	5	8	11	SELL	4	1	2
1307-08 23,080	(stable)	28	27	24	work horses	6	7	12		-2	-7	-4
1309-10 18,251					cart horses	15	23	25				
						59	78	84				
BARLEY Yield	ABBEY	79	66	53	SEED	22	18	23	BUY	14	5	18
1300-01 13,275	Animals	2	1	2	WORKERS	3	3	5	SELL	0	14	14
1307-08 21,028		81	67	55		25	21	28		-14	+9	-4
1309-10 15,968												
RYE Yield	ABBEY	0	0	0	SEED	20	18	22	BUY	0	2	2
1300-01 4,808					WORKERS	95	81	78	SELL	0	7	9
1307-08 5,954						115	99	100		0	+5	+7
1309-10 5,441												

Table 20 (*continued*)

DREDGE (Bushels; figures are % of Yield except yields)

DREDGE	1300–01	1307–08	1309–10
Yield (bushels)	9,463	9,316	7,132
CONSUMPTION (% of Yield)			
Abbey	87	70	58
Animals	2	2	5
	89	72	63
PRODUCTION (% of Yield)			
Seed	27	31	43
	27	31	43
EXCHANGE (% of Yield)			
Buy	0	3	0.05
Sell	1	0	3.0
	+1	−3	+3

LEGUMES (Bushels; figures are % of Yield except yields)

LEGUMES	1300–01	1307–08	1309–10
Yield (bushels)	3,418	6,509	4,950
CONSUMPTION (% of Yield)			
Abbey	0	0	0
Animals	25	52	32
	25	52	32
PRODUCTION (% of Yield)			
Seed	33	21	29
Workers	19	25	29
horses	0	2	0
	52	48	58
EXCHANGE (% of Yield)			
Buy	3	8	8
Sell	12	8	11
	+9	0	+3

Sources: Fitzwilliam Account Rolls, 2388, 233, 2389.

a Where percentage exceed 100 percent, the autumn yield had been supplemented by grain from previous harvest or by purchase.

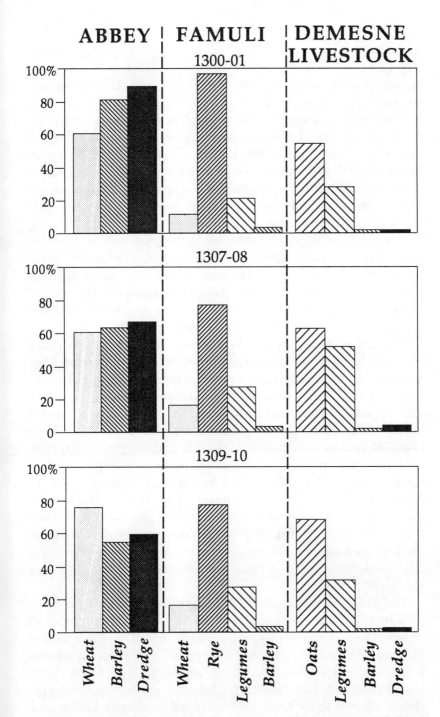

Fig. 8. Consumption of grain on the estate. The graphs depict what percentage of the different cereal grains were consumed by the household of the Abbey, by its famuli (employed agricultural staff), and by the demesne livestock.

inroads of such consumption on marketable yield. During the thirteenth century, Ramsey Abbey and the Bishopric of Worcester sold only 10 percent of its grain harvest. The demesnes and rectories of the prior and convent of Westminster provided by value 40 percent of their grain. Such figures, although crude, show variations in consumption strategies and also emphasize that often less than half of estate harvest made it to the market.[54] The consumption strategies call in question Postan's notion of large estates as "federated grain factories for the production of cash."

Studies of the Abbey's involvement in the grain market show that analysis of sales alone can mislead. The Abbey's purchases of wheat nearly offset its wheat sales. The Abbey followed a policy of selling wheat on its northern manors of Collingham, Fiskerton, Walcot, and Scotere, and purchasing it within its sphere of consumption, the home manors and the manors of Northamptonshire.

The Abbey grew oats as a fodder crop for its horses. Its riding horses ate between one-quarter and one-third of the oat harvest. Cart horses fed on the second highest ration of oats ranging from 15 to 25 percent of the crop. Workhorses received less oats, ranging between 6 and 12 percent of the annual harvest. The Abbey also fed modest portions of its oats to other animals, usually oxen and some young cattle selected by the Abbey for fattening and slaughter. Oats comprised one-third of the total harvest and occupied one-quarter of the sown demesne. Oats did not feed humans but horses used by the Abbey largely for riding and haulage. The Abbey's demands for status and speedy communication thus deflected many acres from human to animal nutrition. Such findings caution against interpreting expansion of acreage sown as a simple response to population pressure. Issues of speed and transport governed decisions about how much oats to plant.

The Abbey brewed its harvest of barley and dredge. To keep up with its household consumption of ale, it sowed one-quarter of its demesne with these malting grains, which yielded over one-third of the total grain harvest. The Abbey brewed ale from the grain left after it reserved seed necessary for the next planting. The Abbey rarely traded dredge. It sold some barley from the northern manors. Purchases of barley on the home manors tended to offset the barley sales. Occasionally it fattened some pigs on barley or the dregs of malted grain.

Rye and legumes occupied a smaller area of the Abbey's fields. The Abbey raised rye as the chief ingredient of *mixtura*, or the mixed grain paid to its famuli. Manorial servants of higher status, such as reeves, received an occasional payment in wheat. The Abbey divided its harvest of legumes between its workers and its pigs. Pigs consumed between one-quarter and one-half of the peas, beans, and vetches raised by the Abbey.

CONCLUSION

A discussion of livestock ratios, yields, and consumption reveals a matrix of interactions between the cereal and pastoral sectors. The changing composition of livestock in the herding economy of the estate characterized a pastoral sector of some complexity. The management within herds of groups with different economic functions (e.g., oxen and cows) required coordination. A study of the demography of the estate herds can offer insight into such complexity. The manner in which the estate governed the reproduction of herd structures over time related to its strategies of production, consumption, and exchange. In the following chapters a discussion of herd demography serves as a starting point for exploring the pastoral economy of a high-farming estate.

Part II

HAVING HERDS

4
THE DEMESNE CATTLE HERDS ON THE PETERBOROUGH ABBEY ESTATE

THE DEMOGRAPHY OF THE ESTATE CATTLE HERD

For the years 1300–01, 1307–08, and 1309–10 there are account rolls preserved for each of the twenty-three manors of the Peterborough Abbey estate, excepting Cottingham and Great Easton in 1300–01. The first decade of the fourteenth century registered a high point of seigneurial high farming.[1] The English medieval population was at its peak. The Great Famine of 1315–17 lay in the future. Inflation and demand for wool exports exerted their most acute influences on agrarian lords.

Over the first decade of the fourteenth century Peterborough Abbey herded over twelve hundred cattle. This chapter explores the economic aspects of husbanding such a cattle herd.[2] It examines the demography of the estate herd and then links its developmental cycle to the Abbey's strategies for producing, consuming, and exchanging traction, meat, milk, hides, and tallow.[3]

The accountants of the Abbey used seven categories to describe the subgroups of the estate cattle-herd: bulls, oxen, cows, older bullocks and heifers (called 3–4-year-olds in the tables), younger bullocks and heifers (called 2–3-year-olds in the tables), yearlings, and calves. Table 21 (see appendix 4 for detailed statistics) summarizes the statistics for the estate cattle-herd in the early fourteenth century. Figure 9 illustrates the proportions of each subgroup in the estate herd. Oxen constituted about one-third and cows one fifth of the estate herd. Each of the four manorial groupings on the estate herded cattle-herds identical in proportional representation of bulls, oxen, cows, and juvenile and immature cattle described in figure 9. The

Table 21. Summary Statistics of the Demesne Cattle Herd: Estate of
Peterborough Abbey

	a	b	c	d	e	f	g
1300–01							
mean	0.75	18.3	12.7	6.6	6.4	8.8	11.1
s.d.	0.78	11.9	12.8	6.9	7.0	9.2	11.0
c.v. as %	104	66	101	103	110	104	93
total	15	367	253	134	128	167	231
1307–08							
mean	1.0	20.2	14.1	5.2	6.9	7.7	10.8
s.d.	0.99	12.3	15.5	5.3	9.1	9.9	13.2
c.v. as %	95	61	109	102	131	130	123
total	25	484	339	124	167	186	258
1309–10							
mean	1.2	20.7	13.5	6.1	7.5	9.7	11.5
s.d.	1.1	13.2	15.0	9.0	10.0	9.9	14.7
c.v. as %	96	64	111	148	133	102	127
total	27	445	309	127	174	156	242

Source: Fitzwilliam Account Rolls, 2388, 233, 2389.
Key to column headings: a = bulls; b = oxen; c = cows; d = 3–4-yr.-olds;
e = 2–3-yr.-olds; f = yearlings; g = calves.
Abbreviations: mean = mean per manor; s.d. = standard deviation; c.v. =
coefficient of variations here expressed as a percentage; total = estate total for that
year.

herd described by figure 9 thus typifies a seigneurial cattle herd of the
high-farming period.

   The coefficients of variation in table 21 show, however, that different subgroups varied in their presence on individual manors. Not all
manorial cattle herds contained the typical proportion of subgroups
already identified. The Abbey's manors specialized in husbanding
different subgroups of the herd to ensure the smooth reproduction of
the estate herd. One type of manorial cattle herd, a microcosm of the
estate herd, did husband subgroups according to the typical proportions of the estate herd. The home manor of Boroughbury managed
such a herd. The Abbey maintained the same mix of subgroups in the

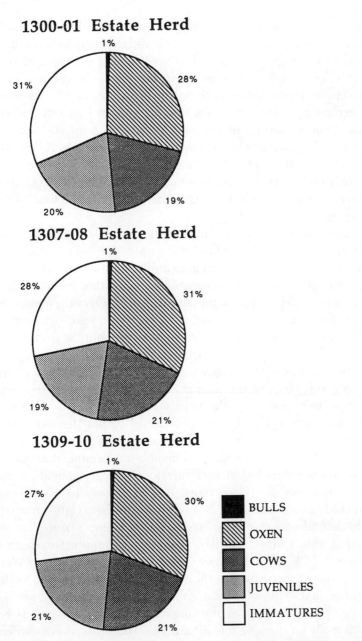

1300-01 Estate Herd

1%
28%
31%
19%
20%

1307-08 Estate Herd

1%
28%
31%
19%
21%

1309-10 Estate Herd

1%
27%
30%
21%
21%

BULLS
OXEN
COWS
JUVENILES
IMMATURES

Fig. 9. The composition of the cattle herd on the estate of Peterborough Abbey in the early fourteenth century.

Boroughbury cattle herd for over a century.[1] Only in the later fourteenth century, after the Black Death, did the composition of the herd
begin to change. Such a typical herd, with few cows and younger
cattle, guaranteed only minimal replacement of that manorial herd.
To ensure reproduction of the estate herd, the Abbey had to rely on
breeding manors, namely the home manor of Eye and the western
manor of Kettering, to husband herds with proportionately fewer
oxen and higher numbers of cows and young animals. A third type of
manorial herd found on the estate kept no cows at all or so few that the
manor had to rely on breeding manors or purchase to stock its oxen.
Such manorial herds were essentially nonreproductive, or "zero-
growth" herds.

The annual cycle of herd management in 1307–08 (figs. 10 and 11)
on the manors of Eye and Castor illustrates the different breeding and
equilibrium strategies found in manorial herds. The circles show the
number of the different subgroups. Arrows within the boxes show the
dynamic stocking cycle of the manorial herd. Over the annual manorial cycle, young calves would stock yearlings, yearlings would stock
2–3-year-olds, and the 3–4-year-olds would join the mature cohorts
of oxen, cows, or bulls. The arrows pointing into the box illustrate the
"external inputs," especially the transfer of cattle from other manors
into a subgroup of the manor herd. Eighteen oxen from another
manor were added to the twenty-eight oxen of the Castor herd.
Arrows pointing out of the box illustrate "output" from the manorial
herd. For instance, Castor butchered three of its oxen in 1307–08.
Eye and Kettering were the only manors on the estate that year where
cows outnumbered oxen, and, therefore, younger animals were more
prominent on the two manors. At Castor only two 3–4-year-olds
stocked its oxen and cows. Not surprisingly, then, eighteen oxen from
another manor were transferred to stock Castor's oxen. Eye, which
kept a much larger herd of young stock, supplied oxen to other
manors. In figure 9 the arrows show that it sent six oxen to Werrington, whence, according to the accounts, they were sent to Walton, a
manor that kept only oxen. As a breeding manor, Eye also kept a
much higher proportion of young females. Of its forty-one 3–4-year-
olds ready for stocking into mature cohorts, eighteen were heifers and
only twelve were bullocks. The sex of the ten 3–4-year-olds butchered
is not known. Given the proportions of males to females in the herd,
one suspects that the cattlemen at Eye had butchered young bullocks,

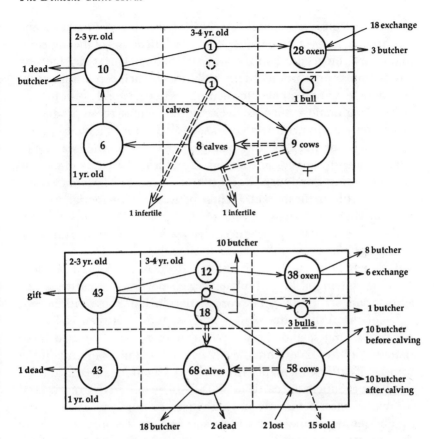

Figs. 10 and 11. Annual cycle of cattle breeding at the manor of Castor (10), where only minimal breeding of oxen occurred, in contrast with the annual cycle at Eye, a breeding manor (11). The numbers in the circles show the different numbers of subgroups of the cattle herd present on each of the manors. The arrows show how the number of subgroups increased or declined through butchery, mortality, intermanorial transfer, stocking, sale, or purchase over the annual cycle of 1307–08.

superfluous to stocking levels of oxen. At Castor, where few cows produced hardly enough stock to maintan the manorial plough oxen, young animals were rarely butchered. The annual butchery rate for young cattle at Eye was much higher; presumably young male calves were also butchered to maintain the high female-sex ratio desired for this breeding manor.

The differences in the composition of the cattle herds and the annual cycle of reproduction, stocking, and butchery at Castor and Eye are striking; yet each manor cultivated demesnes of the same size in the early fourteenth century, and each planted wheat, dredge, and oats in similar proportions.[5] The similarities of their cereal husbandry camouflage real differences in their respective pastoral economies.

Breeding manors, such as Eye, ensured against the reproductive failure on manors with few cows, such as Castor. They also made manorial herds without cows possible elsewhere on the estate. The Abbey used intermanorial transfers to and from breeding manors to correct shortages and surplus of cattle on the estate. The Abbey could also buy cattle on the market. It chose between intermanorial transfers and market purchases depending on the distance of manors from the Abbey. Each strategy produced its own demographic rates for mortality, butchery, and stocking from within the herd.

Figure 12 illustrates how the annual rates of intermanorial transfers, stocking, buying, selling, butchery, and mortality of cattle varied across zones of the estate. The core manors include those within eight miles of the Abbey; the semiperipheral, those between eight and twenty-five miles; and the peripheral manors, those located more than twenty-five miles from the Abbey.[6] The details of intermanorial transfer of cattle from manor to manor are set out in tables 22 and 23. Of all the groups of the cattle herd, the Abbey moved its oxen around the manors most frequently and in the greatest numbers. The greatest number of intermanorial transfers occurred on the home manors of the estate. On the manors of western Northamptonshire fewer transfers of cattle occurred, and Kettering served as the conduit for many of the transfers. Transfers of cattle on the manors of the northern grouping accounted for less than 3 percent of all exchanges.

The Abbey's buying and selling of cattle reversed the pattern just described for intermanorial transfers of cattle. The Abbey bought and sold the most stock at the periphery of the estate where it adjusted manorial herds most infrequently through intermanorial transfer (fig. 12). The Abbey thus used the market differently depending on manorial location. By combining complementary strategies of intermanorial transfer of stock and market sales and purchases, the Abbey conserved the capacity of its estate herd to reproduce itself biologically.

The biological reproduction of the herd also depended on the annual rates at which the Abbey stocked 3–4-year-olds to mature

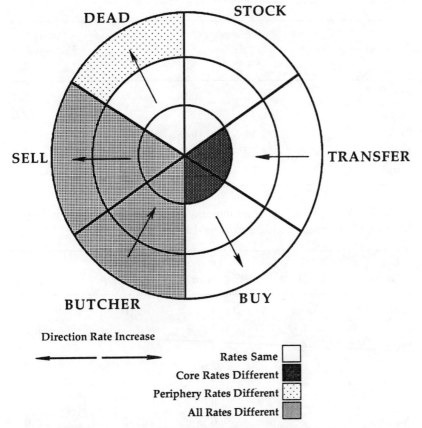

Fig. 12. Vital rates of the estate cattle herd. The concentric rings of the circle represent the home manors (innermost circle), the semi-peripheral manors (middle circle), and the peripheral manors (outermost circle) of the estate. The conventions indicate whether or not the rates of butchery, purchases, intermanorial transfer, stocking of younger cattle into mature cohorts (oxen, cows, bulls), mortality, and sales were similar or different across the different zones of the estate. The arrows indicate the direction of difference; for instance, the rate of butchery, which differed across the three zones of the estate, increased among manorial cattle herds with proximity to the Abbey.

Table 22. Cattle Exchanges Grouped by Cohorts in Cattle Herd Based on Three Accounting Years 1300–01, 1307–08, 1309–10

Cohort	Frequency of Exchanges		Number Exchanged	
	No.	*%*	*No.*	*%*
Bull	8	10.6	8	3.1
Oxen	43	57.3	162	63.0
Cows	14	18.6	49	19.1
Immatures	10	13.3	38	14.8
Total	75		257	

Table 23. Frequency of Intermanorial Transfers of Cattle according to Manorial Groupings (includes total for 1300–01, 1307–08, 1309–10)

In *Out*	*Home*	*West*	*Scarp*	*North*
Home	35	4	0	0
	46.6%	5.3%		
West	6	17	2	0
	8.0%	22.6%	2.6%	
Scarp	0	6	3	0
		8.0%	4.0%	
North	2	0	0	0
	2.6%			
Total number of exchanges = 75				

Source: Fitzwilliam Account Rolls, 2388, 233, 2389.

groups of bulls, oxen, and cows. Butchery and sale of young animals obviously influenced stocking rates too. Everywhere on its estate the Abbey stocked adult groups with young cattle at the same annual rate (fig. 12). When it culled cattle for meat, its choices varied according to manorial location. It butchered the most cattle on its home manors. As distance from the Abbey increased, the Abbey preferred to sell old stock rather than butcher it. Butchery proved to be a highly efficient way for the Abbey to remove older and infertile animals from its herd.

On the peripheral manors, where the Abbey butchered its cattle comparatively infrequently, the mortality rate for cattle was highest. Presumably manorial reeves culled cattle less rigorously on the peripheral manors, where stock often died before market sale.

Patterns of intermanorial transfer and butchery sales illustrate that the Peterborough cattle herd formed one large reproducing herd constituted by a network of manorial herds. The Abbey practiced its different strategies of herd management depending on the geographical location of its manor. The Abbey thus produced its own economic geography for cattle husbandry. Annual fertility and mortality, vital rates not fully controllable by the Abbey, dictated constraints within which the Abbey had to manage its herding strategies.

Annual mortality rates varied for subgroups in the estate herd.[7] The rates lowered with increasing age. For the three accounting years the overall mean mortality rate for oxen was 4.3 percent. Cows died at only a slightly higher rate of 5.2 percent. Only calves died at an average rate (10.4 percent) significantly higher than any of the other subgroups. The mortality rates of the Abbey's cattle herd have interesting economic implications. A 10 percent mortality rate is common with intensive cattle husbandry.[8] Annual death rates of over 15 percent begin to affect the viability of herd management. The Abbey thus enjoyed comparatively low mortality rates for its cattle herd in the first decade of the fourteenth century. Annual mortality rates necessarily influence selection of cattle for butchery. The similar mortality rates among the subgroups, with the exception of calves, meant that the Abbey could cull at will among the subgroups, if it so chose. It is therefore instructive to examine what economic decisions the Abbey made in selecting subgroups for butchery.

Over the first decade of the fourteenth century the Abbey butchered the subgroups of its herds at the following rates: oxen, 8 percent; cows, 12 percent; immatures, 14 percent; calves, 15 percent. To judge from the three accounting years, the overall butchery rates for oxen, cows, and immatures did not differ significantly.[9] The Abbey did, however, butcher its calves at a significantly higher rate than its oxen. Between mortality and butchery the Peterborough cattle herd lost more calves than it did mature animals.

The annual rates at which cows reproduced calves help to determine herd growth and are therefore crucial to herd management. The overall infertility rate for the estate herd, to judge from the three

accounting years, was 28.6 percent.[10] A little more than a quarter of
the cows mated did not produce calves. The infertility rate is inflated,
however, since it includes young heifers which the Abbey had just
stocked among cows, usually without mating them. The mean stocking rate for heifers at this time was 14.3 percent. Without the heifers,
the infertility rate for cows was a respectable 14.4 percent. Medieval
farmers had high expectations for breeding. In his treatise on estate
management, Walter of Henley expected that cows should bear
calves at yearly intervals.[11] With a forty-week gestation period for
calves and an interval of at least three to four weeks from calving to
first heat, cows had only three mating opportunities per year to
maintain yearly production of a calf. The high reproductive rate
indicates the Abbey's successful and intensive management of cattle
breeding.

The Abbey of Peterborough managed its cattle herd as a reproductive unit. It maintained its adult beasts through stocking from its
immature animals bred by estate cows. Some of the Abbey's manors
specialized in breeding cattle, others maintained zero-growth herds
by simply replacing their oxen, the critical members of the estate
herd. Depending on the geographical position of the manor in the
estate, the Abbey relied on different economic strategies for the
maintenance of its cattle herd. The Abbey's practice of buying and
selling cattle more actively on the manors of the northern grouping
distinguished the cattle herd of the peripheral manors from those of
the core of the estate. On the more distant northern manors it made
more sense to sell stock than to herd them into the Abbey for slaughter
and consumption. In contrast, the Abbey involved itself least in
buying and selling cattle on its core manors. It relied on the technique
of intermanorial transfer of stock to adjust the composition of the
manorial herds of the core. It also butchered and consumed the cattle
of its core manors at a much higher rate than at the semiperiphery
or periphery of the estate. It can be said that the demography of
the cattle herd at the periphery was more market-involved and
monetized and at the core more consumption-oriented.

By using the market selectively and relying on breeding manors
that ensured reproduction of the estate herd, the Abbey resisted the
full market penetration of its cattle herding. Its selective use of the
market becomes more evident when one considers the Abbey's production and consumption of the products of its cattle herd.

THE CONSUMPTION AND PRODUCTION OF THE
PRODUCTS OF THE CATTLE HERD

The cattle herd of the estate provided the Abbey with traction, meat, milk, hides, and tallow. The demography of the estate herd indicates that the production of oxen to draw ploughs shaped the basic contours of its demography. The number of oxen continued to correlate with the acreage sown on the estate, even though cows had increased relative to the number of oxen between the twelfth and the fourteenth century.[12] To what extent did the Abbey also rely on its cattle herd for the production of dairy products and meat?

Profits accrued from sale of stock show to what extent the Abbey relied on the production of meat and tallow for income. Figures for selling cattle on the estate in the early fourteenth century are set out in table 24. When comparing income from sales to outlay for purchases of stock, we find that the Abbey actually spent more money on the net purchase of cattle stock in 1300–01 and 1307–08 than it made on sales.

The Abbey exercised caution in marketing certain subgroups of its cattle herd. It never bought bullocks, heifers, or yearlings. Such an economic strategy emphasized the expectation that the estate herd should function as a self-contained reproductive unit. The Abbey separated subgroups most essential to stocking the Abbey's herd from market exchange. Nor did the Abbey sell off cows with calves. Depending on its strategies to maintain reproduction and its equilibrium of oxen and cereal acreage, it selectively sold off cows and calves separately.

The household of the Abbey also consumed beef. No analysis of its cattle marketing can fail to consider the consumption needs of the Abbey. The statistics for beef sent into the Abbey larder are presented in table 25 along with comparative figures for beef consumption available from other ecclesiastical estates. The Peterborough manors sent in sixty-four beasts to the Abbey in 1300–01, 129 in 1307–08, and 147 in 1309–10. The Abbey culled its beef evenly across all the subgroups of its herd excepting calves, which it butchered in slightly greater numbers than it did oxen. Such even culling stresses how the Abbey balanced consumption with a reproductive equilibrium in its demesne herd. The Abbey produced meat as a by-product of its estate herd.

Table 24. Purchase and Sale of Cattle and Dairy Products:
Peterborough Abbey Estate

	Oxen		Cows		Juveniles[a]		Calves	
1300–01								
Autumn #	367		253		425		233	
	#	s.	#	s.	#	s.	#	s.
Buy	36	387	4	26	0	0	2	3
Sell	9	114	10	35	4	15	5	5
Net (s.)		−273		+9		+15		+2
1307–08								
Autumn #	484		339		477		258	
	#	s.	#	s.	#	s.	#	s.
Buy	27	373	8	86	0	0	6	12
Sell	20	256	10	99	4	26	16	16
Net		−117		+13		+26		+4
1309–10								
Autumn #	445		309		462		242	
	#	s.	#	s.	#	s.	#	s.
Buy	18	266	13	197	0	0	1	1
Sell	40	472	33	475	11	78	8	9
Net		+206		+278		+78		+8

	Net Stock Exchange s.	Sales Hides s.	Sales Dairy s.
1300–01	−247	65	426
1307–08	− 74	133	535
1309–10	+570	123	544

Source: Fitzwilliam Account Rolls, 2388, 233, 2389.

[a] Juveniles include bullocks, heifers, and yearlings.

Table 25. Figures for Beef and Dairy Consumption in Selected Cellarer and Household Accounts (figures in parentheses estimated from yearly price averages; all prices in shillings)

Battle Abbey	1275	1278	1306	1319	1320	1351		
Beef consumed number: (market)	7	16	72	77	52	40	(m)[a]	76
Price:	92	193	909	820	795	380	339	

Bishop of Hereford	1289
combination of live cattle and carcasses 102	

Beaulieu	1269	
Beef consumed number:	11 (manors)	1 (market)
Price:	59	2
Cheese from manors (in pounds) consumed:	9,286	
sold:	2,250	

Durham	1307	
Beef consumed number:	228 (hoof)	60 carcasses
Price:	2,101	300
Cheese (pounds)	1,470	
Butter (pounds)	266	

Peterborough	1301	1308	1310
Beef consumed number:	64 (manors)	119 (manors)	146 (manors)
Dairy from manors cheese (pounds)	6,531	5,180	6,590
butter (pounds)	307	945	858

Sources: Eleanor Searle and B. Ross, eds., *The Cellarers' Rolles of Battle Abbey, 1275–1513*, Sussex Record Society, 65 (Sydney, 1967); S. F. Hockey, ed., *The Account-Book of Beaulieu Abbey*, Camden Fourth Series, vol. 16 (London, 1975); J. Webb, ed., *A Roll of the Household Expenses of Richard de Swinfield*, 2 vols., Publications of the Camden Society, 59, 62 (London, 1854–1855); J. T. Fowler, ed., *Extracts from the Account Rolls of the Abbey of Durham*, Publications of the Surtees Society, vols. 99, 100, 102 (Durham, 1898–1901); Fitzwilliam Account Rolls, 2388, 233, 2389.

[a] (m) cattle sent in from manors

Hides contributed comparatively little to the Abbey's income from secondary animal products (table 24). The Abbey sold hides skinned from cattle that had died on its manors. Most of the cattle sent into the Abbey household went in on the hoof. The Abbey undoubtedly marketed the hides from the cattle it slaughtered; however, it is not possible to track these sales without central householding accounts.[13] If it did sell all the hides of its slaughtered cattle, it would have disposed of more hides than all its manors, which marketed only a few hides of dead cattle annually.

The Abbey devoted itself to the production of dairy products. It had increased the proportion of its cows to oxen over the thirteenth century. The bulk of dairy production on the estate occurred on the Abbey's breeding manors, where the ratio of cows to oxen was higher than average. A breakdown of dairy yields on each manor in the year 1307–08 appears in appendix 4. For the manor of Eye and the grange at Northolm near Eye nine accounts are available for the period 1300–1483. Those yields are presented in appendix 5. The study of yields is complicated by the fact that the Abbey occasionally milked its ewes on some manors.[14] With only one exception, however, the yield of sheep milk was not separated from cow milk in the accounts. The table of yields thus indicates the manors for which there is evidence of sheep milking and calculates yields first for dairy cows and then for both cows and milking ewes on the manor.

The adjusted dairy yields ranged from thirty pounds (13.6 kg) to one hundred pounds (45.5 kg) per cow for the milking season of 1307–08. The mean for the estate was ninety-five pounds (43.2 kg) per cow. Surprisingly, dairying on a large scale at Eye, a manor set in the rich summer pasture of the fen, did not produce better dairy yields. The Abbey's largest dairy herd at Eye produced only average dairy yields of ninety-three pounds (42.3 kg) per cow.

The average dairy yields of the estate, equivalent to two-thirds of a gallon a day, or 100–130 gallons of milk during the summer milking season, met the expectations of the husbandry manuals of the thirteenth century:

> And be it known that the dairy woman ought to make cheese from the first day of May until Michaelmas for twenty-two weeks; and each cow ought by right to yield during this time five and one half stone of cheese [69 lb. or 31.3 kg], and of butter in proportion— that is to say that for seven stone [87.5 lb. or 39.7 kg] of cheese one ought to have one stone [12.5 lb. or 5.7 kg] of butter.[15]

Table 26. Dairy Production on the Peterborough Abbey Estate

	a	b	c	d	e	f
Cheese						
1300–01	230	14,736	43.8	308	44.3	
1307–08	247	16,342	50.9	418	31.7	
1309–10	256	15,255	43.5	395	43.2	
Butter						
1300–01	230	2,719	57.3	69	11.3	
1307–08	247	3,290	37.9	91	28.7	
1309–10	256	3,095	67.8	106	27.7	
Milk						
1300–01	230	3,038	31.9	49	17.5	50.9
1307–08	247	2,110	32.2	26	17.4	50.3
1309–10	256	2,893	23.4	43	1.3	61.7

Source: Fitzwilliam Account Rolls, 2388, 233, 2389.
Key to column headings: a = total lactating cows; b = total production in pounds for cheese and butter, in gallons for milk; c = percentage sold; d = total sales in shillings; e = percentage consumed by abbey; f = percentage of milk consumed by lambs and calves.

At the turn of the nineteenth century, four hundred gallons of milk was considered an average yield.[16] The medieval yields are similar to those produced among African pastoralists such as the Nuer, Dinka, and Boran.[17]

The Abbey's cows yielded a total of 19,000 to 23,000 pounds of dairy produce annually during the first decade of the fourteenth century (table 26). The Abbey sold approximately one-half of the yield of its dairy herds. The manors sent in a third of the total yield of cheese and one quarter of the yield of butter into the Abbey for its consumption. Over half of the milk reserved from cheese production nourished lambs and calves. Dairy sales provided small change for the Abbey's purse compared to grain sales. In 1307–08 the proceeds of the Abbey's grain sales (2,580s.) were just short of five times greater than those of its dairy sales (535s.).

It cost the Abbey to maintain its cattle herd and dairies. The Abbey fattened its oxen before butchery with oats reaped from its demesnes. It employed dairymaids who received wages in a combination of cash and grain. The salt, presses, and churns of the dairy were also an expense. The dairy house required maintenance and repair. The wages of the ploughmen on the estate can be considered an expense of cattle husbandry too, since the production of traction necessary to produce grain for consumption was a primary aim of its cattle herding. The Abbey also spent money on cattle stalls. These expenses can be added to upkeep as building costs.

Any effort to quantify costs of upkeep must stumble, since the market did not form the prices for all costs involved.[18] The Abbey drew directly from its own resources, demesne grain, demesne labor, and so on, to meet expenses incurred in its cattle husbandry. The figures in table 27, which do cost all expenses and assign a market value to the meat and dairy produce directly consumed by the Abbey, must be treated with caution. When all items are costed with market prices, the expenses of maintaining the cattle herd matched the annual income in dairy sales and consumption. The Abbey would have realized no profit from its herd if it had not succeeded in limiting its involvement in the market as a consumer. Since it did succeed in containing much of the expense in its consumption sector, it gained some much-needed cash flow from the sale of dairy and other secondary animal products. The "break-even" economics of cattle management underlines again the Abbey's primary interest as a cattle herder in reproducing oxen to work the demesne arable. The Abbey above all conserved its expectation to consume from its estate and ate its own grain and dairy products. It selectively marketed secondary animal products to maintain some cash flow.

As a seigneurial lord the Abbey controlled the pastoral resources of its demesne. It could graze these resources with its own herds or sell them to its peasants. The choice involved decisions about the size of its own cattle herd and the trade-off in money it would receive from sales of pasture. The Abbey's income from sales of pastoral resources in the first decade of the fourteenth century is set out in table 28. The Abbey's sales of pastoral resources produced two to four times more income than its sales of cattle products. The Abbey's capacity to put so much pasture on the market indicates that it enjoyed some slack in matching its cattle herd to its pastoral resources. It chose to sell pastoral resources rather than expand the size of its herd to match its supply of pasture.

Each year the Abbey sold one-fifth of its total pastoral sales in the

Table 27. Income, Consumption, and Expenses: The Cattle Herd of the Peterborough Abbey Estate[a]

| | Income (shillings) | | |
	Net of Stock Exchange	Hides	Dairy	Total
1300–01	−247	65	426	244
1307–08	− 74	133	535	594
1309–10	+570	123	544	1,237

| | Consumption (shillings) | | |
	Carcass	Cheese	Butter	Total
1300–01	257	313	15	585
1307–08	541	248	45	834
1309–10	532	262	56	850

| | Expenses (shillings) | | | |
	Grain	Dairy	Building	Workers	Total
1300–01	215	114	76	536	941
1307–08	328	157	371	547	1,403
1309–10	576	142	87	583	1,388

Source: Fitzwilliam Account Rolls, 2388, 233, 2389.

[a] A note on the computations: The value of beef consumed by the Abbey is based on carcass values for oxen, cows, 3–4-yr.-olds, 2–3-yr.-olds, yearlings, and calves contained in the schedule for the larder appearing in Hockey, *Account-Book of Beaulieu Abbey*, 185. Values for cheese and butter, taken from the tables in volume 1 of James E. Thorold Rogers, *A History of Agriculture and Prices in England* (Oxford, 1866). The grain consumed by cattle is valued according to yearly averages taken from Rogers. Dairy expenses include the wages of dairymaids on the estate (calculated according to an average of 4.5s.) and costs of salt, presses, etc. Workers include ploughmen and cowherds and any other part-time help tending estate cattle. Annual wages calculated at an average of 4.5s.

"processed" form of hay and forage. The Abbey could afford to market hay, since it still collected mowing services from its peasants. The costs of producing hay would have doubled for the Abbey without the labor services of its peasants. The fact that the Abbey still consumed these labor services rendered the sale of its resources even more attractive.

Table 28. Sales of Pastoral Resources and Costs of Hay Production (in Shillings) on the Peterborough Abbey Estate

| | | Pastoral Sales | | | |
	Pasture	Hay & Forage	Stubble	Straw	Total
1300–01	2,842	735	152	30	3,759
1307–08	3,106	799	117	16	4,038
1309–10	2,467	1,189	181	11	3,848

| | Pastoral Costs | |
	Costs of Mowing	Value of Mowing Services[a]
1300–01	259	290
1307–08	416	359
1309–10	408	430

Source: Fitzwilliam Account Rolls, 2388, 233, 2389.

[a] Value of labor services used for mowing, lifting, and carting hay set at 1 pence per labor service.

The expectation of consumption shaped the management of the Abbey's cattle herd in the fourteenth century. The Abbey sought to protect its consumption of grain first. It maintained its herd of oxen to produce traction in the cereal sector. By expanding its dairy herd and marketing half of its dairy surplus, the Abbey made some cash to put toward meeting royal demands and other feudal costs. The Abbey's endowment of pastoral resources could have sustained a much larger herd on the estate, but the Abbey chose instead to sell its pastoral resources to the peasant sector for cash. Such strategies remind us of the difficulties of categorizing an estate as primarily arable or pastoral. The Abbey's endowment of pastoral resources did not automatically translate into bigger herds. With its emphasis on oxen, the Abbey behaved like a "typical" arable lord. It viewed much of its pastoral endowment as a source of cash sales rather than a resource calling for "maximization" of its own pastoral output.

The Abbey's strategies to ensure herd reproduction without the market and its selective use of medieval markets for sales and not for consumption have implications for the study of institutional changes and the emergence of agrarian capitalism in England. Such implications are worthy of broad outline in these concluding remarks. The Abbey carefully marked off its sphere of consumption and reproduction from the market, although it capably used the market to enhance such strategies when it chose. Such institutional behavior helps us to understand better the asymmetrical linkage of consumption and production in medieval regional economies and to appreciate more fully the undoing of such asymmetrical links over the fifteenth century. Recent research suggests that the market increasingly coordinated regional specialization of northern European livestock husbandry over the fifteenth and sixteenth centuries. Different regions, such as Ireland and parts of Scandinavia, specialized in different stages of the herding cycle. By the early modern period in England, the market organized reproduction of livestock and different regions assumed specialized roles in the breeding, finishing, and marketing of livestock and livestock products.[19] Changes in pastoral resource-use accompanied the reorganization of livestock husbandry in the early modern period. New relations of consumption to production unlinked rigid boundaries between permanent pasture and arable through the widespread practice of convertible husbandry or more extensive and regular fodder rotations interspersed with cereal rotations.[20] The dissolution of the boundaries between pasture and arable together with the forging of new links between buying and selling in the late fifteenth century emerges as a locus of transformation in the medieval pastoral economy. This locus requires further study in future work.

5

THE DESMESNE SHEEP FLOCKS

THE DEMOGRAPHY OF THE ESTATE SHEEP FLOCK

English exports of raw wool reached their medieval peak in the first decade of the fourteenth century. In the year 1304–05 England exported 46,382 sacks, or just under seventeen million pounds of wool.[1] Approximately twelve million sheep were shorn to yield such a harvest. The number of sheep in early-fourteenth-century England most certainly belies the claim made for declining numbers of livestock in the high-farming era. Flock numbers increased over the late thirteenth century as many estates adopted centralized organization of the sheep flock under the direction of a head shepherd.[2] The fen abbey of Crowland had centralized its sheep flock by 1276. Peterborough Abbey did so in 1307. With centralized flock management, accounting of sheep shifted from manorial to centralized accounts. Caution must therefore be exercised in handling manorial accounts of this period. Other estates, such as Canterbury Cathedral Priory and Ramsey Abbey, continued to account for their sheep flocks by manor or by manorial grouping. Such large flocks, whether managed centrally or not, required the coordination of lambing and shearing with seasonal availability of pasture. A study of flock management on the estate of Peterborough Abbey illumines the complexities posed by seigneurial sheepherding on a large scale.

The estate of Peterborough Abbey herded flocks numbering between four thousand and nine thousand sheep in the first decade of the fourteenth century. Accountants divided the flock into four subgroups: wethers, ewes, yearlings, and lambs. Table 29 contains the summary statistics for the flock in the first decade of the fourteenth century.[3] The numbers of each subgroup varied significantly from year to year and by manorial grouping. The Abbey doubled flock size in six years. Such growth undoubtedly contributed to the volatility of the figures.

Table 29. Summary Statistics for the Demesne Sheep Flock:
Peterborough Abbey Estate (at opening of accounting year)

	a	b	c	d
1300–01				
Wethers	73.9	99.8	135	1,395
Ewes	63.5	81.7	129	1,207
Yearlings	38.7	61.1	158	735
Lambs	63.5	102.7	162	1,143
1307–08				
Wethers	130.7	143.2	110	2,909
Ewes	114.2	127.0	111	2,585
Yearlings	60.1	101.7	169	1,296
Lambs	97.5	109.2	112	2,145
1309–10				
Wethers	126.8	129.2	102	2,916
Ewes	105.8	106.4	101	2,433
Yearlings	62.7	73.3	117	1,443
Lambs	87.0	93.8	108	2,000

Source: Fitzwilliam Account Rolls, 2388, 233, 2389.
Key to column headings: a = manorial mean (number of manors in 1300–01 = 19,
number of manors in 1307–08 = 22, number of manors in 1309–10 = 23;
b = standard deviation; c = coefficient of variation expressed as a percentage;
d = estate total for subgroup.

The coefficients of variation in table 29 show that the numbers
of each subgroup varied much from manor to manor. The Abbey
managed each subgroup of its sheep flock in a specialized way, and a
discussion of sheep demography must account for such specialization.
During the annual pastoral cycle the Abbey moved the subgroups of
its flock frequently, bought and sold mature stock, and carefully
husbanded its younger stock to ensure reproduction of the herds.

The Abbey managed two types of sheep flocks: an intermanorial
flock on its home and western Northamptonshire manors, and self-
contained manorial flocks on its manors in the northern grouping. It
based its management of the intermanorial flock on its capacity to
shift subgroups to different manors depending on seasonal require-

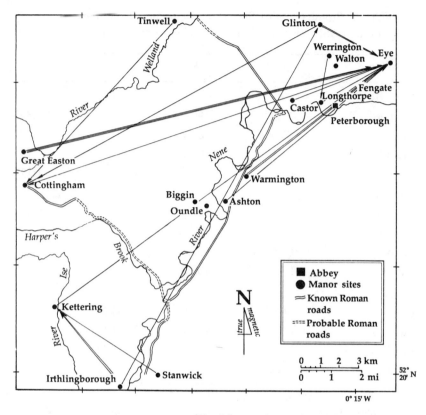

Fig. 13

Figs. 13–16. The movement of different subgroups of the sheep flock around the estate. The figures illustrate the frequency and direction of transfers of subgroups of the sheep flock around the estate in the first decade of the fourteenth century. For the number of animals involved in the transfers see table 30. Fig. 13 shows the movement of ewes; fig. 14 shows the movements of wethers; fig. 15 shows the movement of yearlings; fig. 16 shows the movement of lambs.

ments of each subgroup for pasture and other care.[4] The home manors served as the nursery for the intermanorial flock. They received ewes from the West and Scarp manors in the early spring. The movement of ewes around the manors is illustrated in figure 13. Pregnant ewes in need of good nutrition grazed on the abundant fen pastures attached to the home manors and lambed there. After lambing, the home manors sent out lambs and yearlings to stock the West and Scarp manors (fig. 16).

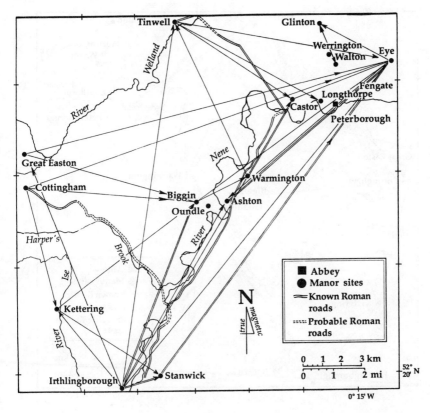

Fig. 14

The Abbey moved yearlings or hoggs according to its strategy for stocking its intermanorial flock. The Abbey herded yearlings less often than ewes but in much larger flocks when it did transfer them among manors (table 30). The Abbey herded the majority of its hoggs to the Scarp manors to increase their stocking levels in the early fourteenth century. The Abbey also pastured a good number of hoggs on the poor pastures of the manor of Irthlingborough (fig. 15). When the yearlings were ready to stock the wethers and ewes, the Abbey moved them to manors specializing in the care of these respective subgroups.

The Abbey moved its wethers, producers of the heaviest and largest fleeces and the greatest amount of manure, most frequently and in the largest numbers (table 30). Manors such as Irthling-borough and Longthorpe served as transfer points for their respective manorial groupings. The wether flock passed through these manors to be dispersed elsewhere in the intermanorial grouping (fig. 14).

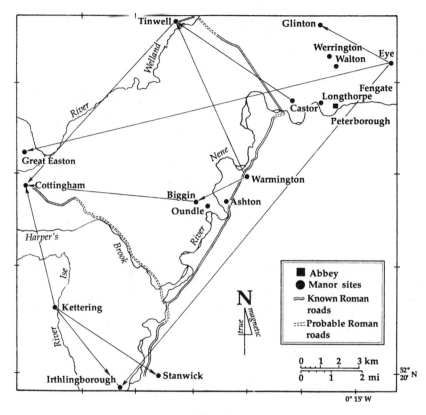

Fig. 15

The Abbey centralized its sale of older mature sheep. The North-amptonshire manors sent in their old and debilitated ewes to the home manors, where the culls could grow fat on the abundant fen pastures before sale. Although the Abbey centralized stock sales on its home manors, it dispersed its purchases of stock. Individual manors maintained contacts with local breeders and purchased fresh stock from them. The Abbey's purchase and sale of sheep thus linked into different market networks, a centralized one for sales and a dispersed one for purchases.

The Abbey probably used the old Roman road system for droving such flocks around its home and western manors. The majority of its Northamptonshire manors were situated along the old Roman road system that bounded the perimeter of Rockingham Forest. The old Roman iron road that cut through the forest connected the Scarp

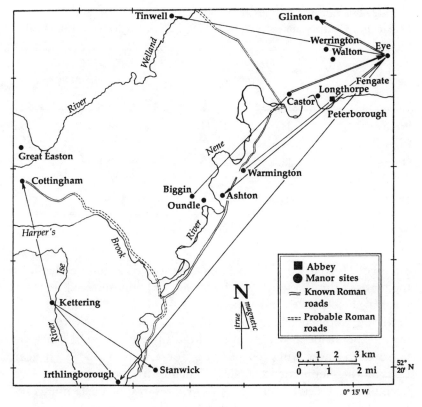

Fig. 16

manors with Northamptonshire manors located along the river Nene.[5]

The flock management of the Abbey on its northern manors contrasted sharply with management of the intermanorial flock just discussed. Each northern manor managed a self-contained flock and engaged in no division of labor in the management of different subgroups of sheep.

The home manors of Longthorpe and Glinton illustrate the different wool and breeding specializations practiced on different manors. Their annual flock cycles are illustrated in figures 17 and 18. Longthorpe, a manor some two miles northwest of the town of Peterborough, specialized in herding wethers. In 1300–01 it kept a herd of ninty-nine wethers. Twenty-five wethers died and four were butchered. Before shearing time, it received sixty wethers from the Scarp

Table 30. Sheep Transfers by Subgroup in the First Decade of the
Fourteenth Century (based on totals from 1300–01, 1307–08, 1309–10)

Subgroup	Frequency of Exchange		Animals Exchanged	
	#	%	#	%
Wethers	34	41	1,000	26.4
Ewes	23	28	813	21.4
Hogs	11	13	767	20.2
Lambs	14	17	1,210	31.9
Total	82		3,790	

Source: Fitzwilliam Account Rolls, 2388, 233, 2389.

manor of Tinwell. Longthorpe typically received wethers culled from
the herds of the West and Scarp manors and administered their last
shearing before sale. After shearing, Longthorpe sold off all of its
surviving wethers, which numbered 133. Longthorpe served as a
transfer point for moving wethers from upland clay and limestone
pastures to lower-lying fen pasture. For a brief period each year,
Longthorpe shepherded a small herd of fifty-five pregnant ewes. Eye,
a fen manor, received the Longthorpe ewes in time for lambing and
shearing. Thus, from early spring through the summer, Longthorpe
herded only wethers. In the winter it tended ewes in their early
pregnancy.

The manor of Glinton overlooked fen pastures from its location on
the gravel terrace of the river Nene and enjoyed access to rich fen
pasture. Breeding ewes were herded at the fen-edge manors of Glinton
and Eye. Glinton specialized in young female sheep and in lambing
(fig. 18). In 1300–01 it kept only nine wethers and received seven
wethers as customary payments from its villagers. Its two yearlings
were added to the wethers and ewes respectively. Glinton received
ewes for lambing and shearing from the western manors of Irthlingborough and Warmington in 1300–01. These ewes bore 301 lambs,
which Glinton kept until they were yearlings. Glinton was the only
home manor to keep its lambs instead of sending them into the West
and Scarp manors. The Abbey used the lambs of Glinton to stock the
herds of the home manors.

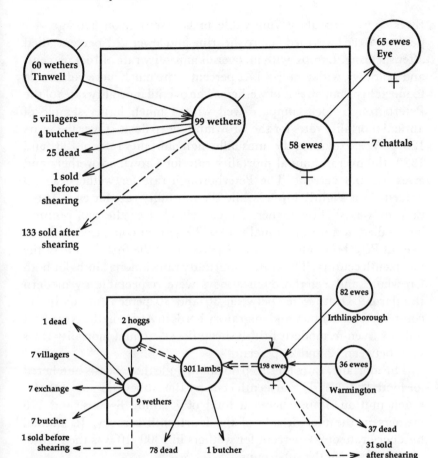

Figs. 17 and 18. Annual cycle of sheep husbandry at the manor of Longthorpe (17), which specialized in caring for wethers, and at the manor of Glinton (18), a breeding manor for the sheep flock. The numbers in the circles show the different numbers of subgroups of the sheep flock present on each of the manors. The arrows show how the number of subgroups increased or declined through butchery, mortality, intermanorial transfer, stocking, sale, or purchase over the annual cycle of 1300–01.

The analysis so far makes it clear that the Abbey managed its flock according to the requirements of each subgroup. Mortality and fertility rates for the flock also varied by age and sex. The accounts of 1300–01, 1307–08, and 1309–10 indicate that ewes and wethers had an overall death rate of 4.9 percent and 6.1 percent respectively.[6]

Ewes were particulary vulnerable in late spring; on average, 4.7 percent of the ewes died before shearing and fewer (2.1 percent) died after shearing. Lambs, with an overall mortality rate of 16.4 percent, and yearlings, with a rate of 14.2 percent, were much more vulnerable to mortality than ewes and wethers. The overall mortality rates of the Peterborough flock compare well with a much larger sample of annual mortality rates for the Crowland sheep flock.[7] Over the years 1267–1327, excluding the unusually high mortality rates of 1281 and 1322, the overall annual mortality rate for Crowland wethers and ewes was 5.8 percent. The Peterborough rate for wethers, at 4.9 percent, was slightly lower, while the mortality rate for ewes at 6.1 percent was slightly higher. At Crowland over the half-century, lambs died at a mean annual rate of 26 percent compared with the overall Peterborough rate of 16.4 percent for the first decade of the fourteenth century. The annual mortality rates among lambs for both Crowland and Peterborough abbeys were respectable by modern standards.[8] Death rates between 30 and 70 percent annually are common for sedentary and migratory herds in Africa in the Near East today.[9] Even in modern British sheep flocks, annual mortality rates vary between 12 and 24 percent.

The mortality rates for sheep do not include those beasts butchered for food. In the early fourteenth century the Abbey did not consume much mutton. It butchered a total of 7 lambs, 8 ewes, and 176 wethers in the first decade of the fourteenth century. Its annual butchery rate of 2.7 percent for wethers in 1309–10 was the highest recorded among the subgroups.

The Abbot of Peterborough and his colleague at Crowland achieved some success as sheep breeders. Over the first decade of the fourteenth century, approximately three-quarters of Peterborough ewes mated annually produced lambs.[10] Crowland Abbey achieved a overall annual fertility rate of 73.8 percent for its ewes in the same decade. Such a success rate shows that both abbeys succeeded in providing ewes with adequate nutrition in early pregnancy, a period of great risk.[11] Inadequate food during that time is a major cause of miscarriage.

The Abbey used the market more frequently in adjusting the demography of its sheep flock than it did for its cattle herd; yet it still husbanded its sheep flock as a reproductive unit. The Abbey conserved its lambs and yearlings, so vital to future herd reproduction. The

Abbey relied on its lambs to stock its flock and sold only thirty-five lambs in the first decade of the fourteenth century. Likewise, the Abbey rarely sold its yearlings or hoggs. It stocked the mature groups of its sheep flock at twice the stocking rate of its cattle herd. The high stocking rate is a measure of the Abbey's reliance on biological reproduction for maintaining its flocks over time.

THE CONSUMPTION AND PRODUCTION OF THE PRODUCTS OF THE SHEEP FLOCK

The Abbey used the market primarily to adjust the numbers of the mature members of its flock, wethers and ewes. The Abbey purchased and sold mature sheep to suit its productive goals. Sheep offer the farmer the products of wool, meat, skins, milk, and manure. To set goals the Abbey had to make complex decisions about the production of such products. The Abbey's productive record for each product will be examined in turn.

Wool production clearly dominated the Abbey's concerns. The Abbey centrally marketed every fleece shorn from its wethers, ewes, and hoggs in the early fourteenth century, and therefore the prices for fleeces do not appear in the accounts. It is possible to estimate the Abbey's income from its fleece sales by multiplying the number of fleeces by an average weight and then by the yearly average price. Table 31 lists the estimated income from the Abbey's fleeces. At its peak in the first decade of the fourteenth century the Abbey produced just under five tons of wool.

Table 31. Estimates of Wool Income: Peterborough Abbey Estate

	Fleeces	Weight[a] (stones)	Price[b] (s.)
1300–01	3,283	398.65	1,873.6
1307–08	6,193	752.0	4,271.3
1309–10	5,471	664.3	3,514.1

Source: Fitzwilliam Account Rolls, 2388, 233, 2389.

[a] An average of 1.70 lb. per fleece used to calculate weight which was then converted into stones at rate of 14 pounds to the stone.

[b] Yearly prices averages taken from Lloyd, *The Movement of Wool Prices in Medieval England*. In 1300–01 yearly price average was 4.7s.; in 1307–08, 5.68s.; in 1309–10, 5.29s.

Table 32. Comparative Receipts from Grain Liveries and Wool
Clips: Peterborough Abbey Estate (in Shillings)

	Grain Liveries[a]	Wool Income	Ratio Wool : Grain
1300–01	15,560	1,873	1 : 8.3
1307–08	17,960	4,271	1 : 4.2
1309–10	17,360	3,514	1 : 4.9

[a] Statistics for grain liveries taken from Edmund King, *Peterborough Abbey,
1086–1310* (Cambridge, 1973), table 8. Estimates of wool income appear in table 31
above.

The economic value of wool production on the estate takes on fuller
meaning when it is compared with the Abbey's grain consumption.
Table 32 compares the estimated income from wool with the estimated
value of the grain sent in from the Abbey's manors for its consumption.
The Abbey consumed four to eight times more in the value of grain
than it earned from its sale of wool. Even in the highly monetized,
market-oriented economy of the early fourteenth century, much of
the worth of the estate still rested in consumption and did not flow
through the market.

As a sheep breeder the Abbey had to make decisions about the
production and consumption of mutton and hides. The Abbey's
purchase and sale of stock, which are used as indicators of its involvement in the mutton trade, are set out in table 33. Over the first decade
of the fourteenth century, the Abbey either lost money or just managed
to break even on buying and selling sheep stock. The exchange of
sheep on the market did not bring money into the Abbey.

The Abbey did not expose all the subgroups of its sheep flock to the
market. Lambs were the subgroup least open to market sales. The one
sale of lambs in 1307–08 involved less than 1 percent of the herd.
The Abbey purchased lambs only to compensate, and to compensate
only partially, for losses of lambs to disease. The Abbey bought lambs
when high mortality among that subgroup threatened the reproductive future of the herd. The purchase of hoggs also compensated
for mortality. The Abbey sold weakened hoggs or female stock in
excess of the requirements for herd reproduction. The Abbey kept
more mature wethers in its flock than it did ewes; wethers yielded

Table 30. Buying, Selling, Expenses, Profits, Peterborough Abbey Sheep Flock (in Shillings)

	Purchase and Sale of Stock							
	Wethers		Ewes		Yearlings		Lambs	
	s.	#	s.	#	s.	#	s.	#
1300–01								
Buy	1,080	574	606	421	144	72	220	227
Sell	845	601	181	164	104	132	0	0
Net	−235s.		−425s.		−40s.		−220s.	
1307–08								
Buy	461	215	56	26	179	103	37	32
Sell	401	250	286	196	45	68	5	20
Net	−60s.		+230s.		−134s.		−32s.	
1309–10								
Buy	2,333	893	219	103	172	89	174	110
Sell	2,109	1,400	1,178	780	28	34	0	0
Net	−224s.		+959s.		−144s.		−174s.	

Stock	Net Exchange s.	Sale^a Wool s.	Sale Pels s.	Flock^b Expenses s.	Net Income s.
1300–01	−920	1,873	199	966	187
1307–08	4	4,271	323	1,147	3,451
1309–10	417	3,514	233	718	3,446

^a See table 31 for estimates of wool income.
^b Expenses include shepherds at average yearly wage of 4s., cost of folds, unguents, housing, feed (including cost of grain and milk), costs of washing, shearing, housing expenses including construction of a new bercaria (sheep house).

heavier fleeces than ewes and were therefore more productive to maintain in a wool-producing economy.

The Abbey exchanged its mature livestock, wethers and ewes, most frequently on the market. The Abbey always lost on the exchange of wethers. It sold more wethers than it purchased and went into the red over purchases. The rough equilibrium between the number of wethers purchased and sold suggests that the Abbey removed at a steady rate animals of declining productivity to replace them with fresh stock. The Abbey bought and sold ewes more erratically. When the Abbey engaged in a strategy to increase herd size in 1300–01, it purchased ewes. In 1309–10 it reversed this strategy, selling proportionately more ewes. Related to this sale was the purchase of more wethers than usual. The trade-off between ewes and wethers that year suggests that the Abbey thought it could make faster gains on wool production by selling off ewes and purchasing wethers, the bearers of heavier fleeces, than by waiting for ewes to increase wool production through biological herd growth. Wool prices were on the rise that year, and the decision made sense. The high figures for stock sales in 1309–10 in fact involve a strategy of financing increased wool production.

The lack of profit on stock exchange with the exception of the unusually high sales of ewes in 1309–10 indicates that the Abbey did not organize its sheep husbandry around mutton production in the early fourteenth century. It directed its sheepherding economy toward the production of a single product, wool. Meat was the by-product rather than the joint product of sheep husbandry on the estate. The Abbey's single-minded pursuit of wool production marks its sheep management as a single-product economy. Its devotion to a single product enabled it to manage its flock on a considerable scale.

The Abbey might not have produced mutton for the market because it consumed mutton in the household. It has already been noted, however, that the Abbey did not butcher more than 3 percent of its wethers in any of the accounting years of the first decade of the fourteenth century. The Abbey never butchered ewes and yearlings and consumed only six of its lambs in 1307–08. The figures for mutton consumption at Peterborough Abbey are surprisingly low in comparison with those for other contemporary households. Comparative figures for mutton consumption selected from cellarer and household accounts are set out in table 34. Assuming that Peterborough shared contemporary ecclesiastical tastes, the figures for mutton consump-

Table 34. Figures for Mutton Consumption Contained in Selected Cellarer and Household Accounts (figures in parentheses based on yearly price averages) (all prices in shillings)

Battle Abbey	1275	1278	1306	1319	1351
Mutton consumed number:	(155)	103	241	(117)	189-manors 264-purchased
Price of mutton price:	182	113	282	275	238 + 307

Beaulieu Abbey	1269
Mutton consumed number:	523
Price of mutton price:	no price

Durham	1307	1317
Mutton consumed number:	232	343
Price of mutton price:	201	no price

Bishop of Hereford	1289	1300
Mutton consumed number:	carcasses 94.5	wethers 29
Price of mutton price:	no price	no price

Peterborough Abbey	1301	1308	1310
Mutton consumed	wethers 29	wethers 30	wethers 117, 3 lambs, 8 ewes
Price of mutton price:	sent in from manors; no price		

Source: See Table 25 for citation of sources.

tion are absurdly low for 1300–01 and 1307–08 and approach contemporaries in 1309–10. Either the Abbey purchased a considerable amount of mutton for household consumption on the market, a transaction that would not register in the manorial accounts, or some of the "sales" of stock on the manors camouflage actual transfers of sheep to the Abbey larder, an accounting practice not unknown during the period. Without central household accounts for the Abbey, the question of the Abbey's alternative procurement of mutton cannot be determined.

The sale of sheepskins was more incidental to the sheep economy of the Abbey than meat production. Stock sold by the Abbey moved on the hoof, and so the Abbey did not sell large numbers of skins. The Abbey marketed only the skins of its dead sheep. In 1300–01 the skins were sold off local manors. In 1307–08 the Abbey sold the woolier skins (*pellis grossa*) of sheep that died before shearing to the merchants purchasing Peterborough Abbey's wool clip. The shorn skins (*peletta*) of the dead sheep of that year were sold locally off manors.

Sheep also produce milk and manure. The Abbey sometimes milked ewes at the nursery manors of the Abbey, Eye and Glinton, where most of the lambing occurred. The reeves on these manors entered on their accounts the expense of hiring dairymaids for milking ewes (and sporadically on several others: 1300–01: Collingham, Scotter; 1307–08: Fiskerton, Warmington, Collingham, Scotter, Great Easton; 1309–10: Fiskerton, Warmington, Kettering, Cottingham, Collingham, Scotter). The accountants did not separate ewe yields from cow yields in their dairy report; therefore, it is impossible to gauge productivity or profit of sheep dairying. The substantial costs the Abbey incurred in purchasing extra milk to sustain newborn lambs, which contributed between one-quarter and one-third of the expenses for maintaining the sheep flock, would have easily offset profits of sheep dairying. The lambs also consumed more than half of the cow milk reserved from cheese making in the Abbey's dairies. The Abbey's large number of lambs thus had considerable impact on its dairying.

The last product of the sheep flock to consider is manure. Accountants did not value manure on the Peterborough account rolls. The Abbey's practice of moving the subgroups of its flock around the core and semiperipheral manors over the year would have ensured at least a fairly even distribution of the product.

The Abbey did manage to make a profit from its sheep flock. The costs of maintaining the sheep herd, which included the construction and maintenance of sheep houses (*bercaria*), the wages in cash and kind paid to shepherds, washers, and shearers, and the costs of unguents, folds, grain, and milk for feed, matched the expenses of keeping the estate cattle herd. Profits from wool sales, however, far exceeded the income earned from the sale of the dairy produce of the cattle herd. The Abbey consumed much less of the product of its sheep herd. Sheep were herded by the Abbey first and foremost to cash-crop wool.

The Abbey produced wool for cash. Its need for cash and the level of wool prices determined flock size. It is not possible to trace the paths that linked the Abbey to the long-distance market for wool, since the household accounts that recorded the centralized sales of its wool clip are not preserved. The Abbey did appear as a buyer of stock, but it bought and sold stock not to make money but to expand wool production. Only with the production of wool did the Abbey fully enter the market as a seller. It did not both consume and sell this product as it did the other products of its herds. Wool production was a full-blown economy of scale on the estate.

6

DEMESNE HORSES, PIGS, AND POULTRY

HORSES

The number of horses tripled on the estate of Peterborough Abbey between the survey of 1125 and the accounts of the early fourteenth century. In 1125 the Abbey kept one horse for every forty demesne oxen. By the fourteenth century the proportion of workhorses rose to 40 to 45 percent of the estate's oxen (table 35). This figure for working horses on the estate easily outstrips the mean proportion of 26.7 percent calculated by John Langdon for a sample of 625 English demesnes during the period 1250–1320.[1] The high proportion of working horses on the Peterborough demesnes comes close to the highest regional representation of working horses found by Langdon for East Anglian demesnes, which employed a mean of 49.4 percent of working horses for the period 1250–1320. The estate of Peterborough Abbey employed far more working horses than demesnes in its own region of the East Midlands, which, according to Langdon, employed working horses at a rate of 27.2 percent.

The growing reliance on horses for speedy haulage had added a new subgroup, cart horses (*equi carectarii*), to the horse population of the estate, since the twelfth century. The Abbey kept horses for transport, traction, and special work in the fields such as harrowing and marling. It also managed a stud farm, which produced riding horses for the Abbey's stable. Summary statistics for horses on the estate in the first decade of the fourteenth century are set out in table 35.[2]

Horses provided the Abbey with no secondary products for consumption other than very cheap horsehide. Freed of its links to the consumption of secondary products, the Abbey departed from its customs of reproduction with its herd of horses. It bought cart horses

116

Table 35. Summary Statistics for Horses on the Peterborough Abbey
Estate[a]

	a	b	c	d	e
1300–01					
mean	2.66	4.33	0.51	2.27	41.5
s.d.	1.64	4.58	0.85	4.36	21.6
c.v. as %	62	105	166	192	52
n	18	18	18	18	16
1307–08					
mean	2.86	4.33	1.00	3.30	40.2
s.d.	1.62	4.61	1.55	3.90	17.1
c.v. as %	57	106	155	118	42
n	21	21	21	21	19
1309–10					
mean	3.19	4.90	1.04	3.38	45.3
s.d.	1.66	5.36	1.53	3.32	22.7
c.v. as %	52	109	147	98	50

Source: Fitzwilliam Account Rolls, 2388, 233, 2389.
Key to column headings: a = equus carectarius; b = affrus; c = iumenta; d =
young horses; e = workhorses (equus carectarius + affrus + iumenta) as % of
number of oxen calculated according to John Langdon, *Horses, Oxen and Technological
Innovation* (Cambridge, 1986), table 11.
[a]The calculations are based on the number of horses at the opening of the
accounting year. I have not included the horses at the breeding park of Eye, which
herd contained between 22 and 24 mares, and twice that number of young stock in
the first decade of the fourteenth century. To calculate column e (% of work horses),
I excluded from calculation those manors with no oxen, or more than a 100%
proportion of workhorses.

on the market and did not breed them. It did, however, replace its
plough horses (*affri* [*auri, averi*]) largely through its own stock. Different marketing and reproductive strategies shaped the demography
of the horse herd depending on the use (transport, ploughing, riding)
to which the Abbey put a subgroup.

The accountants distinguished the following types of horses in the
livestock accounts of the early fourteenth century. They defined cart
horses (*equi carectarii*) by their specialized work of hauling. The cate-

gory was flexible. Cart horses could be moved into the affer category; likewise, affers could be moved into the category of cart horses. On rare occasions three-year-old horses were graduated directly into the category of *equi carectarii*. Only females appeared in the subgroup *iumenta*. The entry appears on manors where mares were bred to stock the horse population. To further distinguish their breeding status, accounts sometimes labeled this group *iumenta affra*. Accountants called the mature subgroup of workhorses of the estate *affers* (*avers*). In the early fourteenth century, accountants used this word to apply to horses only. Accountants distinguished immature horses (*pullani*) by their age. The accounts also mention *runcini*, riding horses, bred in the horse park at the manor of Eye.

In the early fourteenth century, cart horses comprised over one-third of workhorses and one-quarter of all horses, younger horses included, on the estate. The Abbey graduated no more than 3 percent of its young horses into the subgroup of cart horses. The mean stocking rate for the decade, 2.3 percent, indicates that the Abbey did not try to reproduce cart horses on the estate. It bought them on the market as it needed to replace old or dead stock. Cart horses were available in the regional markets at an average price of 25s. 1d. The Abbey paid up to 46s. 8d. for its most expensive cart horse in the early fourteenth century. The average price for a cart horse was twice that of a workhorse. Presumably cart horses cost more because they were larger, heavier, and more trained than workhorses. The accounts do not inform us about who reared and trained cart horses in the regional economy.

Workhorses, or affers, were more numerous than cart horses on the estate. On several manors the accounts refer to *caruce equine*, or horse ploughs; nevertheless, oxen outnumbered workhorses four and three to one in the first decade of the fourteenth century and remained the chief plough animal on the estate.[3]

The Abbey did replace its workhorses at a slow rate. Female affers were mated to ensure a replacement rate of 8 to 10 percent. The Abbey kept as few young horses as possible. In contrast with herds of cattle and sheep, where young animals (newborns to three-year-olds) composed between 40 and 60 percent of the respective herds, young horses never composed more than 30 percent of the horses on the estate. The Abbey sold the young horses that it did not graduate into the subgroup of workhorses.

Table 36. Purchase and Sale of Horses on the Peterborough Abbey Estate

	Cart Horses			Mares & Affers			Young Horses			
	a	b	c	a	b	c	a	b	c	Net
1300–01	8	3	−174.6	1	4	+23.4	0	2	21	−130.3
1307–08	15	3	−296.5	8	10	−72.5	0	4	43.5	−325.5
1309–10	13	2	−290.2	1	9	28.5	0	5	57.5	−204.2

Source: Fitzwilliam Account Rolls, 2388, 233, 2389
Key to column headings: a = number bought; b = number sold; c = net of buying and selling in shillings.

The demography of the herd of riding horses at the horse park at Eye contrasted sharply with the strategies for keeping cart horses and workhorses on the estate. The Abbey bred its own riding horses (*runcini*) at Eye Park. Young horses composed between 60 and 70 percent of the herd. Three-year-old horses stocked the subgroup of breeding mares and riding horses at the rate of 100 percent. The Abbey stocked its riding stable with riding horses from Eye and offered runcini as gifts to friends and officials. The Abbey sold no riding horses in the early fourteenth century.

The Abbey always spent more on the purchase of horses than it made on sales (table 36). Cart horses cost the Abbey the most in purchase and upkeep. The Abbey expended between 15 and 25 percent of its annual oat harvest as fodder for its cart horses (table 37). The horses of the Abbey's stable consumed another 25 percent of the yield of oats. In toto the Abbey expended over 50 percent of its annual harvest of oats on transport animals on the estate. Workhorses, even though more numerous than cart or riding horses, ate only a small portion (6–12 percent) of the oat harvest. So much of the oat harvest went to horses that oats sown on the demesne should be regarded as a fodder rather than a food crop. The Abbey actually bought oats to supplement its supply of fodder on the estate. It sold less oats than it purchased in the first decade of the fourteenth century.

Costs of transport on the estate involved more than the consumption of oats (table 37). The Abbey had to maintain its carts; a new iron-bound cart cost between 16 and 19.5 shillings on the estate in the fourteenth century. It had to shoe cart horses and employ carters for wages in cash and kind. The Abbey's investment in transport is quantified in table 38 and compared with the costs of maintaining its plough horses. The transport costs exceeded the ploughing costs between five and nine times over. The Abbey could defray much of these costs, since it fed its horses with fodder produced on its own demesnes. If all the expenses incurred in transport on the estate had passed through the market, then the Abbey would have actually invested more in cart horses and transport than it made on its wool

Table 37. Consumption of Oats as Fodder on the Peterborough Abbey Estate

	a	b	c	d	e	f	g	h	i
1300–01	2,407	30.5	38.3	28.7	15.0	5.8	0.1	72.5	3.0
1307–08	2,885	27.3	36.8	27.2	22.7	6.8	1.3	181.0	6.2
1309–10	2,281	24.3	36.5	24.7	24.8	11.6	2.4	102.8	4.5

Source: Fitzwilliam Account Rolls, 2388, 233, 2389
Key to column headings: a = yield of oats in quarters; b = % of total acreage planted in oats; c = % of oats reserved as seed; d = % of oats fed to the horses of the Abbot; e = % of oats fed to demesne cart horses; f = % of oats fed to demesne affers; g = % of oats fed to demesne young horses; h = amount of oats bought in quarters; i = oats bought as % of total oats reported on estate.

Table 38. Quantification of Transport and Horse-Ploughing Expenses: Estate of Peterborough Abbey

	Transport					Ploughing		
	a	b	c	d	e	f	g	h
1300–01	2,460	630	56	118	3,264	290	59	349
1307–08	3,926	801	70	152	4,949	535	70	605
1309–10	3,091	807	75	160	4,133	700	73	773

Source: Fitzwilliam Account Rolls, 2388, 233, 2389
Key to column headings: a = value of oats fed to Abbot's riding horses and cart horses in shillings; b = cost of upkeep of carts in shillings; c = cost of shoeing cart horses in shillings; d = wages for carters in shillings; e = total transport expenses costed in shillings; f = value of oats fed to affers in shillings; g = cost of shoeing affers in shillings; h = total horse-ploughing expenses costed in shillings.

sales in the early fourteenth century. Transport, therefore, emerges as a costly investment on the feudal estate. Only the Abbey's non-market ties with consumption made it possible to reduce such costs.

PIGS

The Abbey of Peterborough kept pigs to supply its household of 140 odd members with meat.[4] The Abbey was a consumer and not a marketer of pigs. The annual harvest of pigs from the manors of the estate and from the Abbey's piggery at Peterborough satisfied just under 50 percent of the caloric requirements of the large household.

The sty management of pigs had reached an elaborate state of development on the estate by the early fourteenth century. A study of the accounts of the Abbey's piggery and the manorial accounts offers a detailed picture of pig management and the supply of pork to the Abbey.

The Abbey had doubled the size of its pig herd between the survey of 1125 and the early-fourteenth-century accounts. Summary statistics for the estate herd appear in table 39. The account rolls also report on the demographic makeup of the pig herds at the end of the accounting year (late summer-autumn). These data are listed in table 40 for the accounting year 1300–01. The accountants classified hogs and piglets by terms (*first*, *second*, and *third*) that probably referred to litters born

Table 39. Summary Statistics for Demesne Pigs Peterborough Abbey Estate

	a	b	c	d	e
1300–01	73.6	58.4	79	1,394	19
1307–08	88.4	61.2	69	1,857	21
1309–10	79.8	48.4	61	1,676	21

Source: Fitzwilliam Account Rolls, 2388, 233, 2389

Key to column headings: a = mean number of pigs on manors using the grand total (*summa*) listed in the accounts; b = standard deviation; c = coefficient of variation expressed as a percent; d = total number of pigs on the estate; e = number of manors involved in the calculations.

Table 40. Composition of Pig Herds at the End of the Accounting
Year 1300–01

	a	b
boars	23	2.3
sows	39	4.0
castrates	489	48.8
hogs	158	15.8
weaned	63	6.3
nursing	67	6.7
piglets of different terms	163	16.3
Total	1002	

Source: Fitzwilliam Account Rolls, 2388, 233, 2389
Key to column headings: a = number at the end of the accounting year;
b = percentage of population.

in different terms of the accounting year. They described a small
portion—12.9 percent (130/1002)—of immature pigs as nursing or
just weaned. The subadult and mature animals comprising boars,
sows, and castrates constituted 54.9 percent (551/1002) of the herd.
Mature castrated pigs composed almost half of the population—48.8
percent (489/1002).

The size of a manor's pig herd in the fourteenth century was
significantly associated with the expenditure of grain and legumes on
their sustenance and fattening.[5] The benefits of available forage were
not ignored, but all manors, even Cottingham in Rockingham Forest,
relied on the use of grains and legumes as pig feed in the early
fourteenth century. Table 41 lists the amount of grain and legumes
used in sustaining and fattening demesne pigs. When the number of
pigs on each manor is correlated with the number of bushels of grain
and legumes expended, the correlations are significant. The correlations suggest that the Abbey grew legumes as a fodder crop for its
pigs. Whatever beneficial effects legumes had on soil fertilty appear to
have been secondary to the Abbey's use of legumes as fodder for a
chief source of meat for the Abbey.[6]

The Abbey expended a much smaller proportion of its oats, barley,

Table 41. Summary Statistics of Crops Used to Fatten Pigs: Peterborough Abbey Estate[a]

	a	b	c	d	e
1300–01	78	292	3,246.5	715	24.7
1307–08	16	344	5,585	1,554	28.0
1309–10	80	453	4,667	1,276	31.4

Source: Fitzwilliam Account Rolls, 2388, 233, 2389.
Key to column headings: a = total bushels of oats fed to pigs; b = total bushels of barley and dredge fed to pigs; c = total bushels of legumes produced; d = total bushels of legumes fed to pigs; e = mean percentage of legume crop fed to pigs.

[a] For a breakdown of grain and legumes fed to pigs on the different manors of the estate see Kathleen Biddick, "Pig Husbandry on the Peterborough Abbey Estate," in *Animals and Archaeology*, ed. Juliet Clutton-Brock and Caroline Grigson (Oxford, 1985), table 7.

and dredge as fodder for pigs. Legumes were the crop most commonly fed to pigs. Over the three accounting years of the first decade of the 1300s, approximately one-third of the legume harvest was fed to pigs on the six core manors. The mean percentage of the legume harvest fed to pigs on all the manors over that decade was 28.2 percent. In the accounting year 1309–10, the Abbey planted on average 10 percent of its demesne acres with legumes.

Investment in intensive pig management in the fourteenth century extended beyond the grain expenditures for their sustenance. Every manor employed a swineherd with the exception of Ashton, Irthlingborough, and Tinwell. The Abbey paid these servants in cash and grain. The ubiquity of manorial swineherds on the Peterborough estate is in sharp contrast with the more conservative economic policy advised in the *Seneschaucy*, a tract on estate management composed around the year 1276:

> A swineherd ought to be on those manors where pigs can support themselves and find their own food, without help from the grange, in forest, wood, marsh, or waste... If there are no woods, marsh, or waste where pigs could support themselves without having to be kept entirely with food from the grange, no swineherd ought to be employed, and only as many pigs may be kept on such manors as can be fed in August on stubble and the leavings of the grange when corn for sale is being threshed.[7]

Table 42. The Piggery of the Abbey at Peterborough, 1309–10

Previous Year	Births	Total	Death	No. Butchered	Remain	Subgroups of Herd
81	140	221	1	1 boar	76	4 boars
				60 castrates		6 sows
				83 piglets		10 castrates
						14 hogs
						20 3rd term
						22 weaned

The size of manorial pig herds did not relate to dairy activity, as might have been expected from early modern practices of "finishing" pigs on whey in dairy areas. For instance, the main dairy center of the Abbey, the manor of Eye, kept no pig herd. The delicate drainage of the low-lying fen pastures surrounding Eye could have been a reason for excluding pigs, since their rooting caused damage to the fen dikes.

The Abbey butchered on average 25 percent of its manorial pig herd annually. Its own piggery at Peterborough was as large as the average manor herd. In the year 1309–10 its piggery housed 221 beasts (table 42). The Abbey butchered 144 pigs in its own piggery and consumed an additional 512 sent in from its manors.

From this amount of pork the Abbey harvested an estimated 42,280 pounds (19,218.2 kg) of dressed meat yielding 54,964,000 calories. From this yield the community of 140 men could feed for 157 days at 2,500 calories per day. This proportion of pig meat in the diet is higher, but not much higher, than estimates for the early twelfth century based on the 1125 survey.[8]

Medieval expectations for pig reproduction were high. Walter of Henley stipulated that "the sow ought to bear twice a year, and at each farrowing she ought to bear at least seven pigs."[9] Given a gestation period of sixteen weeks and a probable lactation of four weeks, the sow producing two litters was involved in some aspect of reproduction through the year.[10]

The actual number of sows available in the breeding pool is

difficult to calculate, although this figure is clearly stated in the accounts for cows, ewes, and mares. In the year 1309–10 the Abbey piggery had at least six mature females in the breeding pool. Some younger females in accounting categories other than sow must have been producing as well, since, at the rate of two litters per year and a high average of eight piglets per litter, the six sows would produce 96 piglets—considerably short of the total of 140 piglets known to have been born in that year.

The production of pork for consumption was an important economic strategy for Peterborough Abbey in the early fourteenth century. By satisfying half of its annual caloric requirements with estate-grown pork, the Abbey could avoid the market as a consumer and avoid heavy culling of its cattle and sheep herds of meat. Meat was the main product of pig husbandry. The Abbey's reliance on pork is not surprising. The Abbey consistently opted for single-product herd economies. It used oxen for traction, sheep for wool, horses for transport and some ploughing, and pigs for meat. During the period of seigneurial high farming the Abbey did not pursue the alternative strategy of using one animal for several products at once. Such a strategy grew more typical in regional economies of the fifteenth century.

POULTRY

The accountants enumerated the hens, roosters, capons, chicks, pigeons, geese, ducks, swans, and pheasants on the Abbey's manors. Table 43 lists these poultry along with the renders of poultry and eggs made by the Abbey's peasants for their rents and court fines. The Abbey collected the bulk of its chickens from its peasants. Among the larger poultry the Abbey specialized in keeping geese, herding between 579 and 800 of these birds in the first decade of the fourteenth century. The Abbey had dovecotes on approximately half of its manors and consumed virtually all the offspring of its cotes each year. The number of pigeons consumed annually ranged beetween 1,377 and 2,544. The peasants of the Abbey also contributed enough eggs annually to serve each of the sixty monks of the monastic household three times weekly.

Table 43. Poultry on the Manors of Peterborough Abbey

1300–01	HENS & ROOSTERS Gallinae Galli				CAPONS Capones				PIGEONS Columbe			GEESE Auce			DUCKS Anatre			EGGS Oves				CHICKS Pulcini			
	f.[a]	t.	A.	s.	f.	t.	A.	s.	f.	A.	s.	f.	A.	s.	f.	A.	s.	f.	t.	A.	s.	f.	t.	A.	s.
Walton	6	66	32			8	8					16	12					120	1820	620					
Longthorpe	5	75	61	5					213	181		16	14					100	785	705	100				
Castor	12	78	40	14		5			294	264		45	34	7				140	1140	60	100	14		12	
Werrington	7	68	59			6	6					11	47					60	870	845	45			32	
Glinton	12	71	60		2	8	4					13	33					200	879	900	40	8		12	8
Eye	11	30	30		10	8	4					49	90					360	390	740		15			
Boroughbury	6	168	74	8		6	12		249		60	30	34		25			110	1340	680		18	13		
La Biggin	7		2									15	12	4				150							
Oundle	6					9	7	2	406	346		17	12					160			100	24	10		
Warmington[p]	10	195	124	15	8	3			280	220		64	b	b	39	15	6	162	308	585		24		60	
Tinwell	6	32	29	6	6	19	6	14	170	140		18							550	500					
Stanwick	7	26	25		8	21	18		116	86		20	18					210	220	700		20		12	
Kettering	6	43			28	30	12	19	260	140	30	42	10					2	540	860		28		20	
Irthlingboro'[r]						12																		50	
Cottingham[p]																									
Great Easton																									
Collingham[p]	14	16							414		394	53	18					900			900	20			20
Scotere[s]	6											24						200			200	23			8
Fiskerton[s]	11	102		82								112	36	29								80			24
Ashton												12	6												
Walcot	5	62		53														120	360		320	4			
	137	1032	536	183	62	127	77	35	2402	1377	484	557	364	40	64	15	6	2994	9202	7195	1805	278	23	198	60

Table 43 (*continued*)

1307–08	HENS & ROOSTERS *Gallinae Galli*				CAPONS *Capones*				PIGEONS *Columbe*			GEESE *Auce*			DUCKS *Anatre*			EGGS *Oves*				CHICKS *Pulcini*			
	f.	t.	A.	S.	f.	t.	A.	S.	f.	A.	S.	f.	A.	S.	f.	A.	S.	f.	t.	A.	S.	f.	t.	A.	S.
Walton	15	56	67		6	8	10					66	26					185	785	1000		12			7
Longthorpe	24	75	87						80	80		28	20		7			80	1140	800		18			
Castor	8	78	46		15	9	20		340	340		50	26	2	27	12		80	870	1100		6	20		
Werrington	23	68	66	16	32	10	26					115	94		3	4		159	879	1100		14			
Glinton	4	71	60	4	14	12	6					52	28	17				38	420	800					
Eye	59	30	103		22	4	71															20			
Boroughbury	8	168	124		2	4	12		770	750		12	12					180	1340	70					
La Biggin	8							6	229	140		33		20				200			100	18			6
Oundle	8			1	6	8	8		342	236		28	26	3				160	200	200					
Warmington	11	195	120	8	3	5			943	538		53	146		10	6		267	308	660		18			
Tinwell		32	30		5	23	24		410	320	40	24	10						550	500					
Stanwick	10	30				21	12	5	200	140		38	12					220	60	300		18			
Kettering	8	42	80	19	12	52	52					46	85		9		3	252	540	1400					
Irthlingboro'	9	10			14	6	6					44	13												
Cottingham	8	80	60		2	1						47	6					160	900	700	160				
Great Easton	10	82	60		12	8		8	600		280	50		28				148	752	600	160				
Collingham	14	16		9	10	2			423		340	28		10				900			760	20			14
Scotere	15			16				13						10				260			200	23			5
Fiskerton	9	102		3	28							43										27			
Ashton	7	2		94	16													160	160	320		10			
Walcot	5	62		56	4			4	220		216	43	6		10	6						12			4
	263	1199	903	226	203	173	247	36	4548	2544	876	800	510	90	66	28	3	3449	8904	9550	1380	216	20		36

Table 43 (continued)

1309–10	HENS & ROOSTERS Gallinae Galli				CAPONS Capones				PIGEONS Columbe			GEESE Auce			DUCKS Anatre			EGGS Oves				CHICKS Pulcini			
	f.	t.	A.	s.	f.	t.	A.	s.	f.	A.	s.	f.	A.	s.	f.	A.	s.	f.	t.	A.	s.	f.	t.	A.	s.
Walton	19	56	72		4	8	8	4	202	182		48	12	15				200	820	940		19		19	
Longthorpe	21	75	80				36	2				33	26					80	785	800	100	21			
Castor	12	78	72	52	18	9	20					38	40		25	12		100	1140	680		26		24	
Werrington	4	58	69		14	12	30					56	44					380	870	1400		17		34	
Glinton	12	71	55		0	10	4					38	48					100	879	760		39			
Eye	7	30	29		1	2	12		401	125		125	112					140	380	520		21		54	13
Boroughbury	6	168	90			4	5		480	420		16	13					260	1340	620					
La Biggin	8		20		11		23								6	6		60		60		20		9	
Oundle						3			800	710		38	34			6	8	600		600		16			
Warmington	11	195	121	4	30	7	20	5	410	320	60	60	60					312	307	500		37			
Tinwell	6	32	30		7	23	11		322	182		10	20		27			150	550	560		10		44	
Stanwick	8	30	20		19	19	30		230	160		21	25					130	220	700					
Kettering	7	43	40		10	23	8		270	200		41	15					160	540	1000		20			10
Irthlingboro'	5	4		4	12	8						10	10					500		500					
Cottingham	8	82	60	20		8	8	14	240	60	60	58	11	6	2	10		160	800	1100		24			13
Great Easton				72				6				35	10	17				128	752	1200		20			
Collingham	14	16		16					480		360	32						780			600	24			
Scotere	7								292		228	24		11				200			80	22			4
Fiskerton	8	102		89	22							26						100			20	20			
Ashton	10		24									30	21		6	6		100		600		16			
Walcot	5	62		55					340		320							120	390		90	6			4
	178	1102	782	312	148	128	215	31	4467	2359	1028	739	501	49	66	40	8	4760	9773	12,540	890	378		184	44

a Abbreviation used in table: f. = manorial flock
t. = from tenants
A. = to Abbey
s. = swans

THE LINK THAT SEPARATES

Evidence for the pastoral economy of one medieval estate cannot rewrite our models of medieval agricultural development. The findings do, however, question concepts of productivity and relations of pastoral and cereal agriculture basic to such models. Political reliance on consumption to conserve agrarian lordship and economic reliance on consumption to mitigate market dependence profoundly shaped production on the Peterborough Abbey estate. The centrality of consumption to the Abbey's production indicates the need for further comparative studies of consumption on estates of different size and ownership. Further research on everyday consumption of agricultural products will substantially revise our models of medieval productivity which have neglected household consumption. The study also shows that the pastoral and cereal sector of the estate economy did not oppose each other as posited by our development models. The Abbey linked different livestock and their products with its household economy, the market, and its cereal agriculture along multiple paths. It cleared new paths and linked cereal and pastoral activities in news ways as its political and economic position changed. As a well-endowed Abbey with twenty-three manors, the Abbey coordinated an ensemble of resources to achieve such linkages. On an estate of this scale, the estate economy cannot be reduced to any one of its manorial economies but requires analysis as a network.

Such multiple and changing links between the pastoral and cereal sector complicate methodological efforts to find any one unitary "pastoral" index. In the early twelfth century, when the Abbey had not yet turned to large-scale cash-cropping and direct estate-management, its estimated livestock ratio, or number of cattle, horses, and sheep per one hundred cultivated acres, measured 88.8. At a high-farming peak, its early-fourteenth-century livestock ratio had dropped to 70.8, a ratio that compared well with the estate of the Bishop of Winchester, where a supposed pastoral crisis existed. Peterborough Abbey and Winchester enjoyed livestock ratios almost twice those of Westminster Abbey and demesnes in eastern Norfolk for the same period. Does that mean, then, that Peterborough and Winchester are pastoral estates during this period and Westminster and eastern Norfolk arable demesnes? The risks of simple comparisons of such measures become clearer if we look at the changing composition of Peterborough's livestock ratio. In the early twelfth century, cattle, chiefly oxen, dominated the livestock ratio, by contributing just under two-thirds of the ratio. Sheep and horses together contributed the remaining third of the livestock ratio. By the first decade of the fourteenth century such relationships had reversed. Sheep and horses contributed just under two-thirds of the livestock ratio; cattle, one-third. Presumably the Abbey could have achieved the higher twelfth-century livestock ratio of 88.8 if it had herded more livestock rather than sold its hay and pasture resources, as it chose to do in the fourteenth century. The simple relations between pastoral and cereal husbandry posited by Postan do not adequately account for the comparative commercialization of haulage, dairying, and wool production over the thirteenth century and the trade-offs made between producing such products and selling pastoral resources to others to produce them.

Its commitment to conserving certain consumption strategies did not mean that the Abbey resisted technological innovation or market involvement. It engaged in indebtedness as did large and small lay and ecclesiastical lords of the twelfth century. It adopted Cistercian improvements such as windmills and cereal granges operated by wage labor soon after their introduction into England. The estate herded on average twice the number of workhorses and cart horses as other demesnes in the eastern Midlands. The Abbey had certainly committed itself to investments in speedy haulage. In the instances where the Abbey recorded cereal yields, they were good to excellent, compared to the highyielding Norfolk demesnes. The Abbey used the same strategies observed by Bruce Campbell in Norfolk to achieve such good yields. It spent money on the purchase, hauling, and spreading of manure and hired workers to weed. It applied such strategies near the Abbey where the bulk of the grain went to house-hold consumption and not to the market. Thus, strategies to achieve high yields need not be construed narrowly as market strategies. On the estate of Peterborough Abbey, we find such investments in higher yields occurring in consumption contexts. In Norfolk such strategies occurred on manors producing for the market.

The Abbey selectively participated in medieval markets to conserve its powers to consume. The Abbey did not have to step outside of its household economy to consume basic foodstuffs; nor did it rely on the market to replace the sources of such products. The Abbey did, however, appear on the market as a seller of animal products when it so chose. It thus simultaneously enjoyed the advantages of "costless" everyday consumption of foodstuffs and the profit the market could bring by preventing subsumption of consumption by the market.

The Abbey's strategies of consumption shaped the demography of the estate cattle herd, and therefore its productivity. Its reliance on consuming estate-produced bread and ale as chief sources of nourishment determined that the traction produced by the oxen of its cattle herd became a main, albeit hidden, ingredient of household consumption. The Abbey organized the demography of its cattle herd to furnish the necessary oxen needed for ploughing its demesne. The production of beef and dairy products took second place to the production of traction. The Abbey, in fact, preferred to sell fodder, pasture, and meadow to its peasants rather than expend its herd of dairy cows and young beef cattle. The Abbey's choice not to husband more beef and dairy cattle in order to accumulate capital or, in other words, to maximize profit demonstrates how fundamentally a secure source of consumption motivated the Abbey's household economy.

The Abbey knew how to produce profit but did so selectively. It produced wool for cash and used the market to expand flock size when wool prices rose. It never relinquished, however, its basic control over biological reproduction of its sheep flock. By herding a reproductive flock, the Abbey conserved its ability to shift from cash-cropping to subsistence husbandry. For once interregional markets began to organize herd reproduction, as in the early modern period, sheepherders became irreversibly caught in cash-cropping of livestock products.

The evidence also suggests that the specialized pursuit of cash in seigneurial sheep husbandry, which started in earnest in the late twelfth century, overturned a long-standing practice of consumption which relied on sheep as dairy animals. In the twelfth and early thirteenth century, production shifted from a diversified reliance on dairy and wool to a highly specialized concentration on the production of fine wool. Sheep dairying dropped out of the seigneurial economy of sheep husbandry. Dairy cows grew in importance to the Abbey with such a shift.

The horse husbandry of the Abbey illustrates both the flexibility and the potential instability of its pastoral economy. The Abbey bred its own riding horses, the animals that marked its lordly status, and eschewed the market for their supply. By relying on its stud farm to furnish its riding horses, the Abbey conserved long-standing links between its consumption sphere and its embodiment of agrarian lordship. The Abbey did not breed its own cart horses. It relied on market purchases to replace these animals on the estate. Cart horses gained economic importance as transport animals on the estate in the thirteenth century and embodied the link of the Abbey to the market. The Abbey's commitment to speedier haulage and ploughing was considerable. It kept, on average, almost twice as many workhorses as other demesnes in the East Midlands. Such a contrast reminds us that within a geographical region, such as the East Midlands, different estates pursued different economic policies, which produced variation, much in need of further study. The Abbey's practices of consumption made its investment in workhorses possible. It fed its horses with its own demesne-produced oats, thus defraying the considerable fodder-costs of keeping work-horses.

Pig husbandry long remained central to the Abbey's household consumption. As the Abbey began more intensive management of its woodland resources over the eleventh and twelfth centuries and converted much of this preferred habitat of pigs into fields, it developed sty husbandry and continued to consume pork as an important source of calories in its household diet. Again, its practices of consumption facilitated its sty management of pigs. It fed a substantial portion of its demesne-grown legumes to its pigs.

The Abbey's consumption of poultry also harked back to its oldest practices of consumption. It collected most of its poultry and eggs from its peasants. The use of pigeons to supplement the Abbey's diet grew out of new strategies of production grafted onto the household economy in the thirteenth century.

The one-dimensional concern with production in medieval agricultural history has left consumption invisible in medieval rural economies. The findings of this study show how consumption shaped production, exchange, and reproduction in the pastoral economy of the estate of Peterborough Abbey. Such findings bear on the debate over technological innovation and productivity in medieval agriculture. Postan ascribed the stagnation of English manorial regimes to the low rate of investments in agriculture made by English lords. If lords had been rational economic actors, they would have invested more. Recent research on the high productivity of medieval agriculture in the county of Norfolk has recast the debate on agrarian innovation by emphasizing structural rather than technological differences. Differences in the units of production, fields and farms, not technology, critically influenced agrarian progress and productivity. The links between consumption, production, and reproduction outlined in this study call for widening the debate on agrarian structure to include units of consumption and differences in consumption practices.

The local findings also bear on the debate over the market in the rural economy of medieval England. To reproduce themselves as agrarian lords in a political economy that burdened them with taxation, litigation, and political service, the lords of Peterborough Abbey actively, but selectively, participated in the market at the same time they strove to conserve the "costless" consumption of estate-produced subsistence goods. For them, market and subsistence relations paradoxically intertwined rather than polarized, as some simplistic models of historic markets have led us to expect. The Abbey reproduced agrarian lordship as long as it conserved an asymmetry between consumption and exchange. An almost exclusive concentration on the productive sphere in medieval economic history has obscured the importance of this asymmetry.

The feathers and furs conspicuously consumed by English lords camouflaged the seriousness of everyday consumption of subsistence goods in their estate economies. Their decisions about consuming and marketing resources embodied feudal power, the link that separated them from the peasant farmers among whom they lived and to whom they allocated resources.

APPENDIXES

Appendix 1. Monthly Food Render—Ramsey Abbey c. A.D. 1100

	Value (monthly) s.	d.	Yearly Total (s.)	% Yearly Total	Yearly Amount
Total monthly	335	1	4,021	80.7	
Cash payment	80	0	960	19.2	
			4,981		
GRAIN[a]					
Bread flour	60	0	720		144 q
Grut	24		288		136 q
Malt	32		384		160 q
Oat fodder	12		144		80 q
Loaves	13	4	160		24,000 loaves
Sum			1,696	34.0	
OTHER ARABLE PRODUCTS					
Beans	1.3		16	0.3	24 treiae
ANIMALS					
Lambs	1.2		14		
Piglets	9		108		
Sum			122	2.4	
FOWL					
Chicken	1	8	20		
Geese	0	7	7		
Sum			27	0.5	
SECONDARY[b] PRODUCTS					
Lard	50		600		120 pensae
Cheese	30		360		120 pensae
Eggs	4		48		24,000
Butter	6	8	80		24 treiae
			1,088	21.8	
Honey[c]	5	4	64	1.3	24 sextariae

Source: *Cartularium Monasterii de Rameseia* 3:230–234.

[a] Bread flour listed in quarters (q.). Grut, malt, and *prebendae* (horse fodder) translated from *mittae* into quarters according to schedule published by Raftis in *The Estates of Ramsey Abbey*, 159 n.1.

[b] Lard and cheese are measured in *pensae*. According to W. H. Prior, "Weights and Measures of Medieval England," *Bulletin du Cange: Archivum Latinitatis Medii Aevi* 1 (1924): 88, there are two types of pensae, the regular pensa weighing between 144 and 168 pounds (65.5–76.4 kg) and a "small" pensa of 32 pounds (14.5 kg). The cash valuation for a pensa of lard at 5s. and a pensa of cheese at 3s. suggests that the heavier pensa was the measure used for the monthly renders: David L. Farmer, "Some Price Fluctuations in Angevin England," *Economic History Review*. 2d ser., 9 (1956–57): 34–43.

[c] 24 *sextariae* of honey is equivalent to 13 litres.

Appendix 2. Calculations of Acreage Required to Meet Expectations of Consumption with a Surplus of 50 Percent (Based on Ramsey Abbey Food Farm Schedule)[a]

Net Yields: The following net yields drawn from J. Z. Titow, *English Rural Society* (London, 1969), 81 are used in the calculations:

Wheat: 7 bu per ac

Barley: 10 bu per ac

Oats: 5 bu per ac

Wheat: Ramsey Abbey annually consumed 144 quarters of fine flour (*farinae ad panem monachorum*). Eight bushels of wheat, when cleaned, carefully milled, and sieved, produced 4 bushels of fine flour for monks' bread according to the Beaulieu Abbey accounts. Table for the Bake House and Account for Bake House #77 (pp. 289–304) in S. F. Hockey, *The Account-Book of Beaulieu Abbey*, Camden Fourth Series, vol. 16 (London, 1975).

144 q fine flour = 288 q wheat

288 q × 8 = 2,304 bu / 7 = 329 ac

2 course 329 × 2 = 658 ac (+50% surplus) = 987 ac

3 course 329 × 1.5 = 494 ac (+50% surplus) = 741 ac

Grut: The Abbey consumed 136 quarters of grut annually. Grut is second-grade flour. A quarter of wheat can produce 4 bushels of second-grade flour (*Beaulieu Abbey*, 289–304). There is therefore no reason to add in additional acreage for grut.

Barley: The Abbey consumed 160 quarters of barley annually.

160 q × 8 = 1,280 bu / 10 bu = 128 ac

2 course 128 × 2 = 256 ac (+50% surplus) = 384 ac

3 course 128 × 1.5 = 192 ac (+50% surplus) = 288 ac

Prebendae (oat fodder) = 80 q

80 × 8 bu = 640 / 5 bu = 128 ac

2 course 128 × 2 = 256 ac (+50% surplus) = 384 ac

3 course 128 × 1.5 = 192 ac (+50% surplus) = 288 ac

Source: *Cartularium Monasterii de Rameseia* 3:230–234.

[a] Abbreviations: ac = acre; bu = bushel; q = quarter.

Appendix 3. Calculations of Numbers of Livestock Required to
Produce Secondary Products Consumed by Ramsey Abbey (Based on
Ramsey Abbey Food Schedule)

Lard

According to "The rules and rubrics included in the treatise on accounting
in MS. 79" (Oschinsky, *Walter of Henley*, appendix VIII, 469–475), a
mature pig should produce 2 pounds of lard: De uncto et sepo. Item i
porcus masculus ii annorum respondebit communiter de ii libris uncti que
valebunt ad minus iii d.

In 1208–09 195 pigs killed for the larder of the manor of Downton,
Wilts. yielded 2 weys (*pondera*) of lard (*uncti*) worth 22s. At the rate of
14 stones = 1 wey and 12 1/2 pounds = 1 stone, the pigs produced 350
pounds of lard, which equals 1.8 pounds of lard per pig, a figure reasonably
in line with the accounting guidelines given above (for Downton account
consult Hubert Hall, *The Pipe Roll of the Bishopric of Winchester* [London,
1903], 20). Assuming 2 pounds of lard per pig, 8,640 pigs could produce
the 17,280 pounds of lard collected annually by the Abbey.

CHEESE Oschinsky, *Walter of Henley*, 180

(cows) 1 cow to yield on good pasture during 22 weeks of summer 7 stone
cheese and 1 stone butter or 87.5 pounds cheese and 12.5 pounds butter.
To produce 17,280 pounds cheese Ramsey would have to milk 197 cows.

CHEESE Oschinsky, *Walter of Henley*, 179

(ewes) 10 ewes should produce at the rate of one cow. Therefore, the figure
of 197 cows can be multiplied by 10 to yield 1970 ewes.

Appendix 4. Cattle Cohorts in Manorial Groupings: Peterborough Abbey

CATTLE COHORT	Autumn Tot.	Max Tot.	Manor Transfer	% Max	Stock	% Max	Buy	% Max	Dead	% Max	Sell	% Max	Butcher	% Max	IN Other	% Max
BULLS																
1300–01																
Home	8	13	3	23.1	5	38.4	0		0		0		1	7.6	0	
West	3	7	3	42.8	2	28.5	0		0		2	28.5	0		0	
Scarp[a]	0	1	b		1	100.0	0		0		0		0		0	
North	4	7	0		3	42.8	0		0		0		0		0	
	15	28	6	21.4	11	39.2	0		0		2	7.1	1	3.5	0	
1307–08																
Home	9	12	2	16.6	1	8.3	0		0		0		1	8.3	0	
West	5	6	0		1	16.6	0		0		0		0		0	
Scarp	4	6	0		1	16.6	1	16.6	0		1	16.6	1	16.6	0	
North	7	7	2	28.5	0		0		1	14.3	1	14.3	0		0	
	25	31	4	12.9	3	9.6	1	3.2	1	3.2	2	6.4	2	6.4	0	
1309–10																
Home	11	14	1	7.1	2	14.3	0		0		0		2	14.3	0	
West	5	5	0		0		0		0		0		0		0	
Scarp	4	5	0		1	20.0	0		0		2	40.0	0		0	
North	7	8	0		0		1	12.5	0		3	37.5	0		0	
	27	32	1	3.1	3	9.3	1	3.1	0		5	15.6	2	6.3	0	

OXEN

1300–01

Home	170	261	45	17.2	34	13.0	3	1.1	3	.3	0		37	14.2	5	1.9
West	96	105	9	8.5	00		5	4.8	0		1	11.1	6	5.7	1	9.4
Scarp	9	10	♭	0.0			0		0		0		0		0	
North	92	133	0	0.0	13	9.7	28	21.0	0		8	6.0	4	3.0	0	
	367	509	54	10.6	47	9.2	36	7.0	3	.6	9	1.8	47	9.2	6	1.2

1307–08

Home	235	304	50	16.4	26	8.5	0		4	1.5	1	0.3	20	6.5	1	0.3
West	99	129	3	2.3	12	9.3	15	11.6	1	.7	4	3.1	14	10.8	0	
Scarp	62	69	2	2.9	2	2.9	2	2.8	0		3	4.3	1	1.4	5	7.3
North	88	107	0		8	7.5	10	9.3	5	4.6	12	11.2	5	4.6	0	
	484	609	55	9.0	48	7.9	27	4.5	10	1.6	20	3.3	40	6.6	6	0.9

1309–10

Home	208	275	58	21.1	27	9.8	0		6	2.2	9	3.3	26	9.5	1	0.3
West	83	123	2	1.6	9	7.3	17	13.8	5	4.0	13	10.6	5	4.1	0	
Scarp	61	62	2	3.2	1	1.6	0		0		7	11.2	0		0	
North	93	97	0		3	3.1	1	1.0	1	1.0	11	11.3	1	1.0	0	
	445	557	62	11.3	40	7.2	18	3.2	12	2.2	40	7.2	32	5.7	1	0.1

Appendix 4 (*continued*)

CATTLE COHORT	Autumn Tot.	Max Tot.	Manor Transfer	% Max	Stock	% Max	Buy	% Max	Dead	% Max	Sell	% Max	Butcher	% Max	IN Other	% Max
COWS																
1300–01																
Home	131	178	15	8.4	29	16.3	1		1	0.5	2	1.1	4	2.2	3	1.6
West	63	78	0		13	16.6	0	0.6	0		0		1	1.3	0	
Scarp	1	3	0				0		0		1	33.3	0		2	66.6
North	58	80	0		19	23.7	3	3.7	0	1.3	7	8.8	0		0	
	253	339	15	4.4	61	17.9	4	1.1	2	0.5	10	2.9	5	1.4	5	1.4
1307–08																
Home	188	238	15	6.3	30	12.6	0		0		0		34	14.2	3	1.3
West	71	92	1	1.1	16	17.3	4	4.3	1	1.0	6	2.5	14	15.2	0	
Scarp	16	19	1	5.2	3	15.7	1	5.2	1	5.2	1	5.3	0		0	
North	64	78	0		11	14.1	3	3.8	4	5.1	3	3.8	4	5.1	0	
	339	427	17	3.9	60	14.0	8	1.8	6	1.4	10	2.3	52	12.1	3	0.7
1309–10																
Home	162	207	1	0.4	31	14.9	0		2	0.9	15	7.2	39	18.8	0	
West	70	91	0		9	9.8	12	13.2	0		12	13.1	9	9.8	0	
Scarp	15	17	0		3	17.6	0		1	5.8	0		0		0	
North	62	76	0		10	13.2	1	1.3	0		6	7.9	1	1.3	0	
	309	391	1	.2	53	13.5	13	3.3	3	0.8	33	8.4	49	12.5	0	

3–4-yr.-olds

	N			n	%	n	%	n	%	n	%
1300–01											
Home	70	0	0	0		0		1	1.4	0	
West	27	0	0	0		0		1	3.7	1	3.7
Scarp	2	0	0	1	50.	0		0		0	
North	35	0	0	1	3.	0		0		0	
	134	0	0	2	1.5	0		2	1.4	1	0.7
1307–08											
Home	65	0	0	0		0		13	20.2	0	
West	30	0	0	2	6.6	0		0		0	
Scarp	6	0	0	0		0		0		0	
North	23	0	0	1	4.3	3	13.0	0		0	
	124	0	0	3	2.4	3	2.4	13	10.4	0	
1309–10											
Home	82	0	0	0		0		26	31.7	0	
West	20	0	0	2	10.0	2	10.0	0		0	
Scarp	5	0	0	0		0		0		0	
North	20	0	0	0		7	35.0	0		0	
	127	0	0	2	1.5	9	7.1	26	20.4	0	

Appendix 4 (continued)

CATTLE COHORT	Autumn Tot.	Max Tot.	Manor Transfer	% Max	Stock	% Max	Buy	% Max	Dead	% Max	Sell	% Max	Butcher	% Max	IN Other	% Max
2–3-yr.-olds																
1300–01																
Home	67	69	0		0		0		2	2.8	0		3	4.3	7	10.1
West	23	23	0		0		0		1	4.3	0		0		0	
Scarp	1	2	0		0		0		0		0		0		0	
North	37	37	0		0		0		5	13.5	1	2.7	0		0	
	128	131	0		0		0		8	6.1	1	0.7	3	2.2	7	5.3
1307–08																
Home	99	102	7	6.8	0		0		11	10.7	0		6	5.8	2	1.9
West	32	32	0		0		0		2	6.2	0		0		0	
Scarp	5	5	0		0		0		0		1	20.0	0		0	
North	31	31	0		0		0		6	19.4	0		0		0	
	167	170	7	4.1	0		0		19	11.2	1	.5	6	3.5	2	1.1
1309–10																
Home	110	110	0		0		0		2	1.8	0		5	4.6	0	
West	38	38	0		0		0		2	5.2	2	5.2	0		0	
Scarp	6	6	0		0		0		2	33.3	0		0		0	
North	25	25	0		0		0		3	12.0	0		0		0	
	179	179	0		0		0		9	5.1	2	1.0	5	2.7	0	

1-yr.-olds

1300–01												
Home	88	88	0		0		2	2.2	1	1.1	0	
West	42	42	0		0		1	2.3	0		0	
Scarp	2	2	0		0		0		1	50.0	0	
North	35	35	0		0		4	11.4	0		0	
	167	167	0		0		7	4.2	2	2.0	0	
1307–08												
Home	119	127	8	6.3	0		7	5.5	0		2	1.5
West	37	37	0		0		3	8.1	0		0	
Scarp	6	6	0		0		1	16.6	0		0	
North	24	24	0		0		1	4.2	0		0	
	186	194	8	4.1	0		12	6.1	0		2	1.0
1309–10												
Home	81	82	1	1.2	0		5	6.1	0		0	
West	32	32	0		0		9	28.1	0		0	
Scarp	10	10	0		0		0		0		0	
North	33	33	0		0		2	6.0	0		0	
	156	157	1	0.6	0		16	10.2	0		0	

Appendix 4 (*continued*)

CATTLE COHORT	Autumn Tot.	Max Tot.	Manor Transfer	% Max	Stock	% Max	Buy	% Max	Dead	% Max	Sell	% Max	Butcher	% Max	IN Other	% Max
CALVES																
1300–01																
Home	128	130	0	0	0	0	2	1.5	2	1.5	0		8	6.2	0	
West	53	53	0	0	0	0	0		4	7.5	1	1.8	0		0	
Scarp	1	1	0		0		0		0		0		0		0	
North	49	49	0	0	0	0	0	0	4	8.2	4	8.2	0		0	
	231	233	0	0	0	0	2	0.8	10	4.2	5	2.1	8	3.4	0	
1307–08																
Home	153	166	10	6.0	0	0	5	3.0	12	7.2	0		24	14.4	0	
West	54	54	0		0		1	1.8	4	7.4	7	12.9	0		0	
Scarp	12	12	0		0		0		3	25.0	0		0		0	
North	39	39	0		0		0		5	12.8	9	23.1	0		0	
	258	271	10	3.6	0		6	2.2	24	8.8	16	5.9	24	8.8	0	
1309–10																
Home	141	141	0		0		0		4	2.8	6	4.3	31	21.9	0	
West	51	52	0		0		1	1.9	1	1.9	0		12	23.0	0	
Scarp	14	14	0		0		0		6	42.8	0		2	14.3	0	
North	36	36	0		0		0		1	2.7	2	5.5	0		0	
	242	243	0		0		1	0.4	12	4.9	8	3.3	45	18.5	0	

^a 1300–01—all cohorts; Scarp manors missing Cottingham, Great Easton.
^b Incomplete

Abbreviations used in appendixes 5–7
Appendix 5: ung. = unguent
HOME MANORS

BRBY	Boroughbury
CAST	Castor
EYE	Eye
GLIN	Glinton
LNTP	Longthorpe
NTHM	Northolm
WALT	Walton
WRNG	Werrington

WEST MANORS

ASHT	Ashton
BGGG	Biggin
ILBG	Ithlinborough
KTTG	Kettering
STWK	Stanwick
WARM	Warmington

SCARP MANORS

CTNG	Cottingham
GEST	Great Easton

NORTH MANORS

CLNM	Collingham
FISK	Fiskerton
SCTR	Scotter
TNWL	Tinwell
WLCT	Walcot

Appendix 7: under hogs, w = wethers; e = ewes

Appendix 5. Dairy Yields on the Manors of Peterborough Abbey 1307–08 (1 petra = 14 pounds; 10 ewes = 1 cow)[a]

	Cheese Petra	Sell Petra	% Sell	Milk Lagena	Petra Weight	% Sus.	Petra Pressura	Butter Petra	% Sold	Ung. Petra	Cream	Prod. Petra/Cow	Milk Brght Lagena
BRBY	63			390	28	1.5	0.5	16				4.37	
Cows 23	2.73				.95			0.70					
[b]GLIN	61.5	2	3.2	20	1.25	100		18	8.3			6.72	673
Cows 12	5.12				.10			1.5					
Lambs 256	(1.6)				(.03)			(.478)				(2.1)	
WRNG	93							30				7.23	
Cows 17	5.47							1.76					
LNTP	70			47	3	2		16.5					4
Cows 20	3.5				.15	42.5		.825				4.47	
CAST	23			36	2			6	16.6				
Cows 11	2.09				.181			.545				2.18	
[b]CLNM	112			42	(3)			21	96.4			9.7	40.5
Cows 14	8.0				.214			1.5					
Lambs 140	(1.0)	108	96		(.107)			(.68)				(4.7)	
[c]SCTR	93.25			202	14	79		19.25	100			8.43	241
Cows 15	6.15				.86			1.28					
Lambs 121	(3.41)	90.75	98		(.48)			(.047)				(3.93)	
[b]FISK	39.25			264	16.5	44		9					257

Cows 10	3.93 (1.51)				1.65 (.634)	.90 (.346)	66	22.2	6.48 (2.49)	
Lambs 159		28	71	270						
[b]WARM	47.5				19.5 1.14 (25.5)	11 .64 (.33)	81.8	4.5		255
Cows 17	2.79 (1.43)								4.57 (2.32)	
Lambs 163	(.59)	11.5	24.2	156						
BGGG	103.5				8.5 .53 (.217) 69.2	11 68 (.33)	40.9	40.9		352
Cows 16	6.46 (2.65)								7.67 (3.19)	
Lambs 237		49	47	151						
KTTG	110.5				8 .714 (.348) 68.2	16.5 .785 (.393)	72.7	6.0		266
Cows 21	5.26 (2.56)								6.42 (2.98)	
Ewes 243		56.5	51	95						
CTNG	116.5				5.5 .50 (.19) 100 (.571)	16 1.45	87.5	0		104
Cows 11	10.59 (4.16)								12.54 (6.57)	
Ewes 100		105.0	90.1							
Kids 49										
[b]GEST	14p					5 .030		100		
Cows 0	— (.085)									
Ewes 164		10	71.4						(1.15)	
EYE, NTHM	See appendix 6.									

[a] Number of lactating cows and ewes derived from number of cows and lambs born on the manor for the accounting year.

[b] Evidence for milking ewes.

[c] Petra = 16 pounds.

Appendix 6. Dairy Yields: The Manors of Eye and Northolm 1300–1483 (1 petra = 14 pounds, 10 ewes = 1 cow)

	Cheese Petra	Sell Petra	% Sell	Milk Lagena	Weight	% Milk Sus.	Petra Pressura	Butter Petra	% Sold	Cream Petra	Prod. Petra/Cow
1300–01[a] EYE	149[b]	(1)		473	16.5	61.3		30	65	4	
30 cows	3.95				.55			1		.133	6.65
328 lambs	30 estimated										(.091)
1307–08[a] EYE	221	131	54.1	368	25.5	89		42	54	1.5	4.8
60 cows	3.68				.425			.70			(3.2)
305 lambs	(2.45)				(.283)			(.466)			
1309–10[a] EYE	272	94.5	34.7	459	28.5	91	3	52	71		5.2
68 cows	4.0				.514			.76			
225 lambs[c]			60								
1393–94 NTHM	47.75			.476				10			
9 cows	5.3							1.1			6.8
1407–08 NTHM	46.5			44				12			
12 cows	3.87			.26				1.			5.1
1410–11 EYE	119			111	(22.6)			16.5		1	
19 cows	6.2				.417			.86		.052	7.5

NTHM ?10 cows	5.8		.35		1.3	1.5	7.4
1411–12	108	2	24				
EYE 21 cows	5.14		1.14	101	12	.07	7.4
1411–12	49.5	3	(10)		.8		4.7
NTHM 15 cows	3.3		.66				
1436–37	77		4.5	45	21.25	1.25	6.4
EYE 16 cows[d]	4.8		.281		1.3	.06	
1456–57							
EYE[e] 19 cows	80						5.0
1462–63	68				17		
EYE 17 cows	4				1		5.0
NTHM 15 cows	60				15		5.0
	4				1		
1483 NTHM	68		17		17		5.0
17 cows	4				1		

[a] Evidence for milking ewes.

[b] The sheep cheese estimate has been subtracted.

[c] Sold PT, probably not milked.

[d] An additional 4 cows did not lactate, through sickness.

[e] Leasing arrangement, 1 cow = 1 petra butter; 4 petra cheese; 0 milk.

Appendix 7. Sheep on the Manors of Peterborough Abbey
Wethers: Home Manors

	Autumn Total	Max Total	Manor Transfer	% Max	Stock	% Max	Buy	% Max	Dead	% Max	Sell	% Max	Butcher	% Max
1300–01														
EYE	0	10	0		0		0		0		5	50	3	30
GLIN	0	17	0		1	5.8	0		1	5.8	0		7	41.1
LNTP	99	164	60	36.6	0		0		25	15.2	134	81.7	4	2.4
WALT	159	170	8	4.7	0		0		4	2.3	14	8.2	1	.5
CAST	229	499	15	3.0	21	4.2	175	35.0	16	3.2	106	21.2	5	1.0
WRNG	0	6	0		0		0		0		0		6	100
TOT	487	866	83	9.5	22	2.5	175	20.2	46	5.3	259	29.9	26	3.0
1307–08														
EYE	2	2	0		0		0		0		0		0	
NTHM	0	1	1	100.0	0		0		0		0		0	
GLIN	4	4	0		0		0		0	.9	0		7	63.6
LNTP	0	5	0		0		0		1		1		4	80.0
WALT	281	281	0		0		0		10	3.5	0		0	
CAST	217	257	40	15.5	0		0		28	10.9	0		0	
WRNG	0	6	0		0		0		0		0		6	100.0
TOT	504	556	41	7.3	0		0		39	7.0	1	.2	17	3.0

1309–10														
EYE	3	3	0		0		0				3	100.	0	
NTHM	5	388	280	72.2	6	1.5	96	24.7	13	3.6	280	72.2	0	
GLIN	17	164	0	43.9	67	40.8	80	48.7	5	3.0	14	8.5	1	.6
LNTP	0	5	0		0		0		0		0		5	100.
WALT[a]	348	407	(72)[a]	17.6	0		59	14.5	23	5.6	107	26.2	86	21.1
CAST	197	372	0		175	47.0	0		0		196	52.6	0	
WRNG	0	7	0		0		0		0		1		6	85.7
TOT	570	1,346	352	26.2	248	18.4	235	17.4	41	3.1	601	44.6	98	7.2

Appendix 7 (*continued*)
Wethers: West Manors

	Autumn Total	Max Total	Manor Transfer	% Max	Stock	% Max	Buy	% Max	Dead	% Max	Sell	% Max	Butcher	% Max
1300–01														
WARM	167	227	60	26.4	0		0		8	3.5	217	95.6	0	—
BGGG	351	721	0		50	6.9	320	44.4	24	3.3	20	2.7	1	.1
STWK	0	90	90		90	100.	0		0		0		0	
ILBG	91	91	0		0		0		3	3.3	1	1.1	1	1.1
KTTG	5	16	0		11	68.8	0		0		0		0	
TOT	614	1,145	150	13.1	151	13.1	320	27.9	35	3.1	238	20.8	2	.17
1307–08														
WARM	9	63	0		53	84.1	0		1		59	9.9	1	.16
BGGG	511	593	22	3.7	68	13.3	0		49	8.3	0		0	
ASHT	194	224	30	13.3	0		0		23	10.3	0		0	
STWK	0	157	0		0		0		13	8.3	0		0	
ILBG	252	252	1	0.3	1	.004	0		4	1.6	0		0	
KTTG	12	24	5	20.8	2	8.3	1		0		0		4	16.6
TOT	978	1,313	58	4.4	124	9.4	1	.07	90	6.8	59	4.4	5	.4

1309-10

WARM	17	42	1	2.3	24	57.1	0		2	4.8	0		18	2.6
BGGG	405	677	0		72	10.6	200	29.5	30	4.4	311	45.9	0	
ASHT[b]	181	304	96	31.5	27	8.8	0		5	1.6	0		1	.4
STWK[c]	143	236	84	35.5	8	3.4	0		25	10.6	6	6.7	0	
ILBG	148	197	0		49	24.8	0		(14)	7.1	3	1.5	0	
KTTG[c]	25	28	0		3	10.7	0		0		3	10.7	0	
TOT	919	1,484	181	12.2	183	12.3	200	13.5	76	5.1	323	21.7	19	12.8

[b] Season transfer point.
[c] 47 Wethers given to Staurator—payment.

Appendix 7 (*continued*)
Wethers: North Manors

	Autumn Total	Max Total	Manor Transfer	% Max	Stock	% Max	Buy	% Max	Dead	% Max	Sell	% Max	Butcher	% Max
1300–01														
CLNM	36	130	14	10.8	28	21.5	66	50.8	0		19	14.6	0	
SCTR	158	224	3	1.3	60	26.8	3	1.3	9	4.0	85	37.9	1	.4
FISK	0	131	11	8.4	110	83.9	10	7.6	14	10.7	0		0	0
TOT	194	485	28	5.7	198	40.8	79	16.1	23	4.7	104	21.4	1	.2
1307–08														
CLNM	267	404	0	0	53	13.1	84	20.8	13	3.2	70	17.3	0	
SCTR	(485)[d]	657	0	0	67	10.2	104	15.8	7	1.1	80	12.2	0	
FISK	293	351	0	0	34	9.7	23	9.4	13	3.7	9	2.6	0	
TOT	1045	1,412	0	0	154	10.9	211	14.9	33	2.3	159	11.3	0	
1309–10														
CLNM	242	394	0	0	55	13.9	97	24.6	12	3.0	80	20.3	0	
SCTR	300	615	0	0	40	6.5	280	45.5	8	1.3	280	45.2	0	
FISK	333	447	0	0	52	11.6	62	13.9	25	5.6	96	21.5	0	
WLCT	160	179	0	0			19		2	1.1	19		0	
TOT	1035	1,635	0	0	147	8.9	458	28.0	47	2.9	475	29.1	0	

[d] Discrepancy in account roll.

Wethers: Scarp Manors

	Autumn Total	Max Total	Manor Transfer	% Max	Stock	% Max	Buy	% Max	Dead	% Max	Sell	% Max	Butcher	% Max
1300–01														
TNWL	100	119												
1307–08														
TNWL	143	196	50	25.5	0		3	1.5	13	6.6	31	15.8	0	
GEST	131	279	50	17.9	58	20.7	0		11	3.9	0		3	1.1
CTNG	108	108	0		0		0		0		0		5	4.6
TOT	382	583	100	17.1	58	9.9	3	.5	24	4.1	31	5.3	8	1.4
1309–10														
TNWL[c]	120	158	7	4.4	30	18.9	1	.6	9	5.7	1	.6	0	
GEST[c]	151	176	0	3.9	25	14.2	0		6	3.4	0		0	
CTNG[c]	121	172	0		51	29.6	0		11	6.4	0		0	
TOT	392	506	7	1.3	106	20.9	1		26	5.1	1		0	

[c] 10 Wethers to John Staurator.

Appendix 7 (*continued*)

Ewes: Home Manors

	Autumn Total	Max Total	Manor Transfer	% Max	Stock	% Max	Buy	% Max	Dead	% Max	Sell	% Max	Butcher	% Mcx
1300–01														
EYE	257	339	82	24.2	0		0		28	8.2	0		0	
CAST	0	24	0		0		24		0		0		0	
GLIN	198	317	118	37.2	1	.3	0		37	11.7	31	9.7	0	
LNTP	58	65	0		0		0		0		6		0	
TOT	513	745	200	26.8	1		24	3.2	65	8.7	37	4.9	0	
1307–08														
EYE	349	369	14	3.8	6	1.6	0		34	9.2	14	3.7	0	
GLIN	267	678	0		411	60.6	0		96	14.2	0		0	
NTHM	289	289	0		0		0		23	7.9	0		0	
TOT	905	1,336	14	1.0	417	31.2	0		153	11.4	14	1.0	0	
1309–10														
EYE	222	241	19	7.8	0		0		11	4.6	204	84.6	8	3.3
GLIN	269	327	0		58	17.7	0		15	4.6	10	3.1	0	
NTHM	160	391	201	51.4	20	5.1	20	5.1	16	4.1	345	88.2	0	
TOT	651	959	220	22.9	78	8.1	20	2.0	42	4.3	559	58.2	8	0.8

Ewes: West Manors

	Autumn Total	Max Total	Manor Transfer	% Max	Stock	% Max	Buy	% Max	Dead	% Max	Sell	% Max	Butcher	% Max
1300–01														
WARM	38	278	0		0		240	86.3	0		2	.7	0	
BGGG	128	241	0		113	46.8	0		26	10.8	0		0	
ILBG	122	122	0		0		0		0		0		0	
KTTG	131	221	40	18.1	50	22.6	0		11	5.0	13	5.8	0	
TOT	419	862	40	4.6	163	18.1	240	27.8	37	4.3	15	1.7	0	
1307–08														
WARM	187	244	0		56	22.9	0		9	3.6	0		0	
BGGG	308	387	0		79	20.4	0		43	11.1	26	6.7	0	
ILBG	82	274	0		192	70.0	0		0		0		0	
KTTG	191	277	81	29.2	5	1.8	0		9	3.2	0		0	
TOT	768	1,182	81	6.8	332	28.1	0		61	5.2	26	2.2		
1309–10														
WARM	183	247	0		64	25.9	0		16	6.4	0		0	
BGGG	227	299	4	1.3	72	24.1	0		26	8.7	0		0	
ASHT	63	94	0	67.0	31	32.9	0		0		0		0	
ILBG	85	162	75	46.2	75	46.2	0		0		0		0	
KTTG	223	307	84	27.3	0	46.2	0		14	4.6	0		0	
TOT	781	1,109	163	14.6	242	22.2	0		56	5.0	0		0	

Appendix 7 (*continued*)
Ewes: North Manors

	Autumn Total	Max Total	Manor Transfer	% Max	Stock	% Max	Buy	% Max	Dead	% Max	Sell	% Max	Butcher	% Max
1300–01														
CLNM	122	312	12	3.8	52	16.6	148	44.2	20	6.2	74	23.7	0	
SCTR	153	191	0		38	19.8	0		3	1.6	30	15.7	0	
FISK	0	130	11	8.4	110		9	6.9	13	1.0	0		0	
TOT	275	633	23	3.6	200	14.2	157	23.2	36	5.6	104	16.4	0	
1307–08														
CLNM	236	316	0		60	18.9	20	6.3	22	6.9	60	18.9	0	
SCTR	178	235	0		50	21.2	6	2.5	2	.8	56	23.8	0	
FISK	237	273	0		35	12.8	0		7	2.5	40	14.6	0	
TOT	651	824	0		145	17.6	26	3.8	31	3.8	156	18.9	0	
1309–10														
CLNM	272	344	0		72	20.9	0		15	4.4	80	23.3	0	
SCTR	211	260	0		31	11.9	18	6.9	7	2.7	91	35.0	0	
FISK	219	350	0		66	13.1	65	18.5	15	4.3	50	14.3	0	
TOT	702	954	0		169	17.7	83	8.7	37	3.8	221	23.2	0	

Ewes: Scarp Manors

	Autumn Total	Max Total	Manor Transfer	% Max	Stock	% Max	Buy	% Max	Dead	% Max	Sell	% Max	Butcher	% Max
1300–01														
TNWL	0	10			0		0		0		0		0	
1307–08														
GEST	181	257	0		76	29.5	0		9	3.5	0		0	
CTNG	80	170	40	23.5	50	29.4	0		0		0		0	
TOT	261	427	40	9.3	126	29.5	0		9	2.1	0		0	
1309–10														
GEST	181	233	20	27.4	30	12.8	0		8	3.4	0		0	
CTNG	118	168	12	7.1	50	29.7	0		9	5.4	0		0	
TOT	299	401	32	7.9	80	19.9	0		17	4.2	0	(56)?	0	

Appendix 7 (*continued*)
Hoggs: Home Manors[a]

	Autumn Total	Max Total	Manor Transfer	% Max	Stock	% Max	Buy	% Max	Dead	% Max	Sell	% Max	Butcher	% Max
1300–01														
GLIN	2	2			2e									
CAST	169	169			21e				37	21.8	111	65.6		
LNTP	15	15									15	100.0		
1307–08														
EYE	6	6			6e									
GLIN	411	411			411e									
1309–10														
EYE	5	5			6w									
NTHM	6	79	10		67w		73				5	100.0		
GLIN	174	184			58e				59	32.1				
CAST	191	191			175w				16	8.3				

Hoggs: West Manors

	Autumn Total	Max Total	Manor Transfer	% Max	Stock	% Max	Buy	% Max	Dead	% Max	Sell	% Max	Butcher	% Max
1300–01														
WARM	19	19	0		0		0		0		5	26.3	0	
BGGG	154	206	12	5.8	50w 113e		40	19.4	42	20.4			0	
ILBG	1	1	0		0		0		1	100.0	0		0	
KTTG	153	162	0		11w		9	5.5	0		1	6.7	0	
STWK	90	90	90	100.0	50e		0		0		0		0	
TOT	327	388	102	26.3	224		49	12.6	43	11.1	6	1.5	0	
1307–08														
WARM	126	129	0		53w 56e		3	2.3	20	15.8	0		0	
BGGG	186	246	0		68w 79e		60	32.2	41	22.0	0		0	
ILBG	2	203	201	99.0	1w 192e		0		10	4.9	0		0	
TOT	314	578	201	34.7	449		63	12.2	71	13.7			0	

Appendix 7 (continued)

	Autumn Total	Max Total	Manor Transfer	% Max	Stock	% Max	Buy	% Max	Dead	% Max	Sell	% Max	Butcher	% Max
1309–10														
WARM	131	131	0		24w 64e		0		10	7.6	0		0	
BGGG	185	185	0		72w 72e		0		41	22.2	0		0	
ASHT	63	63	0		27w 31e		0		5	7.9	0		0	
STWK	8	8	0		8w		0		0		0		0	
ILBG	2	128	126	98.4	49w 75e		0		4	3.1	0		0	
KTTG	180	180	0				0		2	6.6	12	6.6	0	
TOT	569	695	126	18.1	422		0		62	8.7	12	1.7	0	

Hoggs: North Manors

	Autumn Total	Max Total	Manor Transfer	% Max	Stock	% Max	Buy	% Max	Dead	% Max	Sell	% Max	Butcher	% Max
1300–01														
CLNM	80	80	0		28w 52e		0		0		0		0	
SCTR	98	98	0		60w 38e		0		0		0		0	
TOT	178	178			178									
1307–08														
CLNM	196	233	0		53w 60e		37	15.8	60	25.7	60	25.7	0	
SCTR	119	119	0		67w 51e		0		3	2.5	8	6.7	0	
FISK	83	83	0		34w 35e		0		14	16.8	0		0	
TOT	398	435			300		37	15.8	77	17.7	68	15.6		
1309–10														
CLNM	130	141	0		55w 72e		11	7.8	3	2.1	0		0	
SCTR	78	78	0		40w 31e		0		7	8.9	0		0	
FISK	143	148	0		52w 66e		5	3.4	13	8.8	17	11.5	0	
TOT	351	367			316		16	4.4	23	6.2	27	4.6		

Appendix 7 (*continued*)
Hoggs: Scarp Manors

	Autumn Total	Max Total	Manor Transfer	% Max	Stock	% Max	Buy	% Max	Dead	% Max	Sell	% Max	Butcher	% Max
1300–01														
TNWL	59	160	100	62.5	0		0		1	6.2	0		0	
CTNG[d]			(58)		0		23		0		0		0	
TOT		158			0		23		1		0		0	
1307–08														
GEST	125	168	40	23.8	58w 76e		3	1.7	34	20.2	0		0	
CTNG	42	100	58	58.0	50e		0		50	50.0	0		0	
TOT	167	268	98	36.5	184			1.1	84	31.3	0		0	
1309–10														
TNWL	0	33	33	100.0	30w		0		3	9.1	0		0	
GEST	74	74	0		25w 32e		0		17	22.9	0		0	
CTNG	73	113	40		51w 50e		0		12	10.6	0		0	
TOT	147	220	73	33.2	188				32	14.5	0		0	

Lambs: Home Manors

	Autumn Total	Max Total	Manor Transfer	% Max	Stock	% Max	Buy	% Max	Dead	% Max	Sell	% Max	Butcher	% Max
1300–01														
EYE	328	408	0		0		80	19.6	50	12.1	0		0	
CAST	0	248	162	65.2	0		0		162	65.3	0		0	
GLIN	301	301	0		0		0		78	25.9	0		0	
TOT	629	957	162	16.9	0		80	8.4	290	30.3	0		0	
1307–08														
EYE	305	305	0		0		0		92	30.2	0		1	.3
NTHM	251	251	0		0		0		80	31.8	0		1	
GLIN	256	289	33	11.4	0		0		129	44.6	0		1	.3
TOT	812	845	33	3.9	0		0		301	35.6	0		3	0.3
1309–10														
EYE	225	225	0		0		0		43	19.1	0		1	.4
NTHM	147	257	0		0		110	70.1	19	7.4	0		0	
GLIN	193	250	57	22.8	0		0		15	6.0	0		1	.4
CAST	0	250	250	100.0	0		0		8	3.2	0		0	
TOT	565	982	307	31.2	0		110	11.2	85	8.6	0		2	0.2

Appendix 7 (*continued*)
Lambs: West Manors

	Autumn Total	Max Total	Manor Transfer	% Max	Stock	% Max	Buy	% Max	Dead	% Max	Sell	% Max	Butcher	% Max
1300–01														
BGGG	111	232	86	37.1			35	15.1	26	11.2	0		0	
STWK	0	50	50	100.0			0		0	2.0	0		0	
ILBG	0	195	195	100.0			0		9	4.6	0		0	
KTTG	165	165	0				11	6.6	45	27.2	0		0	
TOT	276	642	331	51.5			46	7.2	80	12.6	0		0	
1307–08														
WARM	163	163	0				0		22	13.5	0		0	
BGGG	237	269	0				32	11.9	76	28.3	20	7.4	0	
ILBG	6	206	200	97.0			0		2	.9	0		0	
KTTG	243	243	0				0		25	10.3	0		1	.4
TOT	649	881	200	22.7			32	3.6	125	14.2	20	2.2	1	0.1
1309–10														
WARM	154	154	0				0		32	20.7	0		0	
BGGG	203	203	0				0		30	14.8	0		0	
ASHT	60	60	0				0		4	6.6	0		0	
ILBG	3	3	0				0		0		0		0	
KTTG	266	266	0				0		28	10.5	0		0	
TOT	696	686	0				0		94	13.7	0		0	

Lambs: North Manors

	Autumn Total	Max Total	Manor Transfer	% Max	Stock	% Max	Buy	% Max	Dead	% Max	Sell	% Max	Butcher	% Max
1300–01														
CLNM	104	205	0				101	49.2	28	13.6	0		0	
SCTR	118	118	0				0		12	10.2	0		0	
FISK	16	16	0				0		12	75.0	0		0	
TOT	238	339	0				101	29.7	52	15.3	0		0	
1307–08														
CLNM	140	140	0				0		30	21.4	0		0	
SCTR	121	121	0				0		18	14.8	0		0	
FISK	159	159	0				0		28	17.6	0		0	
TOT	420	420	0				0		76	18.0	0		0	
1309–10														
CLNM	170	170	0				0		30	17.6	0		0	
SCTR	120	120	0				0		5	4.2	0		0	
FISK	199	199	0				0		35	17.6	0		0	
TOT	489	489	0				0		70	14.3	0		0	

Appendix 7 (*continued*)
Lambs: Scarp Manors

	Autumn Total	Max Total	Manor Transfer	% Max	Stock	% Max	Buy	% Max	Dead	% Max	Sell	% Max	Butcher	% Max
1300–01														
TNWL	0	65	65		0		0		15	23.0	0		0	
1307–08														
GEST	164	164	0		0		0		44		0		0	
CTNG	100	100	0		0		0		30		0		0	
TOT	264	264	0		0		0		74	28.0	0		0	
1309–10														
TNWL	0	50	50	100	0		0		0		0		0	
GEST	158	158	0		0		0		32	20.3	0		0	
CTNG	105	145	40	27.6	0		0		22	15.2	0		0	
TOT	263	353	90	25.5	0		0		54	15.3	0		0	

[a] The 72 wethers transferred from Glinton to Walton are not mentioned in Walton account.
[b] Season transfer point.
[c] 47 wethers given to Staurator—payment.
[d] Discrepancy in account roll.

NOTES

PREFACE

1. The analyses of faunal material from the Fengate sites may be found in Kathleen Biddick, "Animal Husbandry and Pastoral Land-Use on the Fen Edge, Peterborough, England: An Archaeological and Historical Reconstruction (2500 B.C.–A.D. 1350)" (Ph.D. diss., University of Toronto, 1982) and in the following sections of the publications from the Fengate archaeological sites: Francis Pryor, *Excavation at Fengate, Peterborough, England: The Third Report*, Northampton Archaeological Society Monograph no. 1 = Royal Ontario Museum Archaeology Monograph no. 6 (Leicester, 1980), 217–232; idem, *Excavation at Fengate, Peterborough, England: The Fourth Report*, Northampton Archaeological Society Monograph no. 2 = Royal Ontario Museum Archaeology Monograph no. 7 (Leicester, 1984), microfiche, appendix 6, 245–275.

INTRODUCTION

1. Fernand Braudel, *The Structures of Everyday Life: The Limits of the Possible*, trans. Sian Reynolds (New York, 1981), 105; E. L. Jones, *The European Miracle: Environments, Economies and Geopolitics in the History of Europe and Asia* (Cambridge, 1981), 4; Immanuel Wallerstein, *The Modern World System: Capitalist Agriculture and the Origins of the European World Economy in the Sixteenth Century* (New York, 1976), 56.

2. I discuss later in this Introduction what fragmentary evidence my colleagues, including Bruce Campbell, R. A. Donkin, John Langdon, Mavis Mate, and Martin Stevenson, have gathered for pastoral husbandry. The scattered literature for pastoral husbandry has no counterpart to such classics of cereal husbandry as H. L. Gray, *English Field Systems* (Cambridge, Mass., 1915); Wilhelm Abel, *Agricultural Fluctuations in Europe*, trans. Olive Ordish (New York, 1980); J. Z. Titow, *Winchester Yields: A Study in Medieval Agricultural Productivity* (Cambridge, 1972); Norman Scott Brien Gras, *The Evolution of the English Corn Market from the Twelfth to the Eighteenth Century* (Cambridge, Mass., 1926). Although textbooks commonly recognize that the tradition of northern European agriculture integrated cereal and pastoral activities, the formative research of the early twentieth century treated pastoral and cereal dichotomously and relegated pastoral activities either to marginal geographical areas and ethnic groups or to earlier, less-developed economies of the past. For illustrations consult Cyril Fox, *The Personality of Britain* (Cardiff, 1932); such a limited conceptualization of pastoral economies constrained scholars of livestock husbandry such as Robert Trow-Smith, who restricted his *History of British Livestock Husbandry* (London, 1957) to a narrow consideration of techniques of stock management. Archaeologists have gone much further than historians in questioning current models of

pastoral husbandry. For reevaluations of so-called pastoral and arable zones, see *The Effect of Man on the Landscape: The Lowland Zone*, ed. S. Limbrey and J. G. Evans, Council for British Archaeology Research Report, no. 21 (London, 1978); *The Effect of Man on the Landscape: The Highland Zone*, ed. J. G. Evans, S. Limbrey, and H. Cleere, Council for British Archaeology Research Report, no. 11 (London, 1975). For good reviews of ethnic models of "pastoralists" consult Andrew Fleming, "The Genesis of Pastoralism in Prehistory," *World Archaeology* 4 (1972): 180–191; R. Bradley, "Prehistorians and Pastoralists in Neolithic and Bronze Age England," *World Archaeology* 4 (1972): 192–204; idem, *The Prehistoric Settlement of Britain* (London, 1978). General aspects of the nineteenth-century model of the pastoral come under critical consideration in Talal Asad, "Equality in Nomadic Social Systems (Notes toward the Dissolution of an Anthropological Category)," *Critique of Anthropology* 11 (1978): 57–65, and Paul E. Lovejoy, "Pastoralism in Africa," *Peasant Studies* 8 (1979): 73–85; Eugenia Shankin, "Sustenance and Symbol: Anthropological Studies of Domesticated Animals," *Annual Review of Anthropology* 14 (1985): 375–403.

   3. For estate studies with sections devoted to the pastoral economy consult R. A. L. Smith, *Canterbury Cathedral Priory* (Cambridge, 1943); H. P. R. Finberg, *Tavistock Abbey* (London, 1951); J. A. Raftis, *The Estates of Ramsey Abbey* (Toronto, 1957); Edward Miller, *The Abbey and Bishopric of Ely* (Cambridge, 1951; reprint, 1969); I. Kershaw, *Bolton Priory* (Oxford, 1973); Eleanor Searle, *Lordship and Community: Battle Abbey and Its Banlieu, 1066–1538* (Toronto, 1974); Edmund King, *Peterborough Abbey* (Cambridge, 1973); Barbara Harvey, *Westminster Abbey and Its Estates in the Middle Ages* (Oxford, 1977); Christopher Dyer, *Lords and Peasants in a Changing Society: The Estates of the Bishopric of Worcester, 680–1540* (Cambridge, 1980). The classic work on the techniques of livestock husbandry remains Trow-Smith, *British Livestock Husbandry*. For new work in this area consult John Langdon, "The Economics of Horses and Oxen in Medieval England," *Agricultural History Review* 30 (1982): 31–40; idem, "Horse Hauling: A Revolution in Vehicle Transport in Twelfth- and Thirteenth-Century England," *Past and Present* 103 (1984): 37–66; idem, *Horses, Oxen and Technological Innovation: The Use of Draught Animals in English Farming from 1066 to 1500* (Cambridge, 1986). Specialist studies on Cistercian and other pastoral farming include R. A. Donkin, *The Cistercians: Studies in the Geography of Medieval England and Wales* (Toronto, 1978) (consult his bibliography for further references to his work); John Munro, "Wool Price Schedules and the Qualities of English Wools in the Later Middle Ages," *Textile History* 9 (1978): 118–169; F. M. Page, "'Bidentes Hoylandie' (A Mediaeval Sheep-Farm)," *Economic History (A Supplement to the Economic Journal)* 1, no. 4 (1929): 603–613; M. Stevenson, "Sheep Farming on the Crowland Abbey Estate" (MS, 1978); idem, "Fleece

Yields in Late Medieval England" (Paper delivered at the Historical Geography Research Group Conference on Medieval Economy and Society, Exeter, 1983); Julius Klein, *The Mesta: A Study in Spanish Economic History, 1273–1836*, Harvard Economic Studies, vol. 21 (Cambridge, Mass., 1920).

4. The lack of information on herd demography also plagues contemporary studies of pastoral economies and suggests the deep bias against studying the interactions between humans and animals: Gudrun Dahl and Anders Hjort, *Having Herds: Pastoral Herd Growth and Household Economy*, Stockholm Studies in Social Anthropology, vol. 2 (Stockholm, 1976).

5. The evolutionary model tracing the transitions from savagery and barbarism to civilization echoes in these key texts of the nineteenth century: Karl Marx, *Pre-capitalist Economic Formations*, ed. E. J. Hobsbawm (New York, 1964); Frederick Engels, *The Origin of the Family, Private Property and the State*, ed. Eleanor Burke Leacock (New York, 1972); Lewis Henry Morgan, *Ancient Society; or, Researches in the Lines of Human Progress from Savagery through Barbarism to Civilization*, ed. Eleanor Burke Leacock (New York, 1963); and Henry Sumner Maine, *Dissertations on Early Law and Custom* (London, 1883).

6. Michael Postan, *The Medieval Economy and Society* (London 1975), 63. B. H. Slicher Van Bath develops a similar model in his *The Agrarian History of Western Europe, A.D. 500–1850*, trans. Olive Ordish (London, 1963), 12.

7. Postan, *Medieval Economy*, 65; see also his essay "Medieval Agrarian Society in Its Prime, 7: England," in *Cambridge Economic History of Europe*, vol. 1, 2d ed., ed. M. Postan (London, 1966), 548–632.

8. Mavis Mate, "Profit and Productivity on the Estates of Isabella de Forz (1260–92)," *Economic History Review*, 2d ser., 33 (1980): 326–334. Bridbury has estimated a sheep population in thirteenth-century England numbering between eight and ten million beasts, a number not far from the estimated sheep population of Tudor England, of which Thomas More made his famous complaint: "they consume, destroy, and devour whole fields, houses and cities": A. R. Bridbury, "Before the Black Death," *Economic History Review*, 2d ser., 30 (1977): 393–410. For estimates of the Tudor sheep population consult Peter Bowden, *The Wool Trade in Tudor and Stuart Britain* (London, 1962), 38. The quotation from the *Utopia* of Thomas More is from *The Yale Edition of the Complete Works of St. Thomas More*, ed. Edward Surtz, S. J., and J. H. Hexter, vol. 4 (New Haven, 1965), 67.

9. Bruce M. S. Campbell, "Agricultural Progress in Medieval England: Some evidence from Eastern Norfolk," *Economic History Review*, 2d ser., 36 (1983): 26–46; David L. Farmer, "Grain Yields on Westminster Abbey Manors, 1271–1410," *Canadian Journal of History* 18 (1983): 331–348.

10. Harold Fox, "Some Ecological Dimensions of English Medieval Field Systems," in *Archaeological Approaches to Medieval Europe*, ed. K. Biddick (Kalamazoo, Mich., 1984), 119–158; David Hall, "Fieldwork and Docu-

mentary Evidence for the Layout and Organization of Early Medieval Estates in the English Midlands," ibid., 43–68.

11. Langdon, "Horse Hauling"; idem, *Horses, Oxen and Technological Innovation.*

12. For new technologies of managing sheep flocks consult M. Wretts-Smith, "Organization of Farming at Croyland, 1257–1321," *Journal of Economic and Business History* 4 (1932): 168–192, and David Postles, "Fleece Weights and the Wool Supply," *Textile History* 12 (1981): 96–105.

13. T. H. Lloyd discusses the politics of the wool trade in *The English Wool Trade in the Middle Ages* (Cambridge, 1977). For analysis of wool exports and their peak in the first decade of the fourteenth century consult E. M. Carus-Wilson and Olive Coleman, *England's Export Trade, 1275–1547* (Oxford, 1963).

14. For an excellent introduction to the history of the medieval abbey consult King, *Peterborough Abbey.* My approach to the Peterborough estate as a network within a wider regional economy complements the new methodology based on national samples of manorial accounts described by Bruce M. S. Campbell, "Towards an Agricultural Geography of Medieval England," *Agricultural History Review* 36 (1988): 87–98.

15. For a critique of the categories of "pastoral" and "arable" in the landscape archaeology and history of the East Midlands see Christopher Evans, "Nomads in 'Waterland'? Prehistoric Transhumance and Fenland Archaeology," forthcoming in the *Proceedings of the Cambridge Antiquarian Society.*

16. For a seminal critique of narrow concentration on gross productivity see E. A. Wrigley, "Some Reflections on Corn Yields and Prices in Pre-industrial Economies," in his *People, Cities, and Wealth: The Transformation of Traditional Society* (Oxford, 1987), 92–130.

17. Anthropologists and sociologists in particular have expressed concern over the use of modern economic categories in the study of preindustrial forms of economic activity: for critical discussion see Jean Baudrillard, *The Mirror of Production* (St. Louis, 1975); Michel de Certeau, *The Practice of Everyday Life,* trans. S. F. Rendall (Berkeley, Los Angeles, London, 1984); C. A. Gregory, *Gifts and Commodities* (New York, 1982); and Stephen Gudeman, "Anthropological Economics: The Question of Distribution," *Annual Review of Anthropology* 7 (1978): 347–377.

18. Social theorists are drawing increasing attention to the centrality of resources to institutional history: Anthony Giddens, "Institutions, Reproduction and Socialisation," in his *Central Problems in Social Theory: Action, Structure and Contradiction in Social Analysis* (London, 1979), 96–130.

19. Ecological history is a fledgling field. For review of relevant work in the fields of anthropology and intellectual history see Benjamin S. Orlove,

"Ecological Anthropology," *Annual Review of Anthropology* 9 (1980): 235–273, and Donald Worster, *Nature's Economy: A History of Ecological Ideas* (Cambridge, 1985). The anthropologist Eric Wolf conjoined politics, ecology, and historical anthropology in the early 1970s: "Ownership and Political Ecology," *Anthropological Quarterly* 45 (1972): 201–205. For a more sustained consideration of political ecology, "of the system of relationships between groups possessed of differential access to resources, power and symbols," consult John W. Cole and Eric R. Wolf, *The Hidden Frontier: Ecology and Ethnicity in an Alpine Valley* (New York, 1979), quotation from p. 286.

1. CONSUMPTION AND PASTORAL RESOURCES ON THE EARLY MEDIEVAL ESTATE

1. *The Anglo-Saxon Chronicle*, trans. and ed. G. N. Garmonsway, 2d ed. (New York: E. P. Dutton, 1955), 29. The Chronicle attributes the foundation to the time of Wulfhere. F. M. Stenton believed that the foundation must antedate Abbot Seaxulf's consecration as Bishop of the Mercians, which did not occur later than A.D. 675: F. M. Stenton, " 'Medeshamstede' and Its Colonies," in *Preparatory to Anglo-Saxon England*, ed. D. M. Stenton (Oxford: Oxford University Press, 1970), 179–192. For Wulfhere's probable hegemony over southern England in the mid-seventh century consult Wendy Davies and Hayo Vierck, "The Contexts of Tribal Hidage: Social Aggregates and Settlement Patterns," *Frühmittelalterliche Studien* 8 (1974): 223–293; see also Cyril Hart, "The Kingdom of Mercia," in *Mercian Studies*, ed. Anne Dornier (Leicester: Leicester University Press, 1977), 47 and fig. 2.

2. Stenton, "Medeshamstede." For comparative discussion of pre-Conquest monastic federations see Wendy Davies, *An Early Welsh Microcosm: Studies in the Llandaff Charters* (London: Royal Historical Society, 1978), 139–146.

3. The Nene Valley had undergone radical economic change since the mid-fourth century. Only a few aspects of such change can be treated here. For a fuller discussion consult Biddick, "Animal Husbandry." In brief the region saw a shift toward industry at rural villae: Adrian Challands, "A Roman Industrial Site at Sacrewell, Thornhaugh," *Durobrivae* 2 (1974): 13–16; John Hadman and Stephen Upex, "The Roman Villa at North Lodge, Barnwell, 1973," ibid. 2 (1974): 27–28; "The Roman Villa at Helpston," ibid. 3 (1975): 22–23; John Hadman and Stephen Upex, "The Roman Settlement at Ashton near Oundle," ibid. 3 (1975): 13–15. The pastoral orientation of the later villae and associated cemeteries are discussed in Richard Jones, "A Romano-British Cemetery and Farmstead at Lynch Farm," *Durobrivae* 1 (1973): 13, and John Peter Wild, "Roman Settlement in the Lower Nene Valley," *Archaeological Journal* 131 (1974): 140–170. These

shifts in the economy of the Nene Valley villae are not unlike those discussed by Shimon Applebaum over a decade ago in his contribution "Roman Britain" in *The Agrarian History of England and Wales*, vol. 1, pt. 2 (Cambridge, 1972): "A general trend is elicited in the evolution of the average Romano-British farm : it may be defined briefly as centralization, decentralization, and devolution" (p. 44). The regional centers of Peterborough and their economies shared the fate discussed by Richard Reece, "Town and Country-side: The End of Roman Britain," *World Archaeology* 12(1980): 77–92. At Castor, archaeologists have found evidence of a large building measuring approximately 122 meters by 76 meters, which they speculate might be the seat of the Count of the Saxon Shore. For an interim notice on the building consult the excavation notices in *Britannia* 14 (1983): 303–304. Michael Fulford discusses the demise of the Nene Valley pottery industry: "Pottery Production and Trade at the End of Roman Britain: The Case against Continuity," in *The End of Roman Britain*, ed. P. J. Casey, British Archaeological Reports, British Series, no. 71 (Oxford, 1979), 120–132. The fate of the Christian community offers more evidence for discontinuity in the Peterborough area: Charles Thomas analyzes Nene Valley liturgical hoards in *Christianity in Roman Britain to A.D. 500* (Berkeley, Los Angeles, London: University of California Press, 1981), 114–119, 268, fig. 49. Details on the discovery of the hoards may be found in Catherine Jones and R. Carson, "The Water Newton Hoard," *Durobrivae* 3 (1975): 10–12, and *Current Archaeology*, no. 54 (1976), 199–204. Perhaps the only structures to provide some continuity were the estates or *agri* that began to group themselves along the Nene Valley as early as the second century A.D. (Reece, "Town and Countryside," 88): "What continues through the fourth century and well beyond is not the villa house or even the outbuilding, but the estate, the ager" (Davies, *Welsh Microcosm*, 42).

    4. The fifth-century Saxon occupations excavated at Walton and Orton Hall farm, both located within 5 km of Peterborough, did not continue past the early sixth century. See reports by Donald Mackreth in volumes of *Durobrivae* including: 2 (1974): 19; 4 (1976): 24–25; 5 (1977): 20–21; Nene Valley Research Committee, *Annual Report*, 1981–82, 2; Richard Jones, "A Roman and Saxon Farm at Walton, North Bretton," *Durobrivae* 2 (1974): 29–31.

    5. Carolyn G. Dallas, "The Nunnery of St. Kyneburgha at Castor," *Durobrivae* 1 (1973): 17; Nene Valley Research Committee, *Annual Report*, 1976–77, 10. Unfortunately archaeologists know little about the Mercian church at Peterborough, the foundations of which were deeply disturbed by later medieval building programs. Reports of the most recent excavations of the Nene Valley Research Committee carried out at Peterborough Cathedral may be found in "Medieval Britain and Ireland in 1982," entry

no. 21, *Medieval Archaeology* 27 (1983): 168–169; Donald Mackreth, "Recent Work on Monastic Peterborough," *Durobrivae* 9 (1984): 18–21; idem, "The Monastic Church before 1116," ibid. 8 (1980): 11–12. The recent findings suggest that the plan proposed by H. M. Taylor and Joan Taylor in *Anglo-Saxon Architecture*, vol. 2 (Cambridge: Cambridge University Press, 1965), 491–494 requires modification. The scale and magnificence of the early monastic church at Peterborough most likely rivaled the church at Brixworth, "the largest pre-Conquest church north of the Alps" (David Parsons, "Brixworth and Its Monastery Church," in *Mercian Studies*, 108–114).

6. Peter Addyman, "A Dark Age Site at Maxey, Northants," *Medieval Archaeology* 8 (1964): 20–73. Excavators recovered twelve pounds of iron slag and twenty-five iron objects at Maxey; the report concluded, however, that there was no clear evidence for connecting the iron objects with smelting on the site. Some Saxon iron-smelting did go on in the Soke, but it is difficult to date precisely: David N. Hall, "The Countryside of the South-east Midlands and Cambridgeshire," in *The Romano-British Countryside: Studies in Rural Settlement and Economy*, ed. David Miles, British Archaeological Reports, British Series, no. 103, part 2 (Oxford, 1982), 337–350. Reevaluation of industrial activities, including tanning in pits such as those found at Maxey, is needed.

7. Richard Hodges, *Dark Age Economics: The Origins of Towns and Trade, A.D. 600–1000* (London: Duckworth, 1982), 39–46.

8. The links between monasteries, such as Peterborough Abbey, with its territorial command of grazing, woodland, and arable resources, and provisioning of trading emporia with raw materials such as hides and horn, require further archaeological investigation. For reference to monasteries as reception centers see Hart, "Mercia," 58.

9. Rosemary Cramp, "Schools of Mercian Sculpture," in *Mercian Studies*, 191–231. The distribution of pottery in the Peterborough area also suggests some distinctive regional patterns. Excavation and field-survey so far have found little Ipswich ware, wheel-made domestic pottery of the Saxon period around Peterborough, although it has been found at neighboring monastic sites at Castor and Brixworth, and also at Thrapston and Northampton. At Maxey, archaeologists excavated only handmade wares, which have a distribution up and down the Peterborough fen-edge at Glinton, Peterborough, and Castor and in the silt fens of southern Lincolnshire. The distribution of the handmade ware might mark off some local pastoral activities, associated with lambing, calving, and milking on the fen-edges. Such a hypothesis requires further archaeological testing and excavation. Glenn Foard, "Systematic Fieldwalking and Investigation of Saxon Settlement in Northamptonshire," *World Archaeology* 9 (1978): 357–374; R. Hilary Healey,

"Middle Saxon Pottery in the Fenland Area," *Lincolnshire History and Archaeology* 14 (1979): 80–81.

10. For discussion of the Anglo-Saxon material that appears in garbled form in later charters see Stenton, "Medeshamstede," 141. Grants of precisely bounded estates centered on a settlement belong to political changes in lordship in later-eighth-century England. For an important discussion of the progress of fragmentation of estates in Wales consult Davies, *Welsh Microcosm*, passim.

11. W. T. W. Potts, "The Pre-Danish Estate of Peterborough Abbey," *Proceedings of the Cambridge Antiquarian Society* 65 (1974): 13–27. For a comparative analysis of estates as resource units consult Della Hooke, "Pre-Conquest Estates in the West Midlands: Preliminary Thoughts," *Journal of Historical Geography* 8 (1982): 227–244. Another economic consideration bound the fen-edge Abbey with with its upland holdings, particulary Oundle, center of the double-hundred forming the western portion of the estate. Later sources show that Oundle served as the market of its hundred, a sign of its early importance as an exchange center: R. H. Britnell, "English Markets and Royal Administration before 1200," *Economic History Review*, 2d ser., 31 (1978): 183–196. A ritual center, Peterborough, paired with a trading center, Oundle, resembles the contemporary link of Winchester with Hamwih, the trading emporium of the Kingdom of Wessex: M. Biddle, "Towns," in *The Archaeology of Anglo-Saxon England*, ed. David M. Wilson (London: Methuen, 1976), 114.

12. Local conditions in the fen and the Abbey's use of the fen is by no means certain. The peat fens do seem to have undergone an improved drying phase at the time of the Abbey's foundation. The following references provide a basic introduction to flooding and silting episodes in the silt and peat fens of eastern England in the early first millennium A.D.: David Hall, *The Fenland Project, Number 2: Fenland Landscapes and Settlement between Peterborough and March*, East Anglian Archaeology Report no. 35 (Cambridge, 1987), 32, 35; idem, "The Changing Landscape of the Cambridgeshire Silt Fens," *Landscape History* 3 (1981): 37–49; C. W. Phillips, ed., *The Fenland in Roman Times*, Royal Geographic Society Research Series, no. 5 (London, 1970); B. B. Simmons, "The Lincolnshire Car Dyke: Navigation and Drainage," *Britannia* 10 (1979): 183–196; L. P. Louwe Kooijmans, *The Rhine/Meuse Delta: Four Studies on Its Prehistoric Occupation and Holocene Geology*, Analecta Praehistorica Leidensia, vol. 7 (Leiden, 1974); William TeBrake, *Medieval Frontier: Culture and Ecology in Rijnland* (Austin: Texas A&M University Press, 1985). For regional studies of the medieval fenland see H. C. Darby, *The Medieval Fenland* (Newton Abbot: David and Charles, 1940; reprint, 1975); H. E. Hallam, *Settlement and Society: A Study of the Early Agrarian History of South Lincolnshire* (Cambridge: Cambridge University

Press, 1965); J. R. Ravensdale, *Liable to Floods: Village Landscape on the Edge of the Fens, A.D. 450–1850* (Cambridge: Cambridge University Press, 1974); Joan Thirsk, *Fenland Farming in the Sixteenth Century*, University College of Leicester, Department of English Local History, Occasional Papers, no. 3 (Leicester, 1953).

13. The earliest evidence of feorms on the Peterborough estate contains a privilege of Pope Constantine (709–715) drawn up for Peterborough's daughter houses at Bermondsey and Woking. The privilege mentioned the *monasterialis census*, or the right of the bishop to food rents from monasteries of his diocese. Three-quarters of a century later, the king freed the church of Woking of the its obligation of royal tribute (*regalium tributum*), feorm owed to the king, before he made the church over as a gift to Peterborough. The monastery would then collect the renders of food and service once reserved for the king. Stenton discusses this privilege in "Medeshamstede," 189. Davies provides comparative background on early food rents collected by Welsh bishops in *Welsh Microcosm*, 18–50. For a discussion of consumption in a chiefdom society consult Timothy Earle, *Economic and Social Organization of a Complex Chiefdom*, University of Michigan, Museum of Anthropology, Anthropology Papers, no. 63 (Ann Arbor, 1978). For Celtic arrangements for chiefly consumption see Glanville R. J. Jones, "The Multiple Estate: A Model for Tracing the Interrelationships of Society and Economy and Habitat," in *Archaeological Approaches to Medieval Europe*, ed. K. Biddick, 9–41; William Rees, "Survivals of Ancient Celtic Custom in Medieval England," in *Angles and Britons*, O'Donnell Lectures (Cardiff: University of Wales, 1963), 148–168. Edmund Leach discusses a connection between chiefly office and consumption in *Political Systems of Highland Burma* (Boston: Beacon, 1964), 121–122.

14. C. A. Gregory presents a fundamental discussion of consumption and resources in *Gifts and Commodities*. For further discussion of the organization of resources under complex chiefdoms see Kathleen Biddick, "Field Edge, Forest Edge: Early Medieval Social Change and Resource Allocation," in *Archaeological Approaches to Medieval Europe*, 105–118. See also W. J. Ford, "Some Settlement Patterns in the Central Region of the Warwickshire Avon," in *Medieval Settlement: Continuity and Change*, ed. P. H. Sawyer (London: Edward Arnold, 1976), 274–294. Farmers also paid currency in ninth-century leases: *Anglo-Saxon Chronicle*, 52. The use of such currency does not necessarily mean that mechanisms of price formation operated: Gregory, *Gifts and Commodities*. For Mercian currency consult D. M. Metcalf, "Monetary Affairs in Mercia in the Time of Aethelbald," in *Mercian Studies*, 87–102.

15. A. J. Robertson, ed. *Anglo-Saxon Charters*, 2d ed. (Cambridge, 1956), VII, 12–13.

16. This part of the feorm indicates that a woodland managed by cop-

picing, or the cyclical cutting of underwood, existed on the estate: Oliver Rackham, *Ancient Woodland* (London: Edward Arnold, 1980). Interestingly enough, the woodland of Wulfhere's lease was located in the county of Rutland and detached from his holdings in Lincolnshire.

17. The division of the food rent of the lease between the monastery and the lord of the church, the Abbot, shows that the monastic household had already differentiated into two consumption units, one for the Abbot and one for the monks. The question whether division of consumption units within elite households of the ninth century intensified use of resources requires further exploration. The Abbot certainly developed into a prodigious consumer over time. By the fourteenth century, as subsequent discussion will show, the Abbot consumed more wheat than, and as much barley as, his convent of monks. The horses of the Abbot alone consumed between one-quarter and one-third of the harvest of oats on the estate. For the division of units within monastic households in the ninth century consult Eric John, "The Division of the Mensa in Early English Monasteries," *Journal of Ecclesiastical History* 6 (1955): 143–155.

18. Disruption in the Dark Age world economy accounts for much of this chaos. The long-distance exchange network supporting the Mercian and Carolingian elites faltered in the early decades of the ninth century when Arab silver supplies to the West ceased flowing. The demise of English monasticism over the later ninth and early tenth century, traditionally attributed by historians to the Viking raids, occurred within this changing economic context: Richard Hodges and David Whitehouse, *Mohammed, Charlemagne and the Origins of Europe* (Ithaca, N. Y.: Cornell University Press, 1983); Eric John, "Kings and Monks in the Tenth-Century Reform," in his *Orbis Britanniae* (Leicester: Leicester University Press, 1966), 154–180; Robin Fleming, "Monastic Lands and England's Defence in the Viking Age," *English Historical Review* 100 (April 1985): 247–265.

19. Land tenure took on new importance over the ninth century as elites relied increasingly on the land and its fruits for much-needed revenue. Estates fragmented into smaller units: Patrick Wormald, "The Ninth Century," in *The Anglo-Saxons*, ed. James Campbell (Ithaca, N. Y.: Cornell University Press, 1982), 138–139; A. E. Brown, T. R. Key, and C. Orr, "Some Anglo-Saxon Estates in Northamptonshire," *Northamptonshire Archaeology* 12 (1977): 155–176; Graham Cadman and Glenn Foard, "Raunds: Manorial and Village Origins," in *Studies in Late Anglo-Saxon Settlement*, ed. Margaret L. Faull (Oxford: Oxford University Department for External Studies, 1984), 81–100. Around Peterborough, archaeologists have excavated fortified manorial complexes at Goltho, Lincolnshire; Sulgrave, Northamptonshire; and Water Newton and Little Paxton, Huntingdonshire. Goltho: Guy Beresford, "Goltho Manor, Lincolnshire: The Buildings and

Their Surrounding Defences," in *Proceedings of the Battle Conference on Anglo-Norman Studies IV, 1981*, ed. R. Allen Brown (Woodbridge, Suffolk, and Totowa, N. J., 1982), 13–36; Sulgrave: K. B. Davison, "Excavations at Sulgrave, Northamptonshire, 1960–67: An Interim Report," *Archaeological Journal* 134 (1977), fig. 3; Water Newton: C. Green, "Excavations on a Medieval Site at Water Newton in the County of Huntingdon in 1958," *Proceedings of the Cambridge Antiquarian Society* 56–57 (1962–1963): 68–87; Little Paxton: Peter Addyman, "Late Saxon Settlements in the St. Neots Area, II: The Little Paxton Settlement and Enclosures," ibid. 62 (1969): 59–93.

20. For instance, at Great Paxton, Hunts, just across the river from its berewick Little Paxton, stands the elaborate pre-Conquest church erected by Earl Waltheof (d. A.D. 1076) or his widow Countess Judith: C. A. R. Radford, "Pre-Conquest Minster Churches," *Archaeological Journal* 130 (1973): 133.

21. Peter Addyman, "Late Saxon Settlements in the St. Neots Area, III: The Village or Township of St. Neots," *Proceedings of the Cambridge Antiquarian Society* 64 (1972): 45–100.

22. Beresford, "Goltho," 13–36.

23. John N. Williams, "From Palace to 'Town': Northampton and Urban Origins," *Anglo-Saxon England* 13 (1984): 113–136; Kathy Kilmurry, *The Pottery Industry of Stamford, Lincolnshire, c. A.D. 850–1250*, British Archaeological Reports, British Series, no. 84 (Oxford, 1980); John H. Williams, "Northampton," *Current Archaeology* 79 (1981): 250–259; Christine Mahany, Alan Burchard, and Gavin Simpson, *Excavations in Stamford, Lincolnshire, 1963–69*, Society for Medieval Archaeology, Monograph Series, no. 9 (London, 1982).

24. *Anglo-Saxon Chronicle*, 71.

25. It is difficult not to view the alliance of King Edgar and Bishop Aethelwold in the monastic reform movement as a challenge to local lordship and a reassertion of much-damaged royal power in the East Midlands: John, "Kings and Monks"; D. J. V. Fisher, "The Anti-monastic Reaction in the Reign of Edward the Martyr," *Cambridge Historical Journal* 10 (1952): 254–270.

26. Through the legal process of exchange, and endowment from the king's own landed reserves, and through less savory extralegal means, Aethelwold, "the eagle of Christ," succeeded in creating a land bank which he apportioned to the five monasteries: Eric John, "Some Latin Charters from the Tenth Century," in *Orbis Britanniae*, 181–209; Dorothy Whitelock, foreword to *Liber Eliensis*, ed. E. O. Blake, Camden Third Series, vol. 92 (London, 1962), ix–xviii.

27. "Cuius loci basilicam congruis domorum structuris ornatam et terris

adiacentibus copiose dilatam in honore beati Petri principis apostolorum consecravit": Wulfstan's Life of St. Aethelwold, from Michael Winterbottom, *Three Lives of English Saints* (Toronto: Pontifical Institute of Mediaeval Studies, 1972), 48. As already observed (n. 5 above), later medieval building programs destroyed or rendered very difficult to interpret much of the pre-Conquest remains of the monastic complex at Peterborough. The excavations at Winchester offer some insight into the liturgical and claustral intentions of the building programs of Aethelwold: Martin Biddle, "Excavations at Winchester, 1970: Ninth Interim Report," *Antiquaries Journal* 52 (1972): 116–123, figs. 6–8; idem, "'Felix Urbs Winthonia': Winchester in the Age of Monastic Reform," in *Tenth-Century Studies*, ed. David Parsons (London: Phillimore, 1975), 123–140.

28. David Hill, " Trends in the Development of Towns during the Reign of Ethelred II," in *Ethelred the Unready*, ed. D. Hill, British Archaeological Reports, British Series, no. 59 (Oxford, 1978), 213–253; William C. Wells, "The Stamford and Peterborough Mints," *British Numismatic Journal* 22 (1934–1937): 35–77; 23 (1938–1940): 7–28.

29. King, *Peterborough Abbey*, 9.

30. *Anglo-Saxon Chronicle*, 199.

31. For rankings according to gross Domesday valuations see David Hill, *An Atlas of Anglo-Saxon England* (Toronto: University of Toronto Press, 1981), fig. 248. The following authors have dealt with the problem of interpreting values in the Domesday Book: Reginald Lennard, *Rural England, 1086–1135: A Study of Social and Agrarian Conditions* (Oxford: Clarendon Press, 1959), 156–157; R. Welldon Finn, *The Norman Conquest and Its Effects on the Economy, 1066-1086* (Hampton, Conn.: Archon Books, 1971). In the East Midlands there were large increases in valuation between 1066 and 1086. The worth of Peterborough Abbey increased from 1269*s.* to 2,863*s.* 4*d.*: Welldon Finn, *Norman Conquest*, 238. The worth of Ramsey Abbey, a neighbor of Peterborough, doubled. The increase in valuations must be set, however, in a context of depredation during the Conquest.

32. King, *Peterborough*, 13–34.

33. For a discussion of subinfeudation of properties between 1086 and 1125 see King, *Peterborough*, 13–34. Texts of the Domesday printed in *The Victoria History of the Counties of England* (*VCH*) were used in this study unless otherwise indicated: *VCH Northampton* 1 : 301–356; *VCH Huntingdon* 1 : 337–355; *VCH Leicester* 1 : 306–338; *VCH Nottingham* 1 : 247–288; *VCH Rutland*, 138–142; Lincolnshire: C. W. Foster and T. Longley, eds., *The Lincolnshire Domesday and Lindsey Survey*, Lincoln Record Society, vol. 19 (Lincoln, 1924; reprint, 1976). The text of the 1125 survey contained in the Society of Antiquaries MS. 60 is printed in *Chronicon Petroburgense*, ed. T. Stapleton, Publications of the Camden Society, vol. 47 (London, 1849), 157–168. For

a description of the manuscript consult Janet D. Martin, *Cartularies and Registers of Peterborough Abbey*, Northamptonshire Record Society, Publications, vol. 28 (Peterborough, 1978), 1–7. The survey of 1125 followed upon the death of Abbot John of Peterborough on 14 October 1125. Henry I then seized the revenues of the Abbey during the vacancy (1125–1128) and commissioned his justiciars to carry out an inventory of the "the treasures of the church and all the abbacy, and all that was there, within and without, and this they carried to the King," as the *Peterborough Chronicle* reported. The chronicle of Hugh Candidus may be found in Peterborough Dean and Chapter MS. 1, ff.1–19r. It is printed in Joseph Sparke, *Historiae Anglicanae Scriptores Varii* (London, 1723), pt. 2, 1–94; for a translation see *The Peterborough Chronicle of Hugh Candidus*, trans. Charles Mellows and William Thomas Mellows, 2d ed. (Peterborough: Museum Society, 1966).

34. Battles over the fen were to be fought out fiercely among fen lords and local communities in the courts a century later: Darby, *Medieval Fenland*, 77; H. C. Darby, *The Changing Fenland* (Cambridge: Cambridge University Press, 1983), 24–31; King, *Peterborough*, 84–87; Nellie Neilson, ed., *A Terrier of Fleet, Lincolnshire* (London, 1920); Sandra Raban, The *Estates of Thorney and Crowland: A Study of Medieval Monastic Land Tenure*, University of Cambridge, Department of Land Economy, Occasional Paper, no. 7 (Cambridge, 1977), 54–55; Raftis, *Ramsey Abbey*, 153–155.

35. Both historians and archaeologists have uncritically treated the peat fen as a reedy, sedgy grazing area. For a critique of such treatment see Evans, "Nomads in 'Waterland'?" Sir Harry Godwin first drew attention to the scope for human intervention in the plant communities of the English peat fens: H. Godwin and F. R. Bharucha, "Studies in the Ecology of Wicken Fen, II: The Fen Water Table and Its Control of Plant Communities," *Journal of Ecology* 20 (1932): 157–191; H. Godwin, "Studies in the Ecology of Wicken Fen, III: The Establishment of Fen Scrub (Carr)," ibid. 24 (1936): 82–116; idem, "Studies in the Ecology of Wicken Fen, IV: Crop-taking Experiments," ibid. 29 (1941): 83–106; H. Godwin, D. R. Clowes, and B. Huntley, "Studies in the Ecology of Wicken Fen, V: Development of Fen Carr," ibid. 62 (1974): 197–214. J. R. Ravensdale also provides an excellent discussion of management of fen crops in *Liable to Floods*, 41–69.

36. Grazing and mowing most enhance the pastoral potential of fen vegetation. Botanists have studied the forage potential of managed fen grassland at Woodwalton Fen, a relict fen now preserved by the National Trust. Galloway steers grazed the coarse fen grasses dominated by small woodreed (*Calamagrostis epigejos*) and couch grass (*Agropyron repens*). The grazing of the herd had a marked effect on grassland structure by moving it away from coarse grass toward greater and more palatable botanical diversity. Grazing thus improved the fen fodder. The steers sustained themselves

satisfactorily with the coarse fodder under the environmental conditions of fen grazing: O. B. Williams and T. C. E. Wells, "Grazing Management of Woodwalton Fen: Seasonal Changes in the Diet of Cattle and Rabbits," *Journal of Applied Ecology* 11 (1974): 499–516.

37. For later medieval wet phases and the problem of silting in the fenland river systems consult Hallam, *Settlement and Society*, 155; Darby, *Medieval Fenland*, 156–163; Ravensdale, *Liable to Floods*, 7–8, 114–115; Robert Evans, "The Early Courses of the River Nene," *Durobrivae* 7 (1979): 8–10.

38. H. C. Darby observed that the Domesday Book gives a "very incomplete picture of marshland in England in the eleventh century": *Domesday England* (Cambridge: Cambridge University Press, 1977), 160. Recent research on the Domesday returns for Essex suggests that meadow was a "tax-deductible": J. M. McDonald and G. D. Snooks, "Were the Tax Assessments of Domesday England Artificial? The Case of Essex," *Economic History Review*, 2d ser., 38 (1985): 367; idem, *Domesday Economy: A New Approach to Anglo-Norman History* (Oxford: Clarendon Press, 1986).

39. John Bridges, *The History and Antiquities of Northamptonshire* (London, 1791), 2; *VCH Northampton* 2:472.

40. Darby, *Changing Fenland*, 178–179.

41. For a text of the charter see Cyril Hart, *The Early Charters of Eastern England* (Leicester: Leicester University Press, 1966), 182–183.

42. Kilmurry, *Stamford*, 148–149.

43. The meadow acreage was computed from furlong measurements recorded in Domesday and converted into acres according to the form factor used by Rackham, *Ancient Woodland*, 114. For the twenty-one locations with meadow acreage the descriptive statistics worked out as follows: mean = 72 acres; standard deviation = 90.6 acres; variance = 7,827.5 acres. The minimum holding was 8 acres at the manor of Stanwick and the maximum holding was 380 acres of meadow at Walcot, the manor most distant from the Abbey of Peterborough.

44. Many Lincolnshire manors, such as the Abbey's manors at Fiskerton, Scotter, and Walcot, had unusually high meadow assessments; see Darby, *Domesday England*, 148.

45. Mown meadows and grazed meadows produce distinctive flora which archaeobotanists can distinguish in the archaeological record. In the future it may be possible to reconstruct medieval meadow management in the East Midlands through the study of archaeological seed and plant remains. On grazed and mown meadow flora see H. Baker, "Alluvial Meadows: A Comparative Study of Grazed and Mown Meadows," *Journal of Ecology* 25 (1937): 408–425. For an example of current archaeobotanical methodology used in investigating the economic use of floodplain terraces see Mark

Robinson, "Plants and Invertebrates: Methods and Results; Interpretation," in *Iron Age and Roman Riverside Settlements at Farmoor, Oxfordshire,* ed. George Lambrick and Mark Robinson, Council for British Archaeology Research Report, no. 32 (Oxford and London, 1979), 77–128.

46. E. Duffey, M. G. Morriss, J. Sheail, L. K. Ward, D. A. Wells, T. C. E. Wells, *Grassland Ecology and Wildlife Management* (London: Chapman and Hall, 1974), 34. For early evidence of sophisticated management of water meadows on the river Itchen at Winchester see Martin Biddle, "Excavations at Winchester, 1971 Tenth and Final Interim Report: Part II," *Antiquaries Journal* 55 (1975): 326–328.

47. The statistics for correlating meadow acreage with demesne oxen for sixteen manors where such correlation was possible were as follows: $r = 0.1441$ ($P < 0.59420$); for meadow acreage with estimated peasant oxen (oxen derived from number of ploughs) for thirteen manors: $r = 0.4409$ ($P < 0.1316$); for meadow acreage and total demesne and peasant oxen for thirteen manors: $r = 0.4152$ ($P < 0.1583$). For an excellent discussion of the multiple associations between values on Domesday manors consult McDonald and Snooks, *Domesday Economy.*

48. The acreage for woodland on the Abbey's manors ranged from 1.2 acres to 6,048 acres. There was obviously a great deal of variation in the acreage of woodland on the manors. Calculations of descriptive statistics are as follows: mean = 734 acres; standard deviation = 1,413; variance = 189,999. The acreages were calculated according to Rackham, *Ancient Woodland,* 114.

49. Rackham, *Ancient Woodland,* 114; G. F. Peterken, "Long-Term Changes in the Woodlands of Rockingham Forest and Other Areas," *Journal of Ecology* 64 (1976): 123–146.

50. Edmund King offers an excellent discussion of forest colonization by the Abbey in the twelfth and thirteenth centuries in chapter 4 of his *Peterborough Abbey,* 70–87.

51. Rackham, *Ancient Woodland,* 137–160.

52. Kathleen Biddick, "Pig Husbandry on the Peterborough Abbey Estate from the Twelfth to the Fourteenth Ceutury," in *Animals and Archaeology,* ed. Juliet Clutton-Brock and Caroline Grigson, vol. 4, British Archaeological Reports, International Series, no. 227 (Oxford, 1985), 161–177.

53. Rackham, *Ancient Woodland,* 140.

54. Experimental firings under conditions replicating the Stamford kilns required about sixty to one hundred faggots to reach firing temperature. Archaeologists estimate that at Stamford one kiln-firing produced about two hundred jugs. One carriage of faggots would contain twenty dozen bundles, according to later-thirteenth-century sources: Kilmurry, *Stamford,* 68.

55. Discussion of the soils and arable potential of the Abbey's manors is

based on the volumes in the series *1he Land oj Britain: 1he Report oj the Land Utilisation Survey of Britain*, ed. L. Dudley Stamp (London, 1937–), pt. 58 (1943), *Northamptonshire*; pt. 59 (1943), *Soke of Peterborough*; pt. 53 (1937), *Rutland*; pt. 60 (1937), *Nottinghamshire*; pt. 76–77 (1942), *Lincolnshire*; pt. 69 (1937), *Holland* (*Lincolnshire*); pt. 75 (1941), *Huntingdonshire*.

56. *Land Utilisation Survey, Soke*, 384; *Northamptonshire*, 377.

57. King, *Peterborough Abbey*, 143.

58. Brown, Key, and Orr, "Some Anglo-Saxon Estates in Northamptonshire," 155–176.

59. The estimates for ploughing pace are taken from the late-thirteenth-century agricultural treatise of Walter of Henley: D. Oschinsky, ed., *Walter of Henley and Other Treatises of Estate Management and Accounting* (Oxford: Clarendon Press, 1971), 157.

60. For an excellent discussion of the growing tendency to define work owed by peasants as work units that might be further specified by piecework quotas see Raftis, *Ramsey Abbey*, 193–195.

61. We know very little about the physical plant of manors in the early twelfth century. Little excavation of the ancillary buildings of twelfth-century manor houses has taken place. Archaeologists date the large barn associated with the manor house at Wharram Percy to the thirteenth century: Maurice Beresford and John G. Hurst, *Deserted Medieval Villages* (London: Lutterworth Press, 1971), 132. The wooden barn at Coggeshall Abbey, Essex, measuring 37 ft. (121 m) × 13 ft. (43 m) is the oldest standing wooden construction in Europe and is dated to the twelfth century (Rackham, *Ancient Woodland*, 144–147). Its dimensions easily match those of the great masonry-and-timber tithe barns of the thirteenth century, such as Great Coxwell (Berkshire) and Beaulieu–St. Leonard's (Hampshire). For a magnificent presentation of these barns see Walter Horn and Ernest Born, *The Barns of the Abbey of Beaulieu at Its Granges of Great Coxwell and Beaulieu–St. Leonard's* (Berkeley and Los Angeles: University of California Press, 1965); transcripts of the St. Paul leases may be found in William Hale, *The Domesday of St. Paul's of the Year M.CC.XII*, Publications of the Camden Society, vol. 69 (London, 1858), 122–139.

2. THE SCALE OF CONSUMPTION AND PRODUCTION
ON THE ESTATE OF PETERBOROUGH ABBEY
IN THE DOMESDAY GENERATION

1. For discussion of valuations see chapter 1, n. 31, and below, n. 4. The erection of castles formed a major part of the Norman building program. Before 1100 the Normans had erected ninety-three castles in their colony: D. F. Renn, *Norman Castles in Britain* (London: Baker, 1968). The Normans

built on a much larger scale than contemporary English architecture. For a general discussion of their building program consult H. M. Colvin, "The Norman Kings 1066–1154," in *The History of the King's Works*, ed. Colvin, vol. 1 (London: Her Majesty's Stationery Office, 1963), 19–50. The best case study of regional shifts in town development under the Normans has been provided by Martin Biddle and Derek Keene: "Whatever the doubts regarding any over-all concept in planning or architectural terms, there can be no doubt that the reconstruction of palace and cathedral demonstrated, and were intended to demonstrate, the success and the finality of the Norman acquisition of the Old English state, and in particular the annexation of its royal capital" (*Winchester in the Early Middle Ages*, ed. Martin Biddle, Winchester Studies, 1 [Oxford, 1976], 471). The *Peterborough Chronicle* describes the Abbey's commitment to its own building program. Abbot Ernulf (1107–1114) built a new dormitory and chapter house and began a refectory (p. 47 of Mellows trans.). In 1116 fire struck the monastery and vill, sparing only the chapter house and dormitory. Rebuilding began in 1118 (p. 53 of Mellows trans.). Reorganization of the town and the completion of the chancel of the new church is attributed to Abbot Martin (p. 57 of Mellows trans.). For a discussion of this phase of town development at Peterborough consult Edmund King, "The Town of Peterborough in the Early Middle Ages," *Northamptonshire Past and Present* 6 (1980–81): 187–195; Cyril Hart, "The Peterborough Region in the Tenth Century: A Topographical Survey," ibid., 243–245; Mackreth, "Recent Work on Monastic Peterborough," 18–21. The nature of shifts in the English urban hierarchy after the Conquest is in much need of further study. The preliminary survey of this question in *Winchester in the Early Middle Ages* (pp. 500–506) concluded that London grew in importance and that the East Anglian ports expanded rapidly.

2. See chapter 1 for early evidence of farming on the estate. Reginald Lennard provides a thorough discussion of farming in the Domesday generation in *Rural England*, 105–175. The list of redditus owed by the manors of Peterborough Abbey in the 1125 survey is printed in *Chronicon Petroburgense*, 167–168. See chapter 1, n. 31 for references to Domesday valuations and also H. C. Darby, *Domesday England*, 208–231; Lennard, *Rural England*, 121–125; P. D. A. Harvey, "The Pipe Rolls and the Adoption of Demesne Farming in England," *Economic History Review*, 2d ser., 27 (1974): 345–359; Sally P. J. Harvey, "Recent Domesday Studies," *English Historical Review* 95 (1980): 129–131; idem, "The Extent and Profitability of Demesne Agriculture in England in the Later Eleventh Century," in *Social Relations and Ideas: Essays in Honor of R. H. Hilton*, ed. T. H. Aston et al. (Cambridge, 1983), 45–72; McDonald and Snooks, "Were the Tax Assessments of Domesday England Artificial?"; J. M. McDonald and G. D. Snooks, "The Determinants of

Manorial Income in Domesday England," *Journal of Economic History* 45 (1985): 541–556; idem, *Domesday Economy*.

3. *Leges Henrici Primi*, ed. and trans. L. J. Downer (Oxford, 1972), 175.

4. For insights into the formation of values and their links to consumption consult Mary Douglas, *The World of Goods* (New York, 1979), especially chapter 6 on consumption periodicities. For further contrasts of values formed by methods of consumption and those formed by methods of production based on profits see Gregory, *Gifts and Commodities*; Franco Modigliani, "The Life-Cycle Hypothesis of Saving: The Demand for Wealth and the Supply of Capital," in *The Collected Papers of Franco Modigliani*, ed. A. Abel (Cambridge, Mass.: M.I.T. Press, 1980), 2:323–371, reprinted from *Social Research* 33 (1966): 160–217.

5. Certainly the Abbey of Cluny, under the influence of Henry of Blois, Bishop of Winchester, had begun to calculate consumption *and* further productive potential on its demesne in the mid-twelfth century: Georges Duby, "Une inventaire des profits de la seigneurie clunisienne à la mort de Pierre le Vénérable," *Studia Anselmiana* 40 (1956): 128–140.

6. Lennard, *Rural England*, 176–212. The changing value of money and competition for regional trade are discussed in chapter 3 of the present study.

7. The following manors paid grain in kind (measured in modii): Longthorpe, 4.5 in malt, 4.5 wheat; Castor, 80 malt, 13 wheat; Glinton, 8 oats, 8 wheat; Etton, 3 malt, 1 oats, 4 wheat; Werrington, 4 malt, 4 wheat; Walton, 4 malt, 4 wheat; Fletton, 4 wheat, 4 malt; Alwalton, 4.5 malt, 4.5 wheat; Warmington, 12 wheat, 8 malt; Oundle, 8 malt, 8 wheat. Source: *Chronicon Petroburgense*, 167–168.

8. The data on valuations were taken from texts of the Domesday printed in *The Victoria History of the Counties of England*. The redditus of the 1125 survey are taken from the *Chronicon Petroburgense* (for full references see chapter 1, n. 33). The descriptive statistics for the valuations of 1066, 1086, and 1125 are as follows: 1066 (number of manors = 26): mean, 78.4*s*.; coefficient of variation expressed as a percent, 98.0 percent; 1086 (number of manors = 26): mean, 125.76*s*.; coefficient of variation, 65.9 percent; 1125 (number of manors = 25): mean, 224.7*s*.; coefficient of variation, 71.5 percent. This discussion does not take up the question of hidation; see Cyril Hart, *The Hidation of Northamptonshire*, University of Leicester, Department of English Local History, Occasional Papers, 2d ser., no. 3 (Leicester, 1970). For increasing values on manors over the Domesday generation consult Lennard, *Rural England*, 155–159 and 210–212; Raftis, *Ramsey Abbey*, 53–96; Dyer, *Lords and Peasants*, 51–55; Miller, *Ely*, 94–95.

9. The data for numbers of peasants and their ploughs come from texts of the Domesday and 1125 surveys. The recorded Domesday population of peasants on the estate numbered 802 (number of manors = 24): mean, 33.4; coefficient of variation expressed as a percent, 55 percent. For 1125, recorded

population numbered 1,073 (number of manors = 23): mean, 46.6; coefficient of variation, 55.7 percent.

10. The erection of the motte and bailey of Rockingham Castle under William the Conqueror must have dispossessed some peasants of land. For the castle consult Royal Commission on Historical Monuments, England, *An Inventory of the Historical Monuments in the County of Northampton*, vol. 2, *Central Northamptonshire* (London: Her Majesty's Stationery Office, 1979), 127–129.

11. The monastic system of food farms is discussed by Harvey, *Westminster Abbey*, 80–81; Lennard, *Rural England*, 131–133; Miller, *Ely*, 38–40; Raftis, *Ramsey Abbey*, 153–155. See also Georges Duby, "Économie domaniale et économie monétaire: Le budget de l'abbaye de Cluny entre 1080 et 1155," *Annales: Économies, sociétés, civilisations* 7 (1952): 155–171. The Ramsey foodrent document is discussed by Raftis, *Ramsey Abbey*, 61 and appendix B, 309–313. Raftis argues that the food rent may be attributed to the abbacy of Aldwin (d. A.D. 1111). The text is printed in *Cartularium Monasterii de Rameseia*, ed. W. H. Hart and P. A. Lyons, vol. 3 (London, 1893), 230–234.

12. David Knowles, *The Monastic Order in England*, 2d ed. (Cambridge: Cambridge University Press, 1963), 459–465.

13. The 1185 survey is edited by J. H. Round, *Rotuli de Dominabus et Pueris et Puellis de XII Comitatibus, [1185]*, Publications of the Pipe Roll Society, vol. 35 (London, 1913). I selected those manors for which the surveyors listed demesne stock and indicated how much additional stocking would increase the value of the demesne. I found sixty-five manors that fit these criteria in the *Rotuli de Dominabus*. For tables listing livestock by manor for the 1125 survey consult Biddick, "Animal Husbandry," 458–460.

14. For general discussions of livestock in the Domesday generation consult Trow-Smith, *British Livestock Husbandry*, 65–86. Reginald Lennard provides a survey of twelfth-century livestock leases in his *Rural England*, 189–196.

15. Edmund King discusses the relationship between oxen and demesne ploughs in *Peterborough Abbey*, 143, table 5.

16. For a discussion of oxen on the estate in the fourteenth century see chapter 4.

17. Trow-Smith, *British Livestock Husbandry*, 68–74 discusses the problems of identifying animalia otiosa. He concluded that "a very large part—if not all—of the beasts (animalia) recorded in Domesday as having been present on manors in the less pastoral counties of England were concerned with the plough."

18. The Abbey still relied on ox hauling in the early twelfth century: Langdon, "Horse Hauling," 37–66. Langdon lists the horses on manors surveyed in the *Rotuli de Dominabus* on a county basis in his book *Horses, Oxen and Technological Innovation*, 41. The coefficent of variation (expressed as a

percentage), which I calculated from his county sample, is 122.4 percent, comparable to the variation of horses on the estate of Peterborough (111 percent) and my sample of manors taken from the *Rotuli* (206 percent).

19. Prior to their drainage in the early modern period, the fen pastures were a popular breeding ground for horses. The opponents of drainage in the seventeenth century mentioned horse breeding first in their justification of the fen economy: "for the first the Fens breed infinite number of serviceable horses, mares and colts, which till our land and furnish our neighbors." Cited in Thirsk, *Fenland Farming*, 27.

20. The pattern fits with John Langdon's observations on the rise of horse hauling over the thirteenth century: see above, n. 18.

21. For a discussion of horse husbandry on the estate in the fourteenth century see chapter 6.

22. Biddick, "Pig Husbandry."

23. See chapter 5.

24. Trow-Smith reviews the evidence for the primacy of sheep as milch animals in the twelfth century: *British Livestock Husbandry*, 74–80. The high proportion of lactating ewes in the surveys of the English estates of Holy Trinity, Caen reinforce the economic importance of sheep dairying: Marjorie Chibnall, ed., *Charters and Custumals of the Abbey of Holy Trinity, Caen*, Records of Social and Economic History, n.s., no. 5 (London, 1982), 33–38.

25. Trow-Smith remarks on the association of goat herds with sheep flocks and dairying in *British Livestock Husbandry*, 177.

26. The estimate for wool and cloth production of the demesne sheep flock is based on the following figures. Using an estimate of 1.75 pounds (0.79 kg) per fleece, the average weight of fleeces on the estate at the end of the thirteenth century (King, *Peterborough Abbey*, 159), and including the whole of the flock in 1125, the Abbey could have shorn about 1,950 pounds (88.6 kg) of wool. This amount of wool would fill five sacks of wool (one sack = 364 pounds). To clothe 140 monks and conversi at Beaulieu Abbey in the year 1269–70, the Abbey used eleven sacks and eighteen stone of wool or 4,176 pounds of wool. At the Beaulieu rate, the sixty monks of Peterborough would require 1,754 pounds of wool for their annual clothing allowance. The figures for Beaulieu are taken from S. F. Hockey, *The Account-Book of Beaulieu Abbey*, Camden Fourth Series, vol. 16 (London, 1975), 17, 32.

27. Nellie Neilson has remarked on some of the ancient aspects of the heavy food rent "ad caritatem S. Petri" in her *Customary Rents*, Oxford Studies in Social and Legal History, ed. Paul Vinogradoff, vol. 2 (Oxford, 1910), 191. Ramsey Abbey collected a similar feast-day rent on Saint Benedict's Day: *Cartularium Monasterii de Rameseia* 3:232.

28. There is an interesting document (no. 117, pp. 470–472) printed in Georges Duby, *Rural Economy and Country Life in the West*, trans. Cynthia Postan (Columbia, S.C., 1968) which describes in some detail a cloth render

of twelfth-century date: "his wife must come to the monastery and receive from the provost of the monastery a load of wool or prepared flax and a loaf, like that of the lords, ... and with this she shall prepare a linen or woolen cloth seven ells in length and three in width."

29. The impact of the medieval world economy on regional agriculture in northern Europe is in much need of investigation. For an overview of the medieval world economy consult Fernand Braudel, *The Perspective of the World*, trans. Sian Reynolds (New York, 1984), 91–116.

3. FROM CONSUMPTION TO PRODUCTION: PETERBOROUGH ABBEY IN THE THIRTEENTH CENTURY

1. Richard Fitz Nigel's observation that "money is no less indispensable in peace than in war" epitomizes the transformation of money as a medium of exchange in twelfth-century society: *Dialogus de Scaccario* [1179], ed. and trans. Charles Johnson with corrections by F. E. L. Carter and D. E. Greenway (Oxford, 1983), 2. For an overview of the implications of this transformation consult Jacques Le Goff, "Merchant's Time and Church's Time in the Middle Ages," in his *Time, Work and Culture in the Middle Ages* (Chicago, 1980), 29–42. The changing rhythms of consumption, its "periodicities," and their relation to information are important to consider, as Mary Douglas shows in *The World of Goods*. In such a context see W. Hollister and J. W. Baldwin, "The Rise of Administrative Kingship: Henry I and Philip Augustus," *American Historical Review* 83 (1978): 867–905; B. Lyon and A. Verhulst, *Medieval Finance* (Providence, R. I., 1967). The details of the great English inflation are trenchantly discussed by P. D. A. Harvey, "The English Inflation of 1180–1220," *Past and Present* 61 (1971): 3–30. The study of indebtedness is fragmentary and requires much further work. H. G. Richardson provides a good introduction in *The English Jewry under Angevin Kings* (London, 1960). The best documented financier in England in the twelfth century is the Fleming, William Cade: Hilary Jenkinson, "William Cade, a Financier of the Twelfth Century," *English Historical Review* 28 (1913): 209–227, and "A Money Lender's Bonds of the Twelfth Century," in *Essays in History Presented to R. L. Poole* (Oxford, 1927), 190–209. William Cade owned a house in Winchester in 1148. For some insights into his activities there see Derek Keene, *Survey of Medieval Winchester*, 2 vols., Winchester Studies, no. 2 (Oxford, 1985), 1:292, 324, and 2:116. For an overview of Flemish merchant activity in England consult Gaston Dept, "Les marchands flamands et le roi d'Angleterre (1154–1216)," *Revue du nord* 12 (1926): 303–324.

2. Thomas K. Keefe discusses feudal assessments in his *Feudal Assessments and the Political Community under Henry II and His Sons* (Berkeley, Los Angeles, London, 1983). For tallages in the English boroughs see S. K. Mitchell,

Taxation in Medieval England (New Haven, 1951), 313–315. The changing rank of leading towns in terms of aids and tallages paid is discussed in Biddle, *Winchester in the Early Middle Ages*, 501–505. The rising returns in the court system of Henry II are outlined in Alan Harding, *The Law Courts of Medieval England* (New York, 1973), 54–55. For the shift in the taxation base from land to movable wealth consult Mitchell, *Taxation*. For the arbitrary taxation of local "tyrants" see Edmund King, "The Anarchy of King Stephen's Reign," *Transactions of the Royal Historical Society*, 5th ser., 34 (1984): 133–153, esp. 135–136.

3. J. O. Prestwich, "War and Finance in the Anglo-Norman State," *Transactions of the Royal Historical Society*, 5th ser., 4 (1954): 19–43. Further details on aspects of war and financing may be found in M. Chibnall, "Mercenaries and the 'Familia Regis' under Henry I," *History* 62 (1977): 15–23; Colvin, *History of the King's Works*, vol. 2 (London, 1963), Appendix: Expenditure on Royal Castles, 1155–1215, p. 1023.

4. The best discussion of the change in the medieval trade in the mid-eleventh century remains A. R. Lewis, *The Northern Seas: Shipping and Commerce in Northern Europe, A.D. 300–1100* (Princeton, 1958); Braudel, *Perspective*, 91–116; Pamela Nightingale, "The Evolution of Weight-Standards and the Creation of New Monetary and Commercial Links in Northern Europe from the Tenth Century to the Twelfth Century," *Economic History Review*, 2d ser., 38 (1985): 192–209. The extent of the depression is suggested by David Whitehouse, "Maritime Trade in the Gulf: The Eleventh and Twelfth Centuries," *World Archaeology* 14 (1983): 328–334; also, Philip Curtin, *Cross-Cultural Trade in World History* (Cambridge, 1984), 109–135.

5. Lewis, *Northern Seas*, 455–491; Thomas N. Bisson, *Conservation of Coinage: Monetary Exploitation and Its Restraint in France, Catalonia and Aragon, A.D. 1000–1225* (Oxford, 1979); Philip Grierson, *Monnaies du moyen âge* (Fribourg, 1976), 111.

6. Jenkinson, "William Cade." The Cistercians provide a good example of these transactions: Donkin, *Cistercians*, 148; N. Denholm-Young, *Seignorial Administration in England* (Oxford, 1937), 54; M. Postan, "Credit in Medieval Trade," *Economic History Review* 1 (1927–28): 234–261.

7. Marian Małowist, "A Certain Trade Technique in the Baltic Countries in the 15th to the 17th Centuries," in *Poland at the XIth International Congress of Historical Sciences in Stockholm* (Warsaw, 1960), 103–116.

8. The details of indebtedness can be studied when central treasury records have been preserved on an estate. Such records are not available for Peterborough, but consult Mavis Mate, "The Indebtedness of Canterbury Cathedral Priory, 1215–1295," *Economic History Review*, 2d ser., 26 (1973): 183–197; Knowles, *The Monastic Order*, 300–305.

9. For discussion of loans in the commercial sector see Gérard Sivéry, "Les débuts de l'économie cyclique et de ses crises dans les bassins scaldien

et mosan: Fin du XIIe et début de XIIIe siècle," *Revue du nord* 64 (1982): 667–681; Jenkinson, "William Cade." Much work remains to be done in this area.

10. For the literature on farming of estates see chapter 2, n. 2.

11. *Peterborough Chronicle*, 70.

12. The Book of Robert Swaffham, Peterborough Dean and Chapter Library, MS. 1; citations from printed version of Sparke, *Historiae Anglicanae Scriptores Varii*, pt. 2: "Post ea vero extendit [Abbot Benedict] manum suam ad liberandam ecclesiam suam de debito predecessoris sui Abbatis Willielmi: Cui Romani et in Anglia multi exigebant plus quam mille et quinquagentas marcas. Insuper et ornamenta ecclesiae erant per diversa loca dispersa et invadiata" (p. 98).

13. *Peterborough Chronicle*, 71; for discussion of monastic involvement with vif-gages and mortgages see Robert Genestal, *Le rôle des monastères comme établissements de crédit étudié en Normandie du XIe à la fi du XIIIe siècle* (Paris, 1910), 6–7.

14. Data extracted from the *Publications of the Pipe Roll Society*, [o.s.], vols. 1–2, 4–9, 11–13, 15–16, 21–22, 25–34, 36–38; n.s., vols. 1–9 (London, 1884–1932).

15. For details on Aaron of Lincoln consult Richardson, *The English Jewry*, 74–75.

16. Book of Walter of Whittlesey, B.M. Add. MS. 39758, printed in Sparke, *Historiae Anglicanae Scriptores Varii*, pt. 2, 140; The *Chronicon Petroburgense* mentions the debt faced by Abbot-elect William of Woodford four years after the death of Robert of Sutton (d. 1270): "Electus [William of Woodford] autem facta fidelitate coram consilio domini regis Londoniis, et optenta benedictione, quia ecclesia sua multum fuit onerata ere alieno tempore creacionis sue in Abbatem, videlicet in MMM marcis et amplius ... " (p. 20). The debt of Canterbury Cathedral Priory to Siennese and Florentine merchants is discussed by Mate, "Indebtedness," 187.

17. David L. Farmer, "Some Price Fluctuations in Angevin England," *Economic History Review*, 2d ser., 9 (1956–57): 34–43; Harvey, "The English Inflation"; A. R. Bridbury offers an important reconsideration of the inflation which argues against simple demographic models for explaining it: "Thirteenth-Century Prices and the Money Supply," *Agricultural History Review* 33 (1985): 1–21; Harvey's contention that the inflation was limited to England requires further evaluation in light of the recent study of Sivery, "Les débuts de l'économie cyclique."

18. Swaffham: see above, n. 12. The vacancy accounts come from the Pipe Rolls of 26 Henry III, 12 John, 13 John.

19. P. D. A. Harvey, "The Pipe Rolls and the Adoption of Demesne Farming in England," *Economic History Review*, 2d ser., 27 (1974): 355.

20. Swaffham, 99 and 102; King, *Peterborough Abbey*, 81–82.

21. Donkin, *Cistercians*, 16. Note that Cluniac statutes of 1132 called for the replacement of lay domestic help with *conversi barbati*, illiterate monks, reminiscent of the Cistercian *conversi*: Duby, "Budget," 167.

22. Swaffham, 104. For a discussion of windmills and their use among English Cistercians consult Donkin, *Cistercians*, 173.

23. Donkin, *Cistercians*, 163–170. For the proliferation of stone houses in London in the twelfth century see John Schofield, *The Building of London from the Conquest to the Great Fire* (London, 1984), 52–56.

24. Swaffham, 105.

25. Swaffham, 109.

26. Horn and Born offer a comprehensive discussion of the Cistercian barn tradition in *Barns*.

27. Swaffham, 122: "Reliquit omnem abbatiam omnibus bonis habundantem, scilicet, in stauro de equis, de bobus, vaccis, ovibus, sed et de omnibus pecoribus in maxima multitudine et in multis locis bladum de tribus annis. Sed post decessum eius magister R. de Gosebek, cui dominus rex custodiam abbatiae commiserat per suos fere omnia destruebat, vendebat at asportabat."

28. The estimates in table 10 must be regarded only as rough guidelines to scale.

29. Swaffham, 106: "Item hic dirationavit mariscum, qui est inter Singlesholt et Croyland; unde habemus singulis annis, pro recognitione de Abbate de Croyland, quator petras cerae..." (Pipe Rolls, 11 John). The Abbey's reclamation of areas of the peat fen for pasture are discussed by King, *Peterborough Abbey*, 84–85. A comparative regional context for reclamation may be gained from Raban, *Estates of Thorney and Crowland*, 52–57; Raftis, *Ramsey Abbey*, 154–156.

30. For the allocation of resources favorable to peasants in the early twelfth century consult the following texts: Dyer, *Lords and Peasants*, 98–99; Raftis, *Ramsey Abbey*, 86–95; Chibnall, *Charters and Custumals*, li; Harvey, "Profitability of Demesne Agriculture," 45–72.

31. The 1231 survey is contained in the Black Book (Martin, *Cartularies*, #1) (Society of Antiquaries MS. 60, f. 181–207).

32. Harvey, *Peasant Land Market*; Paul R. Hyams, "The Origins of a Peasant Land Market in England," *Economic History Review*, 2d ser., 23 (1970): 18–31. For an excellent discussion of the later thirteenth-century peasant land market on the Peterborough Abbey estates consult King, *Peterborough Abbey*, 99–125.

33. Pipe Rolls, 16 Henry II. For a fuller discussion of this legal struggle see Paul R. Hyams, *King, Lords and Peasants in Medieval England* (Oxford, 1980).

34. Harvey provides an excellent discussion of changing lord and peasant

land-bonds in *Peasant Land Market*: "Put simply, we might say that in 1100 the lord of a manor was the lord of men who held land of him; in 1200 he was the lord of lands that were occupied by tenants. The change is slight but significant. The tenant's holding could be viewed simply as a standard share in the vill's resources. By 1200 it was far more likely to be viewed as precisely defined in its area of land and other rights" (p. 12).

35. The Abbey of Peterborough was not alone in this strategy. Lords clearly fostered stratification in the early thirteenth century by allowing the tenurial division of customary holdings as Edward Miller observed: "here, it might seem, the virgates of Domesday had simply been divided and two men now stood in the place where one had stood" (Miller, *Ely*, 143–144). For other examples of seigneurial manipulation of customary holdings in the early thirteenth century consult A. J. Raftis, *Tenure and Mobility: Studies in the Social History of the Medieval English Village* (Toronto, 1964), 88; Harvey, *Westminster Abbey*, 210–213; Harvey, *Peasant Land Market*, 1–19.

36. King, "The Town of Peterborough."

37. Peasants ended intercommoning arrangements in areas of the silt fen of Lincolnshire and also reclaimed over fifty square miles of coastline for cropping. Peasants also launched a "sit-in" on the pastures of Crowland Abbey in 1189. For discussion of these episodes see Hallam, *Settlement and Society*, 162–173.

38. The order of magnitude for the increase in the scale of agriculture could be greater. It is not clear when Peterborough Abbey converted from customary to measured acres. The manors of the Bishop of Winchester's estates converted sometime between the account roll of 1226–27 and that of 1231–32. On six manors (Harwell, Berks; Beauworth, Hants; Brightwell, Berks; Meon Church, Hants; Fareham, Hants; and Altclere, Hants) a total of 1,824 customary acres were sown in 1226–27 and a total of 1,054 measured acres in 1231–32. Using the rough ratio that two customary acres approximate one measured acre, we can see that the sown acreage on the six manors actually increased by 15 percent from 1226–27 to 1231–32 (1,824/2,108 expressed as customary acres). My source for the Winchester figures is Winchester Pipe Rolls 159281, 159282 (Hampshire Record Office). See also Titow, *Winchester Yields*, 21.

39. Michael M. Postan uses this framework in his influential essay "Medieval Agrarian Society" and his popular textbook, *Medieval Economy and Society*.

40. Historians have disputed Postan's assumption of buoyant demesnes directly managed prior to the twelfth-century slump: Lennard, *Rural England*, 105–212; Edward Miller, "England in the Twelfth and Thirteenth Centuries: An Economic Contrast?" *Economic History Review*, 2d ser., 24

(1971): 1–14; Professor Harvey certainly upset the Postan framework in his study, "The Pipe Rolls and the Adoption of Demesne Farming."

41. The first use of the label *high farming* that I have been able to locate occurs in Smith, *Canterbury Cathedral Priory*.

42. Postan with his thesis of expansion onto marginal lands and declining yields praises the higher efficiency of management and more rational use of land and accretions of area by agrarian lords in *Medieval Economy and Society*, 65–70.

43. For an introduction to the account rolls see Janet D. Martin, *The Court and Account Rolls of Peterborough Abbey: A Handlist*, University of Leicester, History Department, Occasional Publications, no. 2 (Leicester, 1980), 29–49.

44. Smith, *Canterbury Cathedral Priory*, 141; Harvey, *Westminster Abbey*, 126; Titow, *Winchester Yields*, 67.

45. J. Z. Titow devised the livestock ratio, a ratio of livestock to arable in *Winchester Yields*, 136.

46. Campbell, "Agricultural Progress."

47. The number of oxen remained highly correlated with acreage sown in the fourteenth century, but the number of oxen per acre decreased over the two centuries. The statistics for the correlation of oxen and acreage sown on the manors of Peterborough Abbey are as follows: 1300–01: number of manors in calculation = 17, regression coefficient = 0.743, t = 4.29 > 2.131 probability (0.05 level of significance); 1307–08: number of manors in calculation = 17, regression coefficient = 0.669, t = 3.47 > 2.131 probability (0.05 level of significance); 1309–10: number of manors in calculation = 18, regression coefficient = 0.567, t = 2.75 > 2.131 probability (0.05 level of significance).

48. Bruce M. S. Campbell, "Arable Productivity in Medieval England," *Journal of Economic History* 43 (1983): 387–388.

49. J. S. Drew first called attention to such marginal notes in his article "Manorial Accounts of St. Swithun's Priory, Winchester," *English Historical Review* 62 (1947): 20–41; Bruce Campbell has used such marginal notations: "Arable Productivity."

50. See G. H. Drury, "Crop Failures on the Winchester Manors, 1232–1349," *Transactions of the Institute of British Geographers*, n.s., 9 (1984): 407.

51. Note that the list does not account for 226 works. Sections of the works account were unreadable.

52. Campbell, "Arable Productivity," "Agricultural Progress."

53. On the importance of the position of legumes in rotations see Farmer, "Grain Yields on Westminster Abbey Manors," 344–347; Campbell, "Agricultural Progress," 31.

54. Figures for Ramsey calculated from Raftis, *Ramsey Abbey*, table XXII, p. 114; Dyer, *Lords and Peasants*, 69; Harvey, *Westminster Abbey*, 145–146.

4. THE DEMESNE CATTLE HERDS ON THE PETERBOROUGH ABBEY ESTATE

1. For an overview of conditions in the first decade of the fourteenth century see Ian Kershaw, "The Great Famine and Agrarian Crisis in England, 1315–1322," *Past and Present* 59 (1973): 3–6; Mavis Mate, "High Prices in Early Fourteenth-century England: Causes and Consequences," *Economic History Review*, 2d ser., 28 (1975): 1–16; "Coping with Inflation: A Fourteenth-Century Example," *Journal of Medieval History* 4 (1978): 95–106; Smith, *Canterbury Cathedral Priory*, 114; Bridbury, "Before the Black Death."

2. For a general introduction to the livestock economy of the demesne farm consult Trow-Smith, *British Livestock Husbandry*, 124–129. R. A. Donkin has studied cattle husbandry on Cistercian estates: "Cattle on the Estates of Medieval Cistercian Monasteries in England and Wales," *Economic History Review*, 2d ser., 15 (1962–63): 31–53. See also Wretts-Smith, "Organization of Farming at Croyland Abbey," 186–189.

3. The study of Dahl and Hjort, *Having Herds*, has deeply influenced my approach to herd productivity. For the importance of considering the composition of products in production see Elizabeth E. Bailey and Ann F. Friedlander, "Market Structure and Multiproduct Industries," *Journal of Economic Literature* 20 (1982): 1024–1048. Attention to the development cycle marks the approach of family historians who use the development cycle to understand the intersections between individual time, family time, and the market: Tamara K. Hareven, *Family Time and Industrial Time: The Relationship between Family and Work in a New England Industrial Community* (New York, 1982); see also J. R. Goody, "The Evolution of the Family," in *Household and Family in Past Times*, ed. P. Laslett and R. Wall (Cambridge, 1972).

4. See Biddick, " Animal Husbandry," 367–368.

5. In 1309–10 the Abbey cultivated 293.5 acres at Eye and 322 acres at Castor. The proportion of grain cultivated on each demesne was statistically similar (chi square at 5 degrees of freedom = 4.3 < 11.0 at 0.05 probability).

6. See table VI.20 in Biddick, "Animal Husbandry," 377–378, for the statistical measures of differences for the rates of intermanorial transfers, stocking, buying, selling, butchering, and mortality among the different manorial groupings of the estate.

7. For tables listing the death rates for oxen, cows, immatures, and calves on the Peterborough Abbey estate see Biddick, "Animal Husbandry," table VI.22, p. 388. For a table listing the tests for significant differences of these mean rates see ibid., table VI.21, p. 387. The mean mortality for different subgroups of the herd for the first decade of the fourteenth century were as follows: oxen (number of manors = 13) 4.28 percent, s.d. 3.5; cows (number of manors = 6) 5.2 percent, s.d. = 1.9; immatures (number of manors = 23)

6.2 percent, s.d. = 3.9; calves (number of manors = 23) 10.4 percent, s.d. = 5.4). The percentages were calculated using the *summa* or total number for the subgroup for the accounting year. Immatures include the following subgroups: 3–4-year-olds, 2–3-year-olds, yearlings.

8. Modern rates are discussed in Grahame Williamson and W. J. A. Payne, *An Introduction to Animal Husbandry in the Tropics*, 2d ed. (London, 1965), 211.

9. For tables listing butchery rates for oxen, cows, immatures, and calves on the estate in the first decade of the fourteenth century and tests of differences in the average butchering rates for these cohorts see Biddick, "Animal Husbandry," table VI.23 and table VI.24, pp. 390–391.

10. For a list of infertility rates on the different manors of the estate over the first decade of the fourteenth century see Biddick, "Animal Husbandry," table VI.25, p. 393.

11. Oschinsky, *Walter of Henley*, 425.

12. See chapter 3, n. 47 for the statistics of this correlation.

13. The absence of central householding accounts means that it is not possible to check all the links between the movement of goods from manors to the central household and then to the market, if the goods were marketed. For the problem of sales and central household accounts see Mate, "High Prices," 16; Harvey, *Westminster Abbey*, 133–135; Hockey, *Beaulieu Abbey*.

14. See chapter 5 for further discussion.

15. Oschinsky, *Walter of Henley*, 431; Trow-Smith summarizes the small literature on dairy yields in *British Livestock Husbandry*, 119–123. The yields of the Peterborough herd are slightly lower than Trow-Smith's figure of 120–150 gallons (where one gallon makes one pound of cheese) as a mean yield for medieval cows. See also Slicher Van Bath, *Agrarian History*, 355.

16. G. E. Fussell, *The English Dairy Farmer, 1500–1900* (London, 1966), 282.

17. Dahl and Hjort, *Having Herds*, 145.

18. Witold Kula discusses this important aspect of the feudal economy in *An Economic Theory of Feudalism* (London, 1976), 35–40.

19. For the formation of regional asymmetries in the early modern cattle trade and the emergence of new social groups involved with the economics of cattle production see Christopher Dyer, "A Small Landowner in the Fifteenth Century," *Midland History* 1 (1972): 1–14; Ian Blanchard, "The Continental European Cattle Trades, 1400–1600," *Economic History Review*, 2d ser., 3 (1986): 427–460; P. R. Edwards, "The Cattle Trade of Shropshire in the Late Sixteenth and Seventeenth Centuries," *Midland History* 6 (1981): 72–93; Othmar Pickl, "Routen, Umfang, und Organisation des inner europäischen Handels mit Schlachtvieh im 16. Jahrhundert," in *Festschrift Hermann Wiesflecker*, ed. A. Novotny and O. Pickl (Graz, 1973), 143–166;

Ada K. Longfield, *Anglo-Irish Trade in the Sixteenth Century*, London School of Economics, Studies in Economic and Social History, no. 3 (London, 1929), 107–108; A. Everitt, "The Marketing of Agricultural Produce," in *The Agrarian History of England and Wales*, vol. 4, *1500–1640*, ed. Joan Thirsk (London, 1967), 539–542; Caroline Skeel, "The Cattle Trade between Wales and England from the Fifteenth to the Nineteenth Centuries," *Transactions of the Royal Historical Society*, 4th ser., 9 (1926): 135–158.

20. For a noteworthy example of convertible husbandry in the fourteenth century see Searle, *Battle Abbey*, 272–286; for further comments on convertible husbandry see A. R. Bridbury, "Sixteenth-Century Farming," *Economic History Review*, 2d ser., 27 (1974): 538–556; Christopher Dyer, *Warwickshire Farming, 1349–c. 1520: Preparations for Agricultural Revolution*, Dugdale Society Occasional Papers, no. 27 (Oxford, 1981), 12–14.

5. THE DEMESNE SHEEP FLOCKS

1. Carus-Wilson and Coleman, *England's Export Trade*.

2. Page, "'Bidentes Hoylandie,'" 603–613; King, *Peterborough Abbey*, 156–59; Trow-Smith, *British Livestock Husbandry*, 131–171. The number of sheep continued to rise throughout the fourteenth and fifteenth centuries, as the forthcoming book of Bruce Campbell, *The Geography of Seigneurial Agriculture* (Cambridge University Press), will illustrate.

3. See table F, pp. 469–484 in Biddick, "Animal Husbandry," for a manor-by-manor listing of the intermanorial transfers, purchases, and sales of sheep for the first decade of the fourteenth century.

4. For complete data on the number of sheep involved in the transfers illustrated in figures 13–16 see table G, pp. 490–494 in Biddick, "Animal Husbandry."

5. The Roman roads drawn in figures 13–16 are based on Ivan D. Margary, *Roman Roads in Britain*, 3d ed. (New York, 1973). Sheep from the home group could have moved along the branches of the Fen Road to Water Newton–Thrapston–Irchester Road. Warmington, Ashton, Oundle, and Aldwincle border on or within a mile of this road. The Gartree Road, an old iron road cutting through Rockingham Forest, connected Harper's Brook with Corby and then passed through Cottingham to Leicester. The connection of the southerly Northamptonshire manors of Kettering, Irthlingborough, and Stanwick with the Thrapston-Gartree cross roads could have been along 570 from Thrapston to Kettering, although no Roman road has been recorded by Margary in this area.

6. Overall mortality statistics are based on the manor-by-manor rates for the years 1300–01, 1307–08, and 1309–1310 listed in table F, pp. 469–484 in Biddick, "Animal Husbandry."

7. The rates for Crowland Abbey were calculated from a manuscript kindly shared by Martin Stevenson, "Sheep Farming on the Crowland Abbey Estate." For tabular listing of the Crowland and Peterborough mortality rates see table VI.34 and VI.35 in Biddick, "Animal Husbandry."

8. C. R. W. Spedding, *Sheep Production and Grazing Management*, 2d ed. (London, 1970); Spedding reports on a survey of ewe mortality in England and Wales in 1958 which varied between 5.6 percent and 10 percent depending on region. Intensive grazing experiments monitored over a five-year period showed higher mortality (12.4 percent). Early lamb mortality under modern conditions varied between 16.6 percent and 12.9 percent.

9. Dahl and Hjort, *Having Herds*, 95.

10. For a table listing fertility rates for ewes on Peterborough manors see table VI.38 and for comparative fertility rates for nearby Crowland Abbey see table VI.37 in Biddick, "Animal Husbandry." The overall fertility rate for Peterborough ewes based on the manor-by-manor rates for 1300–01, 1307–08, and 1309–10 was 75.9 percent with a standard deviation of 15.7. These calculations do not include the disaster at Glinton in 1300–01, when 84 percent of ewes did not produce lambs.

11. Spedding, *Sheep Production*, 96.

6. DEMESNE HORSES, PIGS, AND POULTRY

1. For an overview of horses in the medieval agrarian economy see Langdon, "Horse Hauling"; "The Economics of Horses"; *Horses, Oxen and Technological Innovation*; Trow-Smith, *British Livestock Husbandry*, 115–116. For figures on the percentage of working horses on English demesnes between 1250 and 1320 see Langdon, *Horses, Oxen and Technological Innovation*, tables 11, 12.

2. For a list of different types of horses on the Peterborough manors for the three accounting years of the first decade of the fourteenth century see Biddick, "Animal Husbandry," 432–433.

3. Langdon, "Horse Hauling," 39 n. 14.

4. For a detailed discussion of the pig husbandry on the estate consult Biddick, "Pig Husbandry." For an overview of pig husbandry in the medieval agrarian economy consult Trow-Smith, *British Livestock Husbandry*, 117–118.

5. The correlation coefficients for the number of pigs per manor and the bushels of grain and legumes expended on them for fattening are as follows: 1300–01: $r = 0.796$ $t = 9.42$ at 15 degrees of freedom > 2.60 at 0.01 level of probability; 1307–09: $r = 0.579$ $t = 2.93$ at 17 degrees of freedom > 2.56 at 0.01 level of probability; 1309–10: $r = 0.733$ $t = 7.96$ at 17 degrees of freedom > 2.56 at 0.01 level of probability. For further discussion see Biddick, "Pig Husbandry."

6. For another interpretation of the expansion of legumes on demesnes in East Norfolk see Campbell, "Agricultural Progress."

7. Oschinsky, *Walter of Henley*, 285.

8. The details for the calculation of dressed weight and calories are contained in Biddick, "Pig Husbandry."

9. Oschinsky, *Walter of Henley*, 425.

10. V. G. Henry, "Length of Estrous Cycle and Gestation in European Wild Hogs," *Journal of Wildlife Management* 32 (1968): 406–408.

BIBLIOGRAPHY

MANUSCRIPT SOURCES

Peterborough Records

LONDON *British Museum*
Additional MS. 39758.
Additional charter. 737.
Cotton MS.
Nero.C.vii.
Vespasian. E. xxi, xxii.

Society of Antiquaries
MS. 60

PETERBOUROUGH
Dean and Chapter Library
MS. 1

ROCKINGHAM CASTLE
Rockingham A4/33

NORTHAMPTONSHIRE RECORD OFFICE
Fitzwilliam 2388, 231, 232, 233, 2389

Bishop of Winchester Records

HAMPSHIRE RECORD OFFICE
Winchester Pipe Rolls 159281, 159282

PRINTED SOURCES

The Account-Book of Beaulieu Abbey. Edited by S. F. Hockey. Camden Fourth Series, vol. 16. London: Royal Historical Society, 1975.

Anglo-Saxon Charters. Edited by A. J. Robertson. 2d ed. Cambridge: Cambridge University Press, 1956.

The Anglo-Saxon Chronicle. Translated by G. N. Garmonsway. 2d ed. New York: Dutton, 1955.

Bede's *A History of the English Church and People.* Translated by Leo Shirley-Price. Revised by R. E. Latham. Harmondsworth: Penguin, 1968.

Carte Nativorum: A Peterborough Abbey Cartulary of the Fourteenth Century. Edited by C. N. L. Brooke and M. M. Postan. Northamptonshire Record Society, Publications, no. 20. Oxford, 1960.

Cartularium Monasterii de Rameseia. Edited by W. H. Hart and P. A. Lyons. Vol. 3. London, 1893.

The Cellarers' Rolls of Battle Abbey, 1275–1513. Edited by Eleanor Searle and B. Ross. Sussex Record Society, 65. Sydney: Sydney University Press, 1967.

Charters and Custumals of the Abbey of Holy Trinity, Caen. Edited by Marjorie Chibnall. Records of Social and Economic History, n.s., no. 5. London: Oxford University Press, 1982.

Chronicon Petroburgense. Edited by T. Stapleton. Publications of the Camden Society, vol. 47. London, 1849.

Dialogus de Scaccario. Edited by Charles Johnson with corrections by F. E. L. Carter and D. E. Greenway. Oxford: Clarendon Press, 1983.

The Domesday of St. Paul's of the Year M.CC.XII. Edited by William Hale. Publications of the Camden Society, vol. 69. London, 1858.

The Early Charters of Eastern England, by C. R. Hart. Leicester: Leicester University Press, 1966.

Extracts from the Account Rolls of the Abbey of Durham. Edited by J. T. Fowler. Publications of the Surtees Society, vols. 99, 100, 103. Durham, 1898–1901.

Historiae Anglicanae Scriptores Varii. Edited by Joseph Sparke. London, 1723.

Leges Henrici Primi. Edited by L. J. Downer. Oxford: Clarendon Press, 1972.

Liber Eliensis. Edited by E. O. Blake. Camden Third Series, vol. 92. London, 1962.

Lincolnshire Domesday and Lindsey Survey. Edited by C. W. Foster and T. Longley. Lincoln Record Society, vol. 19. Lincoln, 1924. Reprint, 1976.

The Peterborough Chronicle of Hugh Candidus. Translated by Charles Mellows and William Thomas Mellows. Peterborough: Museum Society, 1966.

Pipe Rolls, 5 Henry II–17 John. Publications of the Pipe Roll Society. London, 1884–1964.

A Roll of the Household Expenses of Richard de Swinfield. Edited by J. Webb. 2 vols. Publications of the Camden Society, 59, 62. London, 1854–1855.

Rotuli de Dominabus et Pueris et Puellis de XII Comitatibus, [1185]. Edited by J. H. Round. Publications of the Pipe Roll Society, vol. 35. London, 1913.

A Terrier of Fleet, Lincolnshire. Edited by Nellie Neilson. Records of the Social and Economic History of England and Wales, vol. 4. London: Oxford University Press, 1920.

Walter of Henley and Other Treastises on Estate Management and Accounting. Edited by Dorothea Oschinsky. Oxford: Clarendon Press, 1971.

The Yale Edition of the Complete Works of St. Thomas More. Edited by Edward Surtz, S. J., and J. H. Hexter. Vol. 4. New Haven: Yale University Press, 1965.

SECONDARY WORKS

Abel, Wilhelm. *Agricultural Fluctuations in Europe.* Translated by Olive Ordish. New York: St. Martin's Press, 1980.

Addyman, Peter. "A Dark Age Site at Maxey, Northamptonshire." *Medieval Archaeology* 8 (1964): 20–73.

————. "Late Saxon Settlement in the St. Neots area: II. The Little Paxton Settlement and its Enclosures." *Proceedings of the Cambridge Antiquarian Society* 62 (1969): 59–93.

————. "Late Saxon Settlements in the St. Neots Area, III: The Village or Township of St. Neots." *Proceedings of the Cambridge Antiquarian Society* 69 (1972): 45–100.

Applebaum, Shimon. "Roman Britain." In *The Agrarian History of England and Wales,* edited by H. P. R. Finberg, vol. 1, pt. 2, pp. 3–277. Cambridge: Cambridge University Press, 1972.

Asad, Talal. "Equality in Nomadic Social Systems (Notes toward the Dissolution of an Anthropological Category)." *Critique of Anthropology* 11 (1978): 57–65.

Bailey, Elizabeth E., and Ann F. Friedlander. "Market Structure and Multiproduct Industries." *Journal of Economic Literature* 20 (1982): 1024–1048.

Baker, H. "Alluvial Meadows: A Comparative Study of Grazed and Mown Meadows." *Journal of Ecology* 25 (1937): 408–425.

Baudrillard, Jean. *The Mirror of Production.* Translated by Mark Poster. St. Louis: Telos Press, 1975.

Beresford, Guy. "Goltho Manor, Lincolnshire: The Buildings and Their Surrounding Defences." In *Proceedings of the Battle Conference on Anglo-Norman Studies, IV, 1981,* edited by R. Allen Brown, 13–36. Woodbridge, Suffolk, and Totowa, N. J., 1982.

Beresford, Maurice, and J. G. Hurst. *Deserted Medieval Villages.* London: Lutterworth Press, 1971.

Biddick, Kathleen. "Animal Bones from the Second Millennium Ditches, Newark Road." In *Excavation at Fengate, Peterborough, England: The Third Report,* edited by Francis Pryor, 217–232. Northamptonshire Archaeological Society Monograph no. 1 = Royal Ontario Museum Archaeology Monograph no. 6. Leicester: Northamptonshire Archaeological Society, 1980.

————. "Animal Husbandry and Pastoral Land-Use on the Fen Edge, Peterborough, England: An Archaeological and Historical Reconstruction (2500 B.C.–A.D. 1350)." Ph.D. diss., University of Toronto, 1982.

————. "Animal Bones from Cat's Water Subsite." In *Excavation at Fengate, Peterborough, England: The Fourth Report,* edited by Francis Pryor, microfiche, appendix 6, 245–275. Northamptonshire Archaeological Society Monograph, no. 2 = Royal Ontario Museum Archaeology Monograph, no. 7. Leicester: Northamptonshire Archaeological Society, 1984.

————. "Field Edge, Forest Edge: Early Medieval Social Organization and Resource Allocation." In *Archaeological Approaches to Medieval Europe*, edited by K. Biddick, 105–118. Studies in Medieval Culture, vol. 18. Kalamazoo, Mich.: Medieval Institute Publications, Western Michigan University, 1984.

————. "Pig Husbandry on the Peterborough Abbey Estate from the Twelfth to the Fourteenth Century." In *Animals and Archaeology*, edited by Juliet Clutton-Brock and Caroline Grigson, 161–177. British Archaeological Reports, International Series, no. 227. Oxford: B. A. R., 1985.

————. "Missing Links: Taxable Wealth, Markets and Stratification among Medieval English Peasants." *Journal of Interdisciplinary History* 18 (1987): 277–298.

Biddle, Martin. "Excavations at Winchester, 1970: Ninth Interim Report." *Antiquaries Journal* 52 (1972): 93–131.

————. "Excavations at Winchester, 1971 Tenth and Final Interim Report: Part II." *Antiquaries Journal* 55 (1975): 295–337.

————. "'Felix Urbs Winthonia': Winchester in the Age of Monastic Reform." In *Tenth-Century Studies*, edited by David Parsons, 123–140. London: Phillimore, 1975.

————. "Towns." In *The Archaeology of Anglo-Saxon England*, edited by David M. Wilson, 99–150. London: Methuen, 1976.

————, ed. *Winchester in the Early Middle Ages*. Winchester Studies, 1. Oxford: Oxford University Press, 1976.

Bisson, Thomas N. *Conservation of Coinage: Monetary Exploitation and Its Restraint in France, Catalonia and Aragon, A.D. 1000–1225*. Oxford: Oxford University Press, 1979.

Blanchard, Ian. "The Continental European Cattle Trades, 1400–1600." *Economic History Review*, 2d ser., 3 (1986): 427–460.

Bloch, Marc. *French Rural History*. Translated by Janet Sondheimer. Berkeley and Los Angeles: University of California Press, 1966.

Bowden, Peter. *The Wool Trade in Tudor and Stuart Britain*. London: Macmillan, 1962.

Bradley, Richard. "Prehistorians and Pastoralists in Neolithic and Bronze Age England." *World Archaeology* 4 (1972): 192–204.

————. *The Prehistoric Settlement of Britain*. London: Routledge and Kegan Paul, 1978.

Braudel, Fernand. *The Perspective of the World*. Translated by Sian Reynolds. New York: Harper and Row, 1984.

————. *The Structures of Everyday Life: The Limits of the Possible*. Translated by Sian Reynolds. New York: Harper and Row, 1981.

Bridbury, A. R. "Sixteenth-Century Farming." *Economic History Review*, 2d ser., 27 (1974): 538–556.

———. "Before the Black Death." *Economic History Review*, 2d ser., 30 (1977): 393–410.

———. "Thirteenth-Century Prices and the Money Supply." *Agricultural History Review* 33 (1985): 1–21.

Bridges, John. *The History and Antiquities of Northamptonshire*. 2 vols. Oxford and London, 1791.

Britnell, R. H. "English Markets and Royal Administration before 1200." *Economic History Review*, 2d ser., 31 (1978): 183–196.

Brown, A. E., T. R. Key, and C. Orr. "Some Anglo-Saxon Estates in Northamptonshire." *Northamptonshire Archaeology* 12 (1977): 155–176.

Cadman, Graham, and Glenn Foard. "Raunds: Manorial and Village Origins." In *Studies in Late Anglo-Saxon Settlement*, edited by Margaret L. Faull, 81–100. Oxford: Oxford University Department for External Studies, 1984.

Campbell, Bruce M. S. "The Regional Uniqueness of English Field Systems? Some Evidence from Eastern Norfolk." *Agricultural History Review* 29 (1981): 16–28.

———. "Agricultural Progress in Medieval England: Some Evidence from Eastern Norfolk." *Economic History Review*, 2d ser., 36 (1983): 26–46.

———. "Arable Productivity in Medieval England: Some Evidence from Norfolk." *Journal of Economic History* 43 (1983): 379–404.

———. "Towards an Agricultural Geography of Medieval England." *Agricultural History Review* 36 (1988): 87–98.

———. *The Geography of Seigneurial Agriculture*. Cambridge: Cambridge University Press, forthcoming.

Carus-Wilson, E. M., and Olive Coleman. *England's Export Trade, 1275–1547*. Oxford: Clarendon Press, 1963.

Certeau, Michel de. *The Practice of Everyday Life*. Translated by Steven Rendall. Berkeley, Los Angeles, London: University of California Press, 1984.

Challands, Adrian. "A Roman Industrial Site at Sacrewell, Thornhaugh." *Durobrivae* 2 (1974): 13–16.

Chibnall, Marjorie. "Mercenaries and the 'Familia Regis' under Henry I." *History* 62 (1977): 15–23.

Cole, John W., and Eric R. Wolf. *The Hidden Frontier: Ecology and Ethnicity in an Alpine Valley*. New York: Academic Press, 1979.

Colvin, Howard Montagu, ed. *The History of the King's Works*. 2 vols. London: Her Majesty's Stationery Office, 1963.

Cramp, Rosemary. "Schools of Mercian Sculpture." In *Mercian Studies*, edited by Anne Dornier, 191–231. Leicester: Leicester University Press, 1977.

Curtin, Philip. *Cross-Cultural Trade in World History*. Cambridge: Cambridge University Press, 1984.

Dahl, Gudrun, and Anders Hjort. *Having Herds: Pastoral Herd Growth and Household Economy*. Stockholm Studies in Social Anthropology, no. 2. Stockholm: University of Stockholm, Department of Social Anthropology, 1976.

Dallas, Carolyn G. "The Nunnery of St. Kyneburgha at Castor." *Durobrivae* 1 (1973): 17.

Darby, H. C. *The Medieval Fenland*. Newton Abbot: David and Charles, 1940. Reprint, 1975.

———. *Domesday England*. Cambridge: Cambridge University Press, 1977.

———. *The Changing Fenland*. Cambridge: Cambridge University Press, 1983.

Davies, Wendy. *An Early Welsh Microcosm: Studies in the Llandaff Charters*. London: Royal Historical Society, 1978.

Davies, Wendy, and Hayo Vierck. "The Contexts of Tribal Hidage: Social Aggregates and Settlement Patterns." *Frühmittelalterliche Studien* 8 (1974): 223–293.

Davison, K. B. "Excavations at Sulgrave, Northamptonshire, 1960–67: An Interim Report." *Archaeological Journal* 134 (1977): 105–114.

Denholm-Young, N. *Seignorial Administration in England*. Oxford: Oxford University Press, 1937.

Dept, Gaston. "Les marchands flamands et le roi d'Angleterre (1154–1216)." *Revue du Nord* 12 (1926): 303–324.

Donkin, R. A. "Cattle on the Estates of Medieval Cistercian Monasteries in England and Wales." *Economic History Review*, 2d ser., 15 (1962–63): 31–53.

———. *The Cistercians: Studies in the Geography of Medieval England and Wales*. Toronto: Pontifical Institute of Mediaeval Studies, 1978.

Douglas, Mary. *The World of Goods*. New York: Basic Books, 1979.

Drew, J. S. "Manorial Accounts of St. Swithun's Priory, Winchester." *English Historical Review* 62 (1947): 20–41.

Drury, G. H. "Crop Failures on the Winchester Manors, 1232–1349." *Transactions of the Institute of British Geographers*, n.s., 9 (1984): 401–418.

Duby, Geoges. "Économie domaniale et économie monétaire: Le budget de l'abbaye de Cluny entre 1080 et 1155." *Annales: Économies, sociétés, civilisations* 7 (1952): 155–171.

———. "Une inventaire des profits de la seigneurie clunisienne à la mort de Pierre le Vénérable." *Studia Anselmiana* 40 (1956): 128–140.

———. *Rural Economy and Country Life in the West*. Translated by Cynthia Postan. Columbia, S.C.: University of South Carolina Press, 1968.

Duffey, E., M. G. Morriss, J. Sheail, L. K. Ward, D. A. Wells, and T. C. E. Wells. *Grassland Ecology and Wildlife Management*. London: Chapman and Hall, 1974.

Dyer, Christopher. "A Small Landowner in the Fifteenth Century." *Midland History* 1 (1972): 1–14.

————. *Lords and Peasants in a Changing Society: The Estates of the Bishop of Worcester, 680–1540*. Cambridge: Cambridge University Press, 1980.

————. *Warwickshire Farming, 1349–c. 1520: Preparations for Agricultural Revolution*. Dugdale Society Occasional Papers, no. 27. Oxford: Dugdale Society, 1981.

Earle, Timothy. *Economic and Social Organization of a Complex Chiefdom*. Anthropological Papers, no. 63. Ann Arbor, Mich.: Museum of Anthropology, University of Michigan, 1978.

Edwards, P. R. "The Cattle Trade of Shropshire in the Late Sixteenth and Seventeenth Centuries." *Midland History* 6 (1981): 72–93.

Engels, Frederick. *The Origin of the Family, Private Property and the State*. Edited by Eleanor Burke Leacock. New York: International Publishers, 1972.

Evans, Christopher. "Nomads in 'Waterland'? Prehistoric Transhumance and Fenland Archaeology." *Proceedings of the Cambridge Antiquarian Society*, forthcoming.

Evans, J. G., S. Limbrey, and H. Cleere, eds. *The Effect of Man on the Landscape: The Highland Zone*. Council for British Archaeology Research Report, no. 11. London: Council for British Archaeology, 1975.

Evans, Robert. "The Early Courses of the River Nene." *Durobrivae* 7 (1979): 8–10.

Everitt, Alan. "The Marketing of Agricultural Produce." In *The Agrarian History of England and Wales, vol. 4, 1500–1640*, edited by Joan Thirsk, 539–542. Cambridge: Cambridge University Press, 1967.

Farmer, David L. "Some Price Fluctuations in Angevin England." *Economic History Review*, 2d ser., 9 (1956–57): 34–43.

————. "Grain Yields on the Winchester Manors in the Later Middle Ages." *Economic History Review* 2d. ser., 30 (1977): 555–566.

————. "Grain Yields on Westminster Abbey Manors, 1271–1410." *Canadian Journal of History* 18 (1983): 331–348.

Finberg. H. P. R. *Tavistock Abbey*. Cambridge: Cambridge University Press, 1951.

Finn, R. Welldon. *The Norman Conquest and Its Effects on the Economy: 1066–1086*. Hampton, Conn.: Archon Books, 1971.

Fisher, D. J. V. "The Anti-monastic Reaction in the Reign of Edward the Martyr." *Cambridge Historical Journal* 10 (1952): 254–270.

Fleming, Andrew. "The Genesis of Pastoralism in Prehistory." *World Archaeology* 4 (1972): 180–191.

Fleming, Robin. "Monastic Lands and England's Defence in the Viking Age." *English Historical Review* 100 (1985): 247–265.

Foard, Glenn. "Systematic Fieldwalking and Investigation of Saxon Settle ment in Northamptonshire." *World Archaeology* 9 (1978): 357–374.

Ford, W. J. "Some Settlement Patterns in the Central Region of the War-wickshire Avon." *In Medieval Settlement: Continuity and Change*, edited by P. H. Sawyer, 274–294. London: Edward Arnold, 1976.

Fox, Cyril. *The Personality of Britain*. Cardiff: University of Wales Press, 1932.

Fox, Harold. "Some Ecological Dimensions of English Medieval Field Systems." In *Archaeological Approaches to Medieval Europe*, edited by Kathleen Biddick, 119–158. Studies in Medieval Culture, vol. 18. Kalamazoo, Mich.: Medieval Institute Publications, Western Michigan University, 1984.

Fulford, Michael. "Pottery Production and Trade at the End of Roman Britain: The Case against Continuity." In *The End of Roman Britain*, edited by P. J. Casey, 120–132. British Archaeological Reports, British Series, no. 71. Oxford: B.A.R., 1979.

Fussell, G. E. *The English Dairy Farmer, 1500–1900*. London: F. Cass, 1966.

Génestal, Robert. *Le rôle des monastères comme établissements de crédit étudié en Normandie de XIᵉ à la fin du XIIIᵉ siècle*. Paris, A. Rousseau, 1910.

Giddens, Anthony. *Central Problems in Social Theory: Action, Structure and Contradiction in Social Analysis*. London: Methuen, 1979.

Godwin, Harry. "Studies in the Ecology of Wicken Fen, III: The Establish-ment of Fen Scrub (Carr)." *Journal of Ecology* 24 (1936): 82–116.

———. "Studies in the Ecology of Wicken Fen, IV: Crop-taking Experi-ments." *Journal of Ecology* 29 (1941): 83–106.

Godwin, Harry, and F. R. Bharucha. "Studies in the Ecology of Wicken Fen, II: The Fen Water Table and Its Control of Plant Communities." *Journal of Ecology* 20 (1932), 157–191.

Godwin, Harry, D. R. Clowes, and B. Huntley. "Studies in the Ecology of Wicken Fen, V: Development of Fen Carr." *Journal of Ecology* 62 (1974): 197–214.

Goody, J. R. "The Evolution of the Family." In *Household and Family in Past Times*, edited by Peter Laslett and R. Wall, 103–124. Cambridge: Cam-bridge University Press, 1972.

Gras, Norman Scott Brien. *The Evolution of the English Corn Market from the Twelfth to the Eighteenth Century*. Cambridge, Mass.: Harvard University Press, 1926.

Gray, H. L. *English Field Systems*. Cambridge, Mass.: Harvard University Press, 1915.

Green, Charles. "Excavations on a Medieval Site at Water Newton in the County of Huntingdon in 1958." *Proceedings of the Cambridge Anti-quarian Society* 51–52 (1962–63): 68–87.

Gregory, C. A. *Gifts and Commodities*. New York: Academic Press, 1982.

Grierson, Philip. *Monnaies du moyen âge*. Fribourg: Office du Livre, 1976.

Gudeman, Stephen. "Anthropological Economics: The Question of Distribution." *Annual Review of Anthropology* 7 (1978): 347–377.

Hadman, John, and Stephen Upex. "The Roman Villa at North Lodge, Barnwell, 1973." *Durobrivae* 2 (1974): 27–28.

Hall, David N. *The Fenland Project, Number 2. Fenland Landscapes and Settlement between Peterborough and March*. East Anglian Archaeology Report no. 35 Cambridge: 1987.

———. "The Roman Settlement at Ashton, near Oundle." *Durobrivae* 3 (1975): 13–15.

———. "The Changing Landscape of the Cambridgeshire Silt Fens." *Landscape History* 3 (1981): 37–49.

———. "The Countryside of the South-east Midlands and Cambridgeshire." In *The Romano-British Countryside: Studies in Rural Settlement and Economy*, edited by David Miles, 2:337–350. British Archaeological Reports, British Series, no. 103. Oxford: B.A.R., 1982.

———. "Fieldwork and Documentary Evidence for the Layout and Organization of Early Medieval Estates in the English Midlands." In *Archaeological Approaches to Medieval Europe*, edited by Kathleen Biddick, 43–68. Studies in Medieval Culture, vol. 18. Kalamazoo, Mich.: Medieval Institute Publications, Western Michigan University, 1984.

Hallam, H. E. *Settlement and Society: A Study of the Early Agrarian History of South Lincolnshire*. Cambridge: Cambridge University Press, 1965.

Harding, Alan. *The Law Courts of Medieval England*. New York: Barnes and Noble, 1973.

Hareven, Tamara K. *Family Time and Industrial Time: The Relationship between Family and Work in a New England Industrial Community*. New York: Cambridge University Press, 1982.

Hart, Cyril. *The Hidation of Northamptonshire*. University of Leicester, Department of English Local History, Occasional Papers, 2d. ser., no. 3. Leicester: Leicester: University Press, 1970.

———. "The Kingdom of Mercia." In *Mercian Studies*, edited by Anne Dornier, 43–61. Leicester: Leicester University Press, 1977.

———. "The Peterborough Region in the Tenth Century: A Topographical Survey." *Northamptonshire Past and Present* 6 (1980–81): 243–245.

Harvey, Barbara. *Westminster Abbey and Its Estates in the Middle Ages*. Oxford: Clarendon Press, 1977.

Harvey, P. D. A. "The English Inflation of 1180–1220." *Past and Present* 61 (1971): 3–30.

———. "The Pipe Rolls and the Adoption of Demesne Farming in England." *Economic History Review* 2d. ser., 27 (1974): 345–359.

————, ed. *The Peasant Land Market in Medieval England.* Oxford. Clarendon Press, 1984.

Harvey, Sally P. J. "Recent Domesday Studies." *English Historical Review* 95 (1980): 129–131.

————. "The Extent and Profitability of Demesne Agriculture in England in the Later Eleventh Century." In *Social Relations and Ideas: Essays in Honor of R. H. Hilton,* edited by T. H. Aston, P. R. Coss, Christopher Dyer, and Joan Thirsk, 45–72. Cambridge: Cambridge University Press, 1983.

Healey, R. Hilary. "Middle Saxon Pottery in the Fenland Area." *Lincolnshire History and Archaeology* 14 (1979): 80–81.

Henry, V. G. "Length of Estrous Cycle and Gestation in European Wild Hogs." *Journal of Wildlife Management* 32 (1968): 406–408.

Hill, David. "Trends in the Development of Towns during the Reign of Ethelred II." In *Ethelred the Unready,* edited by D. Hill, 213–253. British Archaeological Reports, British Series, no. 59. Oxford: B.A.R., 1978.

————. *An Atlas of Anglo-Saxon England.* Toronto: University of Toronto Press, 1981.

Hilton, Rodney. "Medieval Market Towns and Simple Commodity Production." *Past and Present* 109 (1985): 3–23.

Hodges, Richard. *Dark Age Economics: The Origins of Towns and Trade, A.D. 600–1000.* London: Duckworth, 1982.

Hodges, Richard, and David Whitehouse. *Mohammed, Charlemagne, and the Origins of Europe.* Ithaca, N.Y.: Cornell University Press, 1983.

Hollister, Warren, and J. W. Baldwin. "The Rise of Administrative Kingship: Henry I and Philip Augustus." *American Historical Review* 83 (1978): 867–905.

Hooke, Della. "Pre-Conquest Estates in the West-Midlands: Preliminary Thoughts." *Journal of Historical Geography* 8 (1982): 227–244.

Horn, Walter, and Ernest Born. *The Barns of the Abbey of Beaulieu and Its Granges of Great Coxwell and Beaulieu St. Leonards.* Berkeley and Los Angeles: University of California Press, 1965.

Hyams, Paul. "The Origins of a Peasant Land Market in England." *Economic History Review,* 2d ser., 23 (1970): 18–31.

————. *King, Lords and Peasants in Medieval England.* Oxford: Clarendon Press, 1980.

Jenkinson, Hilary. "William Cade: A Financier of the Twelfth Century." *English Historical Review* 28 (1913): 209–227.

————. "A Money Lender's Bonds of the Twelfth Century." In *Essays in History Presented to R. L. Poole,* edited by H. W. C. Davis, 109–209. Oxford: Clarendon Press, 1927.

John, Eric. "The Division of the Mensa in Early English Monasteries." *Journal of Ecclesiastical History* 6 (1955): 143–155.

————. "Some Latin Charters from the Tenth Century." In his *Orbis Britanniae*, 181–209. Leicester: Leicester University Press, 1966.

Jones, Catherine, and Richard Carson. "The Water Newton Hoard." *Durobrivae* 3 (1975): 10–12.

Jones, E. L. *The European Miracle: Environments, Economics and Geopolitics in the History of Europe and Asia.* Cambridge: Cambridge University Press, 1981.

Jones, Glanville R. J. "The Multiple Estate: A Model for Tracing the Interrelationships of Society, Economy and Habitat." In *Archaeological Approaches to Medieval Europe*, edited by K. Biddick, 9–41. Studies in Medieval Culture, vol. 18. Kalamazoo, Mich.: Medieval Institute Publications, Western Michigan University, 1984.

Jones, Richard. "A Romano-British Cemetery and Farmstead at Lynch Farm." *Durobrivae* 1 (1973): 13.

————. "A Roman and Saxon Farm at Walton, North Bretton." *Durobrivae* 2 (1974): 29–31.

Keefe, Thomas K. *Feudal Assessments and the Political Community under Henry II and His Sons.* Berkeley, Los Angeles, London: University of California Press, 1983.

Keene, Derek. *Survey of Medieval Winchester.* Winchester Studies, 2. Oxford: Clarendon Press, 1985.

Kershaw, Ian. *Bolton Priory.* Oxford: Oxford University Press, 1973.

————. "The Great Famine and Agrarian Crisis in England, 1315–1322." *Past and Present* 59 (1973): 3–50.

Kilmurry, Kathy. *The Pottery Industry of Stamford, Lincolnshire, c. A.D. 850–1250.* British Archaeological Reports, British Series, no. 84. Oxford: B.A.R., 1980.

King, Edmund. *Peterborough Abbey, 1086–1310: A Study of the Land Market.* Cambridge: Cambridge University Press, 1973.

————. "The Town of Peterborough in the Early Middle Ages." *Northamptonshire Past and Present* 6 (1980–81): 187–195.

————. "The Anarchy of King Stephen's Reign." *Transactions of the Royal Historical Society*, 5th ser., 34 (1984): 133–153.

Klein, Julius. *The Mesta: A Study in Spanish Economic History, 1273–1836.* Harvard Economic Studies, vol. 21. Cambridge, Mass.: Harvard University Press, 1920.

Knowles, David. *The Monastic Order in England.* 2d ed. Cambridge: Cambridge University Press, 1963.

Kula, Witold. *An Economic Theory of Feudalism.* Translated by L. Garner. London: N.L.B., 1976.

Langdon, John. "Horse Hauling: A Revolution in Vehicle Transport in Twelfth- and Thirteenth-Century England." *Past and Present* 103 (1984): 37–66.

————. *Horses, Oxen and Technological Innovation: The Use of Draught Animals in English Farming from 1066 to 1500*. Cambridge: Cambridge University Press, 1986.

————. "The Economics of Horses and Oxen in Medieval England." *Agricultural History Review* 30 (1982): 31–40.

Leach, Edmund. *Political Systems of Highland Burma*. Boston: Beacon, 1964.

LeGoff, Jacques. "Merchant's Time and Church's Time in the Middle Ages." In his *Time, Work, and Culture in the Middle Ages*, translated by Arthur Goldhammer, 29–42. Chicago: University of Chicago Press, 1980.

Lennard, Reginald. *Rural England, 1086–1135: A Study of Social and Agrarian Conditions*. Oxford: Clarendon Press, 1959.

Lewis, A. R. *The Northern Seas: Shipping and Commerce in Northern Europe, A.D. 300–1100*. Princeton: Princeton University Press, 1958.

Limbrey, S., and J. G. Evans, eds. *The Effect of Man on the Landscape: The Lowland Zone*. Council for British Archaeology Research Report, no. 21. London: Council for British Archaeology, 1978.

Lloyd, T. H. *The Movement of Wool Prices in Medieval England*. Economic History Review, Supplement, no. 6. Cambridge: Cambridge University Press, 1973.

————. *The English Wool Trade in the Middle Ages*. Cambridge: Cambridge University Press, 1977.

Longfield, Ada, *Anglo-Irish Trade in the Sixteenth Century*. London School of Economics, Studies in Economic and Social History, no. 3. London: G. Routledge and Sons, 1929.

Louwe Kooijmans, L. P. *The Rhine/Meuse Delta: Four Studies on Its Prehistoric Occupation and Holocene Geology*. Analecta Praehistorica Leidensia, vol. 7. Leiden: Leyden University Press, 1974.

Lovejoy, Paul. "Pastoralism in Africa." *Peasant Studies* 8 (1979): 73–85.

Lyon, B., and A. Verhulst. *Medieval Finance*. Providence, R.I.: Brown University Press, 1967.

Mackreth, Donald. "The Monastic Church before 1116." *Durobrivae* 8 (1980): 11–12.

————. "Recent Work on Monastic Peterborough." *Durobrivae* 9 (1984): 18–21.

Mahany, Christine, Alan Burchard, and Gavin Simpson. *Excavations in Stamford, Lincolnshire, 1963–69*. Society for Medieval Archaeology, Monograph Series, no. 9. London: Society for Medieval Archaeology, 1982.

Maine, Henry Sumner. *Dissertations on Early Law and Custom*. New York: H. Holt, 1883.

Małowist, Marian. "A Certain Trade Technique in the Baltic Countries in the Fifteenth to the Seventeenth Centuries." In *Poland at the XIth*

International Congress of Historical Sciences in Stockholm, 103–116. Warsaw, 1960.

Margary, Ivan D. *Roman Roads in Britain*. 3d ed. New York: Humanities Press, 1973.

Martin, Janet D. *Cartularies and Registers of Peterborough Abbey*. Northamptonshire Record Society, Publications, vol. 28. Peterborough: Northamptonshire Record Society, 1978.

————. *The Court and Account Rolls of Peterborough Abbey: A Handlist*. University of Leicester, History Department, Occasional Publications, no. 2. Leicester: University of Leicester, History Department, 1980.

Marx, Karl. *Pre-capitalist Economic Formations*. Edited by E. J. Hobsbawm. New York: International Publishers, 1964.

Mate, Mavis. "Monetary policies in England, 1271–1307." *British Numismatic Journal* 41 (1972): 34–79.

————. "The Indebtedness of Canterbury Cathedral Priory, 1215–1295." *Economic History Review*, 2d ser., (1973): 183–197.

————. "High Prices in Early-Fourteenth-Century England: Causes and Consequences." *Economic History Review*, 2d ser., 28 (1975): 1–16.

————. "Coping with Inflation: A Fourteenth-Century Example." *Journal of Medieval History* 4 (1978): 95–106.

————. "Profit and Productivity on the Estates of Isabella de Forz (1260–92)." *Economic History Review*, 2d ser., 33 (1980): 326–334.

Mayhew, Nicholas. "Numismatic Evidence and Falling Prices in the Fourteenth Century." *Economic History Review*, 2d ser., 27 (1974): 1–15.

————, ed. *Edwardian Monetary Affairs (1279–1344)*. British Archaeological Reports, no. 36. Oxford: B.A.R., 1977.

McDonald, J. M., and G. D. Snooks. "Were the Tax Assessments of Domesday England Artificial? The Case of Essex." *Economic History Review*, 2d ser., 38 (1985): 352–372.

————. "The Determinants of Manorial Income in Domesday England." *Journal of Economic History* 45 (1985): 541–556.

————. *Domesday Economy: A New Approach to Anglo-Norman History*. Oxford: Clarendon Press, 1986.

Metcalf, D. M. "Monetary Affairs in Mercia in the Time of Aethelbald." In *Mercian Studies*, edited by Anne Dornier, 87–102. Leicester: Leicester University Press, 1977.

Miller, Edward. *The Abbey and Bishopric of Ely*. Cambridge: Cambridge University Press, 1951. Reprint, 1969.

————. "England in the Twelfth and Thirteenth Centuries: An Economic Contrast?" *Economic History Review*, 2d. ser., 24 (1971): 1–14.

Mitchell, S. K. *Taxation in Medieval England*. New Haven: Yale University Press, 1951.

Modigliani, Franco. "The Life-Cycle Hypothesis of Saving: The Demand for Wealth and the Supply of Capital." In *The Collected Papers of Franco Modigliani*, edited by Andrew Abel, 2: 323–371. Cambridge, Mass.: M.I.T. Press, 1980.

Morgan, Lewis Henry. *Ancient Society; or, Researches in the Lines of Human Progress from Savagery through Barbarism to Civilization.* Edited by Eleanor Burke Leacock. New York: World Publishing Co, 1963.

Munro, John. "Wool Price Schedules and the Qualities of English Wools in the Later Middle Ages." *Textile History* 9 (1978): 118–169.

Neilson, Nellie. *Customary Rents.* Oxford Studies in Social and Legal History, vol. 2. Oxford: Clarendon Press, 1910.

Nene Valley Research Committee. *Annual Report.* 1976–1982.

Nightingale, Pamela. "The Evolution of Weight-Standards and the Creation of New Monetary and Commercial Links in Northern Europe from the Tenth Century to the Twelfth Century." *Economic History Review*, 2d ser., 38 (1985): 192–209.

North, Douglass C., and R. P. Thomas. *The Rise of the Western World: A New Economic History.* New York: Cambridge University Press, 1973.

Orlove, Benjamin S. "Ecological Anthropology." *Annual Review of Anthropology* 9 (1980): 235–273.

Page, Frances M. "'Bidentes Hoylandie' (A Mediaeval Sheep-Farm)." *Economic History (A Supplement to the Economic Journal)* 1, no. 4 (1929): 603–613.

Parsons, David. "Brixworth and Its Monastery Church." In *Mercian Studies*, edited by Anne Dornier, 108–114. Leicester: Leicester University Press, 1977.

Peterken, G. F. "Long-Term Changes in the Woodlands of Rockingham Forest and Other Areas." *Journal of Ecology* 64 (1976): 123–146.

Phillips, C. W., ed. *The Fenland in Roman Times.* Royal Geographical Society, Research Series, no. 5. London: Royal Geographical Society, 1970.

Pickl, Othmar. "Routen, Umfang, und Organisation des inner europäischen Handels mit Schlactvieh im 16. Jahrhundert." In *Festschrift Hermann Wiesflecker*, edited by A. Novotny and O. Pickl, 143–166. Graz: Historisches Institut der Universität Graz, 1973.

Postan, Michael. "Credit in Medieval Trade." *Economic History Review* 1 (1927–28): 234–261.

———. "Medieval Agrarian Society in Its Prime, 7: England." In *The Cambridge Economic History of Europe*, vol. 1, 2d ed., edited by M. M. Postan, 548–632. Cambridge: Cambridge University Press, 1966.

———. *The Medieval Economy and Society.* Harmondsworth: Penguin Books, 1975.

Postles, David. "Fleece Weights and the Wool Supply." *Textile History* 12 (1981): 96–105.

Potts, W. T. W. "The Pre-Danish Estate of Peterborough Abbey." *Proceedings of the Cambridge Antiquarian Society* 65 (1974): 13–27.

Prestwich, J. O. "War and Finance in the Anglo-Norman State." *Transactions of the Royal Historical Society*, 5th ser., 4 (1954): 19–43.

Prior, W. H. "Weights and Measures of Medieval England." *Bulletin du Cange: Archivum Latinitatis Medii Aevi* 1 (1924): 77–170.

Pryor, Francis. *Excavation at Fengate, Peterborough, England.* 4 vols. Royal Ontario Museum Archaeology Monographs, nos. 3, 5, 6, 7. Toronto: Royal Ontario Museum, 1974–1984. Third and fourth vols. (vols. 6 and 7 of Royal Ontario Museum Archaeology Monographs) copublished by Northampton Archaeological Society, Leicester, as vols. 1 and 2 of its Monographs.

Raban, Sandra. *The Estates of Thorney and Crowland: A Study in Medieval Monastic Land Tenure.* University of Cambridge, Department of Land Economy, Occasional Paper, no. 7. Cambridge, 1977.

Rackham, Oliver. *Ancient Woodland.* London: Edward Arnold, 1980.

Radford, C. A. R. "Pre-Conquest Minster Churches." *Archaeological Journal* 130 (1973): 120–140.

Raftis, J. Ambrose. *The Estates of Ramsey Abbey.* Toronto: Pontifical Institute of Mediaeval Studies, 1957.

———. *Tenure and Mobility: Studies in the Social History of the Medieval English Village.* Toronto: Pontifical Institute of Mediaeval Studies, 1964.

———. *A Small Town in Late Medieval England, 1278–1400.* Toronto: Pontifical Institute of Mediaeval Studies, 1982.

Ravensdale, J. R. *Liable to Floods: Village Landscape on the Edge of the Fens, A.D. 450–1850.* Cambridge: Cambridge University Press, 1974.

Reece, Richard. "Town and Countryside: The End of Roman Britain." *World Archaeology* 12 (1980): 77–92.

Rees, William. "Survivals of Ancient Celtic Custom in Medieval England." In *Angles and Britons*, 148–168. O'Donnell Lectures. Cardiff: University of Wales Press, 1963.

Renn, D. F. *Norman Castles in Britain.* London: Baker, 1968.

Richardson, H. G. *The English Jewry under Angevin Kings.* London: Methuen, 1960.

Robinson, Mark. "Plants and Invertebrates: Methods and Results and Interpretation." In *Iron Age and Roman Riverside Settlements at Farmoor, Oxfordshire*, by George Lambrick, Mark Robinson, et al., 77–128. Council for British Archaeology Research Report, no. 32. Oxford: Oxfordshire Archaeological Unit; London: Council for British Archaeology, 1979.

Rogers, James E. Thorold. *A History of Agriculture and Prices in England, 1259–1793.* 7 vols. Oxford: Clarendon Press, 1866–1902.

Rowley, Trevor, ed.. *The Origins of Open Field Agriculture.* London: Croom Helm, 1981.

Royal Commission on Historical Monuments, England. *An Inventory of the Historical Monuments in the County of Northampton.* Vol. 2, *Central Northamptonshire.* London: Her Majesty's Stationery Office, 1979.

Schofield, John. *The Building of London from the Conquest to the Great Fire.* London: Colonnade, 1984.

Searle, Eleanor. *Lordship and Community: Battle Abbey and Its Banlieu, 1066–1538.* Toronto: Pontifical Institute of Mediaeval Studies, 1974.

Shankin, Eugenia. "Sustenance and Symbol: Anthropological Studies of Domesticated Animals." *Annual Review of Anthropology* 14 (1985): 375–403.

Simmons, B. B. "The Lincolnshire Car Dyke: Navigation and Drainage." *Britannia* 10 (1979): 183–196.

Sivéry, Gérard. "Les débuts de l'économie cyclique et de ses crises dans les bassins scaldien et mosan: Fin du XIIe et debut du XIIIe siècle." *Revue du Nord* 64 (1982): 667–681.

Skeel, Caroline. "The Cattle Trade between Wales and England from the Fifteenth to the Nineteenth Centuries." *Transactions of the Royal Historical Society,* 4th ser., 9 (1926): 135–158.

Slicher Van Bath, B. H. *The Agrarian History of Western Europe, A.D. 500–1850.* Translated by Olive Ordish. London: Edward Arnold, 1963.

Smith, R. A. L. *Canterbury Cathedral Priory.* Cambridge: Cambridge University Press, 1943.

Spedding, C. R. W. *Sheep Production and Grazing Management.* 2d ed. London: Ballière, Tindall and Cassel, 1970.

Stamp, L. Dudley, ed. *The Land of Britain: The Report of the Land Utilisation Survey of Britain.* London, 1937–.

Stenton, Frank Merry. " 'Medeshamstede' and Its Colonies." In *Preparatory to Anglo-Saxon England,* edited by D. M. Stenton, 179–192. Oxford: Oxford University Press, 1970.

Stevenson, Martin. "Sheep Farming on the Crowland Abbey Estate." MS, 1978.

———. "Fleece Yields in Late Medieval England." Paper delivered at the Historical Geography Research Group Conference on Medieval Economy and Society, Exeter, 1983.

Taylor, H. M., and Joan Taylor. *Anglo-Saxon Architecture.* Vol. 2. Cambridge: Cambridge University Press, 1965.

TeBrake, William. *Medieval Frontier: Culture and Ecology in Rijnland.* Austin: Texas A&M University Press, 1985.

Thirsk, Joan. *Fenland Farming in the Sixteenth Century.* University College of Leicester, Department of English Local History, Occasional Papers, no. 3. Leicester: University College, 1953.

Thomas, Charles. *Christianity in Roman Britian to A.D. 500.* Berkeley, Los Angeles, London: University of California Press, 1981.

Titow, J. Z. *English Rural Society, 1200–1350.* London: George Allen and Unwin, 1969.

———. *Winchester Yields: A Study in Medieval Agricultural Productivity.* Cambridge: Cambridge University Press, 1972.

Trow-Smith, Robert. *History of British Livestock Husbandry.* London: Routledge and Kegan Paul, 1957.

The Victoria History of the County of Huntingdon. Vols. 1–4. Edited by William Page, Granville Proby, and S. Inskip Ladds. London, 1926–1938.

The Victoria History of the County of Leicester. Vols. 1–5. Edited by William Page, W. G. Hoskins, R. A. McKinley, and J. M. Lee. London, 1907–1964.

The Victoria History of the County of Northampton. Vols. 1–4. Edited by W. Ryland, D. Adkins, R. M. Serjeantson, William Page and L. F. Salzman. London, 1902–1937.

The Victoria History of the County of Nottingham. Vols. 1–2. Edited by William Page. London, 1906–1910.

The Victoria History of the County of Rutland. Vols. 1–2. Edited by William Page. London, 1908–1935.

Wallerstein, Immanuel. *The Modern World System: Capitalist Agriculture and the Origins of the European World Economy in the Sixteenth Century.* New York: Academic Press, 1976.

Wells, William C. "The Stamford and Peterborough Mints," parts 1–3. *British Numismatic Journal* 22–23 (1938–1940).

Whitehouse, David. "Maritime Trade in the Gulf: The Eleventh and Twelfth Centuries." *World Archaeology* 14 (1983): 328–334.

Wild, John Peter. "Roman Settlement in the Lower Nene Valley." *Archaeological Journal* 131 (1974): 140–170.

Williams, John N. "From Palace to 'Town': Northampton and Urban Origins." *Anglo-Saxon England* 13 (1984): 113–136.

Williams, O. B., and T. C. E. Wells. "Grazing Management of Woodwalton Fen: Seasonal Changes in the Diet of Cattle and Rabbits." *Journal of Applied Ecology* 11 (1974): 499–516.

Williamson, Grahame, and W. J. A. Payne. *An Introduction to Animal Husbandry in the Tropics.* 2d ed. London: Longmans, 1965.

Winterbottom, Michael, ed. *Three Lives of English Saints.* Toronto: Pontifical Institute of Mediaeval Studies, 1972.

Wolf, Eric. "Ownership and Political Ecology." *Anthropological Quarterly* 45 (1972): 201–205.

Wormald, Patrick. "The Ninth Century." In *The Anglo-Saxons,* edited by James Campbell, 132–159. Ithaca, N. Y.: Cornell University Press, 1982.

Worster, Donald. *Nature's Economy: A History of Ecological Ideas.* Cambridge: Cambridge University Press, 1985.

Wretts-Smith, M. "Organization of Farming at Croyland, 1257–1321." *Journal of Economic and Business History* 4 (1932): 168–192.

Wrigley, E. A. "Some Reflections on Corn Yields and Prices in Pre-industrial Economies." In his *People, Cities, and Wealth: The Transformation of Traditional Society*, 92–130. Oxford and New York: Blackwell, 1987.

Yelling, J. A. *Common Field and Enclosure in England, 1450–1850*. London: Macmillan, 1977.

INDEX

Designer: U.C. Press Staff
Compositor: Asco Trade Typesetting Ltd.
Text: 11/13 Baskerville
Display: Baskerville
Printer: Edwards Bros.
Binder: Edwards Bros.